Abandoned in the Wasteland

Abandoned in the WASTELAND

CHILDREN, TELEVISION, AND THE FIRST AMENDMENT

Newton N. Minow and Craig L. LaMay

HILL AND WANG

A division of Farrar, Straus and Giroux / New York

Designed by Fritz Metsch
First edition, 1995
First Hill and Wang paperback edition, 1996

LIBRARY OF CONGRESS CATALOGING-IN-PUBLICATION DATA
Minow, Newton N.
Abandoned in the wasteland : children, television, and the First
Amendment / Newton N. Minow and Craig L. LaMay.—1st ed.
p.   cm.
Includes index.
1. Television programs for children—Law and legislation—United
States.   2. Television advertising—Law and legislation—United
States.   3. Violence in television—Law and legislation—United
States.   4. Sex in television—Law and legislation—United States.
I. LaMay, Craig L.   II. Title.
KF2840.M56 1995 343.73099'46—dc20 [347.3039946] 95-1113 CIP

A study conducted for the American Academy of Arts and Sciences

This book is based on a project conducted under the auspices of the
American Academy of Arts and Sciences and supported by the Carnegie Corporation of New York. The opinions expressed are those of
the authors only, and do not necessarily reflect the views of the American Academy or the supporting foundation.

To Benjamin, Rachel, and Mira,
Ellis and Owen

Acknowledgments

This book is the result of thirty-four years of work and contemplation of a medium, television, that since mid-century has transformed the world, the nation, the community, the family. The idea for the book first took shape in May 1991, when I was invited by the Freedom Forum Media Studies Center at Columbia University, and its fine director, Everette Dennis, to analyze the thirty years of television that had passed since my first speech to the nation's broadcasters as a young FCC chairman. When I did, I was both dismayed and alarmed to find that while television certainly offered many more choices in 1991 than it had in 1961, in several key respects the wasteland had only grown vaster, the prospects for serving the public interest even dimmer. What could be done?

At the urging of Carnegie Corporation president David Hamburg and American Academy of Arts and Sciences president Leo Beranek, I enlisted the help of a young communications scholar and journalist, Craig LaMay, to find out. This book is the result of that collaboration. I thank Everette Dennis, Carnegie and the Academy for bringing Craig and me together and giving us this opportunity to study, reflect, and share our work with everyone interested in television's future.

Like all books of this type, the collaboration is bigger than the names on the cover suggest. Although we alone are responsible for the contents of this book, many people took the time to share their opinions and expertise. At the Carnegie Corporation, Dr. Hamburg, Barbara Finberg, Vivien Stewart, Fred Hechinger, and Avery Russell provided us with encouragement and intellectual support; at the American Academy of Arts and Sciences, Dr. Beranek, Dr. Jaroslav Jan Pelikan, and Joel Orlen helped both in the administration of the project and in guiding its progress.

Special thanks go to those who read early drafts of the manuscript and gave us their advice and comments during a conference in May 1994 at the American Academy of Arts and Sciences in Cambridge. They are Jonathan Alter, of *Newsweek*; Ellen Hume and Stephen Bates, of the Annenberg Washington Program in Communications Policy Studies of Northwestern University; Professors Margaret Blanchard and Jane Brown, of the University of North Carolina School of Journalism; the communications lawyer and former FCC general counsel Henry Geller; the former NBC and PBS president Lawrence Grossman; one of *Sesame Street*'s creators, Gerald Lesser, of the Harvard University Graduate School of Education; Kathryn Montgomery, of the Center for Media Education; Willard Rowland, dean of the University of Colorado Journalism School; and Elizabeth Thoman, of the Center for Media Literacy.

Several other people provided us with invaluably wise counsel and were instrumental in turning our focus to the needs of America's children. They include Joan Ganz Cooney, chair of the executive committee at the Children's Television Workshop, and CTW president David Britt; Markle Foundation president Lloyd Morrisett; the former CBS president Frank Stanton (who is my definition of a public-interest broadcaster); PBS president Ervin Duggan; Bill McCarter, president of WTTW-Chicago; the late Merrill Panitt, the first editor of *TV Guide*; former FCC commissioner Henry Rivera; University of Chicago law professor Cass Sunstein; James Fellows, president of the Central Educational Network; the television critic Les Brown; the FCC's chief of plans and policy, Robert Pepper;

Adam Clayton Powell III, director of technology for the Media Studies Center at Columbia University; Stanley Frankel, a writer and thinker who has advised me on children and television for more than thirty years; Ruth Caplin, an exceptional and thoughtful therapist in Washington, D.C.; James Carey, the former dean of the communications school at the University of Illinois; Marcy Kelly, president of Mediascope; Squire Rushnell, former head of children's television for ABC; the writer, scholar, and social commentator Amitai Etzioni; Robert Larson, former president of WTVS-Detroit; RAND economist Walter Baer; U.S. senator Paul Simon; and the veteran broadcaster Ward Quaal.

Northwestern University, my alma mater, gave the Public-Service Television Project a home while this book was written. We owe our warm reception there to Arnold Weber, who recently retired as the university's president; Michael Janeway, dean of the Medill School of Journalism; and Burton Weisbrod, director of the university's Center for Urban Affairs and Policy Research.

We owe a unique debt to the talented staff of the Public-Service Television Project, Kathy Schultz, Gina Fattore, and Alison Siegler, without whom this book would never have been completed and who, along the way, benefited the project with their good sense and good humor. Also, at my law firm of Sidley & Austin, we thank Howard Trienens and Eden Martin, each of whom read and commented on the manuscript, and Carol S. Clark, who helped us pull together the First Amendment case law for Chapter 3.

Every book benefits from having a good editor, and we were fortunate to have one of the very best in Elisabeth Sifton. While we take full responsibility for the ideas and arguments in these pages, we thank Elisabeth first for her belief in the importance of this book, and second for her wise guidance and counsel.

And I owe an immeasurable debt of appreciation to Ambassador Walter H. Annenberg, whose imaginative and creative philanthropy advanced the uses of television for education in our country. It has been my privilege to direct the Annenberg Washington Program in Communications Policy Studies in our nation's capital since 1987 and to serve as the Walter H. Annenberg Professor of Communications Law and Policy at Northwestern.

My largest debt is to my family. My wife, Jo, and our daughters, Nell, Martha, and Mary, read and commented on every draft of this book and supplied us with original research and ideas. Jo, my wife of almost forty-six years, always had the best idea and the last word, both of which are in this book.

A word about my colleague, Craig LaMay. A gifted journalist, scholar, and author, Craig moved from New York to the Chicago area to work with me in 1992, right after his wife, Karrie, had their second child, Owen, to add to Ellis, then four years old. Karrie developed Hodgkin's disease and became critically ill, but with excellent medical care and Craig's rocklike support and total dedication, she is now thriving, full of energy and spirit. Craig never wavered or faltered in our project, despite this harrowing experience. I salute him for his courage and faith; he is the same age as my youngest daughter, and I learned so much from him that he became not only my friend but also my teacher.

Finally, this book was in many ways born and nurtured in the lives of the small children closest to me. They are my grandchildren, Benjamin, Rachel, and Mira. It is to all of America's children and grandchildren that we dedicate this book.

Newton N. Minow

I have had the benefit of counsel from all the people whom Newt has acknowledged above, many of whom I knew before starting this book and others I did not, but who in every case helped renew my own faith in the possibilities of public life. I thank them for their help and, many of them, for their friendship. I owe special thanks to those at Northwestern University—Dean Michael Janeway and Professors Larry Lichty, Robert Entman, and Burton Weisbrod—who, though their views are in many cases different from ours, made this a better book through their willingness to share ideas and through their encouragement. I also thank Everette Dennis, executive director of the Freedom Forum Media Studies Center at Columbia University, a valued teacher and mentor who urged me to pursue this project.

And I owe an unpayable debt to Newton Minow, who taught

me much more than he knows. I became a journalist in the first place because I believed it to be a profession with a public purpose; many journalists and scholars I know are either cynical about that idea or, if they believe in it, weary of defending it. Many have settled into what can only be described as a kind of apologetic discourse. Newton Minow continues to believe in the public interest without apology. But most remarkable to me is that behind the icon is a man who personifies the values he espouses. He treats everyone with utmost courtesy and respect; he is never cynical or even discouraged, but sees in every setback a new opportunity to advance the public good; and his greatest treasure in life is his family. He is, as Murray Kempton once described, a true gentleman: "all of a seam, on camera and off." I hope, as a father and a citizen, to live up to his example.

If I do, it will be in no small part because of the example my parents, Edward and Virginia LaMay, set for me when I was young, and which my wonderful young sons, Ellis and Owen, require of me now. I thank my parents for their love, and for the enormous help they were to me and my family during the writing of this book. I thank God for my children, every day.

And finally I thank my wife, Karrie, whom I love deeply. Without her sweet nature, her confidence and encouragement—without her—this book would never have been possible.

Craig L. LaMay

Contents

Abandoned in the Wasteland

Introduction

NEWTON N. MINOW

IN 1961, SHORTLY AFTER PRESIDENT JOHN F. KENNEDY APPOINTED me chairman of the Federal Communications Commission, I told the nation's broadcasters, the people who in those days ran the television business, that they had made television into a "vast wasteland."

Almost overnight, those two words became television's first enduring sound bite. For decades, they have been used, over and over and over again, to describe what Americans find when they come home after work in the evenings and turn on their television sets, what our children find there after school or on Saturday morning. "Vast wasteland" appears in newspaper headlines, in book titles, in magazine articles, in Bartlett's *Familiar Quotations*, even as the answer to a Trivial Pursuit question. My wife and our three daughters threaten to inscribe my tombstone, "On to a Vaster Wasteland."

But the last straw came when our daughter Mary showed me a

reading comprehension test for prospective law students that included five multiple-choice questions about a paragraph in my vast-wasteland speech. Imagine my shock when I got three of the answers wrong! At that point, I realized that my too-quoted speech had been a failure. The two words I wanted people to remember from that speech were not "vast wasteland." The two words I cared about were "public interest."

The law governing radio and television broadcasting, the Federal Communications Act of 1934, gives broadcasters free and exclusive use of broadcast channels on condition that they serve the "public interest, convenience and necessity." When I arrived at the FCC, I sought out the man who had drafted the law twenty-seven years earlier, Washington's former senator Clarence C. Dill, long retired by then. I asked him what he had meant by the "public interest." Senator Dill told me that he and his colleagues had been of two minds: on the one hand, it was the middle of the Great Depression and they wanted to encourage people to risk their money in the new medium; on the other hand, they knew they had to have some legal standard with which to award licenses to some people while rejecting others, because there were not enough channels to go around. "A young man on the committee staff had worked at the Interstate Commerce Commission for several years," Dill recalled, "and he said, 'Well, how about "public interest, convenience and necessity"? That's what we used there.' That sounded pretty good, so we decided we would use it, too."

The plan backfired. No one in Congress defined what the public-interest clause was supposed to mean in broadcasting. It had been developed to regulate the railroads and later the telegraph and telephone services, industries that the law deemed public utilities subject to detailed rate and public-service regulation. But the Federal Communications Act specifically exempted broadcasters from obligations as public utilities, which meant that they had the best of both worlds—all the benefits of a utility monopoly but none of the rate and public-service obligations. In the absence of a clear, specific definition of the public interest, broadcasters had the *quid*—exclusive, free use of the public airwaves—without the *quo*. So it has remained for sixty years.

Today, the Communications Act stands as a monument to the mistake of writing into law vaguely worded quid pro quos. Because the act did not define what the public interest meant, Congress, the courts, and the FCC have spent sixty frustrating years struggling to figure it out.

For more than half of those years, I've been privileged to participate in this debate and to observe it from a ringside seat. It has been my good luck to serve our government, public television, commercial broadcasting, advertising, and telephone, publishing, and cable companies, to help organize televised presidential debates, to teach students who now are leaders in communications and law, and to direct think tanks and foundations concerned with communications policy. I've seen every side of the elephant from every angle: as a chairman of a leading public television station (WTTW in Chicago); as a chairman of the Public Broadcasting Service (PBS); as a director of a commercial network (CBS); as a director of independent commercial broadcasting stations (of the Tribune Company); as a director of a leading advertising and communications company (Foote, Cone & Belding); and as a professor at the Annenberg Washington Program of Northwestern University. After these decades, to me the answer is clear. The public interest meant and still means that we should constantly ask: What can television do for our country, for the common good, for the American people?

Most important, I believe, the public interest requires us to ask what we can do for our children. By the time most Americans are eighteen years old, they will have spent 15,000 hours in front of a television set, about 4,000 hours more than they have spent in school, and far more than they have spent talking with their teachers, their friends, or even their parents. If we can't figure out what the public interest means with respect to those who are too young to vote—the youngest of whom are illiterate, who are financially, emotionally, and even physically dependent on adults—then we will never figure out what it means anywhere else. Children above all know this. They hear us talk incessantly about broken schools, broken homes, and broken values, and they watch as we do nothing about their broken spirits.

Why haven't we acted to give our children a healthier television environment? For half a century, anyone who has questioned the American commercial television system has been shouted down as a censor. Instead of talking seriously about how to improve television for our children, Americans argue to a stalemate about broadcasters' rights and government censorship. We neglect discussion of moral responsibility by converting the public interest into an economic abstraction, and we use the First Amendment to stop debate rather than to enhance it, thus reducing our first freedom to the logical equivalent of a suicide pact.

We have become accustomed to using the First Amendment to avoid asking ourselves hard questions which might require uncomfortable answers. For example, when I served on the CBS board of directors, I was concerned about the practice our television networks had of announcing the predicted results of elections before the polls were closed. After I asked for a review of this policy at a CBS board meeting, CBS News executives presented the methodology that the network used—with its exit-poll interviews, computerized databases, and comparisons with prior election data from carefully selected precincts. On this basis, they defended their announcing likely election results while polls were still open.

I asked, "But why do this?" The answer was, "We have a right to do this under the First Amendment."

I asked again, "But why do we do it?" The answer again was, "We have a right to do this under the First Amendment."

I said, "Perhaps my question is not clear. My question is, *Why* do we do it?" For a third time, the answer was, "We have a right to do this under the First Amendment."

To say I was bothered is to put it mildly. So I asked, "Acknowledging that the First Amendment gives us the right to do it, my question is *Why* do it? For competitive reasons, so ABC and NBC won't beat us?" The answer was no.

So, I asked again, "If we don't do it to beat ABC and NBC, then why?" This time the answer was, "We must share immediately with the public all the information we have. We can't sit on information and keep the public in the dark when we know the election results. We must inform the public at once!"

"Then why," I asked, "do we say, 'We have an important announcement for you, but first, a commercial'? If it's so important, why wait for the commercial?"

I never got an answer to that one. I expect that the answer would have been, It is our right to do this under the First Amendment.

This example dramatized for me how correct Justice Potter Stewart was when he said that we confuse the right to do something with whether it is the right thing to do.

We should be asking ourselves whether what we do is the right thing. In 1961, when I called television a "vast wasteland," I was thinking of an endless emptiness, a fallow field waiting to be cultivated and enriched. I never dreamed that we would fill it with toxic waste. If I had it to do over again, I would concentrate every effort on improving children's television. For, as Gabriela Mistral, the Chilean poet who won the Nobel Prize, wrote: "We are guilty of many errors and many faults, but the worst crime is abandoning the children."

If I had to do it over again, that's where I would draw the battle line.

My interest in television's effect on children began in 1956, when Robert Kennedy and I traveled together, often as roommates, as members of Adlai Stevenson's presidential campaign staff. Bob and I had a lot in common, especially because my wife, Jo, and I have three children the same ages as three of Bob and Ethel's children. When the Stevenson campaign reached Springfield, Illinois, Bob asked if we could skip the speeches and go visit Abraham Lincoln's home. On the way, Bob said something I've never forgotten: he said that when he grew up, the three great influences on children were home, school, and church, but in observing his own children, he believed that there was now a fourth major influence, television.

In the thirty-eight years since that walk in Springfield, more than 3,000 sociological studies have confirmed Bob Kennedy's observation. Television's influence on our children is staggering. Even those who do not accept the link described in 1972 by the Surgeon General between screen violence and aggressive behavior in children concede that television teaches our children that guns and violence solve problems, that it affects the way they perceive people of other races, that it regards them as consumers rather than as citizens, and that it shapes their fears and expectations about the future. Every afternoon when they come home from school, millions of American children turn on their television sets to see what the adult world holds for them. What do they find there?

During one randomly selected week, January 31 through February 4, 1994, my daughter Nell recorded what they saw: programs about a thirteen-year-old girl who has slept with twenty men and a seventeen-year-old who has slept with more than a hundred (both girls carried beepers); about transsexual prostitutes; about parents who hate their daughters' boyfriends; about men whose girlfriends want too much sex; about white supremacists who hate Mexicans; about a woman who tried to kill herself nine times; about a sadomasochistic couple who explained that instead of putting a ring on her finger at their wedding, they had his penis pierced; about a man who fathered four children by three women and who "couldn't stop cheating"; and programs called "Dad by Day, Cross-Dresser by Night" and "Using Sex to Get What You Want."

Peggy Noonan described the difference between what children see on television now and what they saw a generation ago:

> When I was a kid there were kids who went home to empty houses, and they did what kids do, put on the TV. There were game shows, cartoons, some boring nature show, an old movie, *The Ann Sothern Show*, Spanish lessons on educational TV, a soap opera.
>
> Thin fare, boring stuff; kids daydreamed to it. But it was better to have this being pumped into everyone's living room than, say, the Geto Boys on channel 25, rapping about killing women, having sex with their dead bodies and cutting off their breasts.
>
> Really, you have to be a moral retard not to know that this is harmful, that it damages the young, the unsteady, the unfinished. You have to not care about anyone to sing these words and to put this song on TV for money.

In an ideal world, no American children would be left alone for long periods of time with only television for companionship. In an ideal world, every parent would be responsible, every parent would have the time and financial resources to control his or her child's television viewing, and every parent would be as vigilant as *Miami Vice* producer Dick Wolf, who says that he won't allow his own children to see the shows he has produced. In an ideal world, the people who work in television would have to take an oath like the Hippocratic oath, the first tenet of which would be, "Do no harm." In an ideal world, the people who use the airwaves to send toxic programming into our living rooms would be forced to sit down with their *own* children and explain to them why it is they are proud of what they do. I think then producers and programmers would come out from behind the First Amendment and try to do better for all our children.

They started off with the best intentions. In the early 1950s, when television was still new, broadcasters, in the hope of inducing people with children to purchase television sets, aired exemplary, high-quality children's programs. My friend Burr Tillstrom created Chicago's own *Kukla, Fran and Ollie*. A decade later, when more than 90 percent of American homes had sets, most commercial broadcasters stopped thinking about what was best for children and shifted their emphasis to selling products for advertisers. Indeed, the most important children's program in the United States might not have come about at all except for a string of lucky coincidences.

Late in 1968, Dean Burch (whom I knew from our service together on a bipartisan commission) called me in Chicago from Tucson and asked for some advice. President-elect Richard M. Nixon had offered him the appointment of chairman of the FCC. Dean had turned it down and was having second thoughts. I advised him to call immediately and accept.

A few months later, he invited me to dinner in Washington. "Okay, big shot," he said. "You talked me into this. You told me I could do good in the world. Any ideas?" I told Dean about a new program not yet on the air, funded in part by the Carnegie Corporation and which I had heard described by an exceptionally talented, dedicated broadcaster named Joan Cooney at a meeting of the board of National Educational Television—NET, the precursor to the Public Broadcasting Service.

"Is she married?" Dean asked. "Do you think her maiden name

might be Ganz?" When I said that she had indeed been introduced at the meeting as Joan Ganz Cooney, Dean smiled.

"That must be Joanie Ganz," he said. "I asked her to marry me when we both were students at the University of Arizona."

When Dean got in touch with Joan, she told him that she was having problems getting additional funding approved by the Department of Health, Education and Welfare. Dean, who had managed Barry Goldwater's 1964 presidential campaign, went with Joan to meet with the Arizona senator. The minute Senator Goldwater was introduced to her, he said, "Ganz, from Phoenix. Are you related to Harry Ganz?" When Joan said yes, the senator replied, "Harry was my dear friend and the first to encourage me to run for office. How can I help you?" Not long after that, HEW approved the necessary funding. Twenty-five years later, it remains the best example of how television can be used to help and nurture all children. Since it went on the air in 1969, *Sesame Street* has been seen by billions of children in more than one hundred countries.

Why aren't there more *Sesame Street*s? Apart from public television, our television system is a business attuned exclusively to the marketplace. Children are treated as a market to be sold to advertisers at so many dollars per thousand eyeballs. In such a system, children are not seen as the future of democracy, nor does the television industry consider that it has a special responsibility for their education, values, and nurturing. When Congress wrote the Communications Act in 1934, it took great pains to ensure equal time for only one group of Americans: politicians. Children were not on the agenda, because Congress did not think about connecting broadcasting with the needs of children. In the years after World War II, when television exploded into American homes and transformed American culture, Congress again did not think about children.

The Children's Television Act, a small step in the right direction, did not become law until 1990. The act marked the first time Congress recognized children as a special audience, and it requires commercial broadcasters to provide "educational and informational" programs for children. Until recently, however, broadcasters all but ignored the law. After researchers discovered that stations throughout the country were claiming that cartoons and old episodes of *Leave It to Beaver* and *The Jetsons* met the law's requirements, the FCC began a proceeding to make them clean up their act. There are more good children's television shows today than there have been in more than a decade, but even now 60 percent of the programs broadcasters claim meet the minimal requirements of the Children's Television Act air between 5:30 a.m. and 7 a.m.

We have only one *Sesame Street* and a few programs like *Ghostwriter, Mister Rogers' Neighborhood,* and *The Magic School Bus.* But the reason we have so few is that we have only whatever the sponsors think the market will bear, and there is a clear market failure. For millions of children, that means talk shows and violent cartoons which are often nothing but thinly disguised commercials. Ask any commercial television executive what the key to success is in children's television, and he will tell you that it's not the show but the merchandising that surrounds it—the millions of dollars' worth of toys, video games, canned spaghetti, lunch boxes, and other products the show was created to sell.

Anyone who doubts this merchandising imperative should read an issue of *Broadcasting and Cable,* the television industry's trade magazine. In a special August 1992 issue devoted to "Children's TV," the Fox and Buena Vista production studios were fighting to "carve out at least three-quarters of the kids' viewing pie," the magazine reported, while smaller suppliers were "battling for the remaining fringe availabilities." Said one executive of his company's strategy for children's programming: "We have to be sharpshooters to pick off time periods we can get into." This image—of sharpshooters gunning for our children—perfectly sums up the American approach to children's television.

All this illustrates Fred Friendly's wise observation about the American television system: broadcasters make so much money doing their worst that they cannot afford to do their best. While producers try to re-create runaway merchandising hits like *Teenage Mutant Ninja Turtles, Mighty Morphin Power Rangers,* or *Beavis and Butt-Head,* good programs like *Cro* or *Beakman's World* struggle to gain an audience in the worst possible time slots.

This system is what television executives, writers, and producers call, with no sense of irony, the "marketplace of ideas." As the term is used today, this is a crude caricature of the metaphor first used by John Stuart Mill and later by Supreme Court Justice Oliver Wendell Holmes, Jr. But in one respect the caricature is accurate: the ideas that matter the most in the television marketplace are those that make the most money.

When it could be serving the best interests of children, our system chooses to serve the best interests of advertisers. Unless we correct this, unless we make explicit provisions for what the "public interest" truly means with regard to children, we shall repeat—in the digital era of "telecomputers" and information-on-demand—the worst mistakes that plagued the age of analog broadcasting. In 2054, some future FCC chairman will look back at us from the vantage point of a much vaster wasteland and wonder why, when we had a second chance, we failed to seize it.

Law and public policy usually lag behind new technologies. The Constitution is subject to amendment only through specific, prescribed procedures, but I suggest to you that sometimes the Constitution and the law are amended without any of us realizing it. Sometimes this happens through the evolution of political practices—as in the case of the electoral college—and sometimes when the Constitution is amended by technology, silently and instantly.

For example, consider political jurisdictions. When the technology of television developed, the television and advertising industries quickly saw that television signals did not correspond with political boundaries. A television signal spreads through the air in a circle with a radius of about sixty miles. Viewers of a signal broadcast from my hometown of Chicago live in the city of Chicago, the suburbs in Cook County, five other counties in the metropolitan area of Chicago, and in other parts of Illinois, Wisconsin, Indiana, and Michigan. The same situation exists throughout the United States and across our national boundaries into Canada and Mexico.

When this became apparent, the broadcasting and television industries quickly drew their own map of the United States, ignoring city, county, state, and national boundary lines, and dividing the country into DMA's—designated marketing areas. They didn't call for a constitutional convention or persuade Congress to change any laws. They simply threw away the official governmental maps and boundaries and began defining their business in terms of DMA's instead of cities, counties, states, and the nation. Today there are 211 DMA's, the ten largest of which cover a third of the nation's population. And thus communities became markets, citizens became customers, and children became fair game.

During World War II, the Army battalion in which I served built the first telephone lines along the Burma Road, miraculously connecting the ancient civilizations of India and China with modern communications technology. This was an early version of the information superhighway of the future. After World War II, I entered college and then law school, all the while intensifying my interest in communications. I met Marshall McLuhan when he participated in a panel discussion at Northwestern University in 1960. When President Kennedy asked me to serve as chairman of the Federal Communications Commission, I knew this was the one government job I had to take.

My first day on the job at the FCC, I received a visit from one of the senior commissioners, T.A.M. Craven, a crusty ex-Navy engineer who had been appointed by President Dwight D. Eisenhower. Commissioner Craven asked, "Young man, do you know what a communications satellite is?" I said no. He groaned, "I was afraid of that."

When I said I'd like to learn, he told me of his unsuccessful efforts to get the FCC to approve a test launch of Telstar, an experimental communications satellite developed by the American Telephone and Telegraph Co. with the encouragement of the National Aeronautics and Space Administration. Commissioner Craven convinced me that this was the one part of the space race with the Soviet Union where we were far ahead, but that our own government was standing in the way. The FCC quickly approved the Telstar experiment, and to this day I treasure a picture of Tam Craven with me in Bangor, Maine, where Telstar was successfully launched on July 10, 1962.

The development of communications satellites like Telstar in the 1960s led to the development of CNN, C-SPAN, HBO, and countless other cable networks in the 1970s and 1980s, to cheaper long-distance telephone rates, and to the explosion of global communications in the 1990s. Through communications satellites, we learned that modern technology has no respect for political boundaries, or Berlin Walls, or Tienanmen Squares, or dictators in Iraq.

Today, we are finding that the things we did a generation ago have led to another communications revolution, fueled by the technologies not only of satellites but of digitization and fiber-optic cable. This revolution is going on not just here in the United States but around the world. In most countries it is especially challenging to the not-for-profit, public telecommunications systems established in the early days of broadcasting, such as the BBC in Britain, the CBC in Canada, or NHK in Japan. All these national systems are having to meet new competition, much of it originating with programmers outside their borders, and all are having to ask what their function should be as public servants in a multichannel marketplace.

Their officials recognize that the meaning of the public interest will change—indeed, must change—in a new communications environment in which viewers rather than programmers choose what to watch and when, and in which viewers may one day even produce and distribute programs themselves. There are few firm points of agreement on how this new communications environment should be structured or whom it should serve. My daughter Martha often reminds me that, particularly in the United States, the public is much more cynical and divided now than during the years of the Kennedy administration, when it was much easier to agree on the meaning of the public interest.

But everyone everywhere, even in 1995, can agree on one precept: the public interest requires us to put our children first. Left to the marketplace, children will receive either very bad service or none at all. Policymakers in every country know this is true because they have the example of American broadcast television to show them it is true. For that reason, all of them are working to make special provisions for children in their national communications policies.

Now, after sixty-one years of missed opportunities, Congress should seize the opportunity to do the same. In the midst of the current technological revolution, as we build a new communications capacity undreamed of in human history, Congress has a second chance to define what Americans mean by the public interest, a second chance to give meaning to the public interest as the information superhighway enters our lives.

Second chances are rare in life, and are often—as Samuel Johnson said of second marriages—a "triumph of hope over experience." But there should be little argument that if we are wisely to take advantage of our gift of a second chance, Congress should concentrate on children. The time to act is now, not later. Later will be too late. By not specifying what it meant by the public interest in the Communications Act of 1934, Congress gave license to a broadcast system that sees children not as human beings but as financial opportunities. It is a bad system, and many good men and women in television must be liberated from it. If we want to change it, we should not be deterred by false choices. The choice is not between free speech and the marketplace on the one hand, and governmental censorship and bureaucracy on the other. The choice is to serve the needs of children and use the opportunities presented by the superhighway in the digital age to enrich their lives. If we turn away from that choice, the consequences of our inaction will be even greater educational neglect, more craven and deceptive consumerism, and inappropriate levels of sex and violence—a wasteland vaster than anyone can imagine, or would care to. Let us do for our children today what we should have done long ago.

I am reminded of a story President Kennedy told a week before he was killed. The story was about French Marshal Louis-Hubert-Gonzalve Lyautey, who walked one morning through his garden with his gardener. He stopped at a certain point and asked the gardener to plant a tree there the next morning. The gardener said, "But the tree will not bloom for one hundred years." The Marshal looked at the gardener and replied, "In that case, you had better plant it this afternoon."

1 : Strangers in the House

Shall we just carelessly allow children to hear any casual tales which may be devised by casual persons, and to receive into their minds ideas for the most part the very opposite of those which we should wish them to have when they are grown up? —*Plato*

EVERY DAY, MILLIONS OF AMERICANS LEAVE THEIR CHILDREN IN the care of total strangers. Many do so reluctantly. Child care is hard to come by and they take what they can get. Fortunately, many of the strangers are good company. They know something about the needs of children, and are caring, even loving, in trying to meet them. But because the financial rewards for child care are few, these people rarely stay. Those who do stay usually neglect the children altogether. When they do pay attention, they hustle the children for money, bribing them with toys and candy. They bring guns to the house, and drugs, and they invite their friends over; sometimes they use the house for sexual liaisons. Often things get out of hand. Fights break out, and frequently someone gets hurt or killed.

Many parents eventually catch on. Some are horrified; some don't care. Amazingly, however, most accept the situation, believing it beyond their power to change. They may be right. Better care is expensive and hard to find, and the strangers, once there, refuse to leave. Like drug dealers on the corner, they control the life of the neighborhood, the home, and, increasingly, the lives of the children in their custody. Unlike drug dealers, they cannot be chased away or deterred: they claim a constitutional right to stay.

This is not a horror story from the tabloids. Nor, upon meeting the parents of these children, would most of us think them criminal, unfit, or even irresponsible. The fact is, if you own a television set, there is a good chance that this is *your* family, and these are *your* children. Every day, all across the United States, a parade of louts, losers, and con men whom most people would never allow in their homes enter anyway, through television. And every day the strangers spend more time with America's children than teachers do, or even in many cases the parents themselves. "If you came home and you found a strange man . . . teaching your kids to punch each other, or trying to sell them all kinds of products, you'd kick him right out of the house," says Yale psychology professor Jerome Singer. "But here you are; you come in and the TV is on, and you don't think twice about it."[1]

We should. Those strangers are raising and educating our children. They occupy a special place in our children's lives, as important for what they teach them as the family, the school, or the church is. By the time most American children begin first grade, they will have already spent the equivalent of three school years in the tutelage of the family television set. Between the ages of six and eighteen they will spend more time each week in front of that set than they will engaged in any other activity, whether schoolwork, playing, or talking with friends and family. For millions of them, television is not only the first but also the most enduring educational and social institution they will know. For those in unstable or abusive families, a television set may be the nearest thing to a parent they can hope for, providing whatever intellectual nourishment they are likely to get during the critical developmental period between birth and their sixth birthday. For millions of other children in loving families, whose lives are more stable, television still occupies more of their waking time than their parents do. Nearly 70 percent of the day-care facilities at which their parents leave them have a television on for several hours each day.[2]

In the 1930s and 1940s, television's creators expressed their hope that the new medium would be the greatest instrument of enlightenment ever invented, a blessing to future generations. They were wrong. Broadcasters and politicians have turned it instead into an instrument of child exploitation and abuse. In the American system, children are not primarily to be educated, nurtured, or even entertained; like everyone else, they are simply chattel to be rounded up and sold to advertisers. The Fox Children's Network, for example, boasts to advertisers that "we deliver more young viewers than anyone."[3] That is how American television works: the sponsors and advertisers are its real public; the viewers are the "product" it can "deliver"; and programs are merely the bait, the means to obtain the product. To lure children, television's main bait is cheaply produced and frequently aired cartoons, many of which look like advertisements and are: the success of these programs is determined not by who watches and likes them but by the revenues generated through the sale of merchandise related to them, from toys to breakfast cereals.* As a European broadcasting executive once observed to an American audience, "Your system trains children to be consumers; ours trains children to be citizens."

No other major democratic nation in the world has so willingly turned its children over to mercenary strangers this way. No other democratic nation has so willingly converted its children into markets for commercial gain and ignored their moral, intellectual, and social development. Psychologists and social scientists know both that this system does measurable harm and that, used wisely, television can do measurable good; teachers and parents know the

---

* Cynics often argue that where merchandising is concerned there is no difference between a program like *Mighty Morphin Power Rangers* and *Sesame Street*, which licenses toys, vitamins, and other products. The comparison is easy to make because it is so facile. *Mighty Morphin Power Rangers* exists to support a product, the success of which is measured in sales; *Sesame Street* products exist to support the program, the success of which is measured in educational research. To argue that the programs have the same purpose in merchandising is like comparing the fundraising goals of a PTA bake sale with the marketing strategy of RJR Nabisco.

same things from experience. But broadcasters know that the existing system makes money for them, and because it does they assert that it serves the public interest.

This belief—that the public interest can best be expressed in the language of dollars and cents—has been a part of American broadcast history since the 1920s and the earliest days of radio, as we shall see. But until very recently, that belief was balanced against another: that the public interest requires broadcasters actually to do good, to consider the needs of their listeners before their own. This is especially true where children are concerned, because while adults can take full responsibility for themselves, children typically cannot. They do not have the skills, resources, or knowledge to make the normal market mechanism related to consumer choice meaningful, which means that others—parents, educators, physicians, judges, librarians, and so on—must play a role in making meaningful choices for them.[4] Broadcasters, whose exclusive use of the public airwaves gives them unique access to children in their homes, until recently shared some of this moral and social obligation. It was only in the late 1970s that Congress and the Federal Communications Commission began to openly question this public-interest rationale and suggest that it infringed unreasonably on the First Amendment rights of the broadcast media. And it was only in the early 1980s that the FCC effectively jettisoned its public-interest mandate altogether, declaring that thereafter the market-place, with its preference for economic efficiency, would determine the public interest.*

Significantly, the FCC's decision was based less on economics than on the First Amendment. Too many of the public-interest regulations borne by broadcasters, the agency argued, unduly restricted their right to determine the content of their broadcasts; as a judge of the public interest, the market was more precise, less arbitrary, and far less intrusive. The market itself was imperfect, the commission acknowledged, but its failings were best remedied

---

* The FCC cannot overrule an act of Congress, of course, but it can interpret the 1934 Communications Act as it sees best. The only traditional public-interest requirement that the FCC has chosen to honor since the 1980s is that broadcasters air programs that concern issues in their local communities.

through market adjustments, not through government regulation of private broadcasters.

The effect of this argument, and of the FCC's decision, was to unleash competitive tensions in the television industry that had been held in check since the earliest days of broadcast radio in the 1920s. The new economic environment transformed all areas of television programming, none more so than news and children's programs, both of which had traditionally produced slim or even no profits and had depended instead on the broadcasters' own sense of public obligation and on regulatory attention. Children's programming, a focus of reform at the FCC throughout the 1970s, was dropped from the agency's list of concerns almost overnight. It was quickly overrun by toy and food companies eager to create programs that featured their products. News, educational programs, and other types of TV broadcasting for children virtually disappeared, re-placed by programs that commanded higher advertising rates. Many, such as *GI Joe*, were intended to sell toys, while others were intended primarily for adult audiences. Violence in children's pro-grams increased considerably; so, too, did the number and fre-quency of commercials.

A second effect of the FCC's marketplace theory was to turn the effort to reform children's television into a debate not about children and their needs but about the rights of broadcasters to make money. Whether this was intended or not, the meaning of free speech came to be measured exclusively in dollars. So exploitative did children's programming practices become as a result that in 1990 Congress passed the Children's Television Act, restoring time limits on com-mercials in children's programs and requiring broadcasters to air at least some "educational and informational" fare suitable for children. The act became law without the signature of President George Bush, who said it violated the First Amendment and that the market should determine what children see on television. Mak-ing the same argument, President Ronald Reagan had vetoed similar legislation in 1988. Broadcasters had objected to the Children's Television Act since it was first proposed in 1983. Testifying before Congress that year, National Association of Broadcasters senior vice president for research John Abel said, "The nation's broadcasters do not need the government to be their programming part-ner. The Commission's proposal is very intrusive in a sensitive First Amendment area."[5] By the time the law was finally enacted in 1990, the NAB had succeeded in greatly weakening it, so much so that broadcasters paid it little mind.

Then, in November 1992, the Center for Media Education in Washington, D.C., an organization that monitors children's pro-gramming practices, reported that dozens of broadcasters around the country had listed in their FCC filings thirty-year-old reruns of cheerful commercial programs like *Yogi Bear* and *The Jetsons*, or afternoon talk shows, as the "educational and informational" com-ponent of their children's programming. The center's study, which quoted some of the artful descriptions that broadcasters had used to justify these listings, led the commission to announce that it would begin scrutinizing broadcasters' compliance with the law more closely.[6] Many broadcasters, led by *Broadcasting and Cable*, complained that all this violated the First Amendment. Later, when the Center for Media Education urged Congress to *require* one hour of educational programming a day in time periods when children are watching, the Media Institute, a think tank in Washington, D.C., complained, "The Children's Television Act represents an attempt by government to coerce video publishers to offer up a certain class of government approved programming . . . Endorsing certain pro-grams and discrediting others are clear examples of forbidden gov-ernment conduct."[7]

At about the same time, Congress began to give new attention to the question of whether television did children actual harm. In the winter of 1993, Illinois senator Paul Simon and Massachusetts representative Edward Markey opened hearings on the subject of television violence and its effects on children. Senator Simon led the initiative; in 1990 he had persuaded Congress to offer the major broadcast networks a three-year reprieve from the antitrust laws so that they could together discuss television violence, but he was disappointed, since the networks had failed to so much as acknowl-edge the issue in the first two years of his reprieve. The hearings drew enormous press attention, bringing together top executives from the broadcasting and entertainment industries in New York and Hollywood, leading social scientists, pediatricians, parents, and many others. But the hearings seemed to have virtually no effect on the networks' nightly schedules, particularly during the so-called sweeps periods, when broadcasters seek the highest audiences possible as a benchmark for establishing advertising rates. In the midst of the hearings, for example, ABC aired a two-evening special movie called *Murder in the Heartland*, about Nebraska mass murderer Charles Starkweather—a montage of shotgun blasts and bloodied victims that was followed in many television markets with local news items about the killer, his crimes, and his 1959 execution.

In June 1993 the three major broadcast networks announced that they would begin labeling programs for their violent content, which would give a warning to parents that certain shows were not children's fare. By August, when a nationally televised "summit meeting" convened in Hollywood to discuss television violence, the Fox Television Network, the Turner Broadcasting System, and several independent broadcasters had said that they, too, would begin labeling violent programs. Several cable programmers, many of whom, like Home Box Office and Showtime, had always preceded the showing of feature films and special programs with some type of content rating, also clarified their policies with respect to parental advisories.

These labeling plans were greeted with skepticism by children's advocates, who argued that labels alone might make matters worse. Labels would work, they argued, only if augmented by some sort of computer chip built into the television set that would allow parents actually to screen out the shows they found offensive. This suggestion for what were soon known as "v-chips" was derided by entertainment executives, many of whom argued that the labeling system itself had been "coerced" and that, used in conjunction with a screening chip, it would be unconstitutional. CBS president Howard Stringer said, "A chip for violence might be followed with a chip . . . for political correctness, soon, chips with everything. Without care, the chip could be the curse of the First Amendment."[8]

Sensing the depth of public frustration, Congress refused to drop the issue and by late 1993 was considering several bills, any one of which, Attorney General Janet Reno told a congressional committee, would meet constitutional muster. Almost immediately every major newspaper in the United States published an editorial rebuking the Attorney General, agreeing implicitly, if not explicitly, with the television industry's defense that *any* congressional action to curb television violence—even keeping records and reporting publicly on the issue—was censorship. Most opined, as the *Chicago Tribune* did, that Reno had prescribed "a dangerous cure for TV violence." *The New York Times* warned against "Janet Reno's heavy hand," while in *USA Today* former NBC News president Michael Gartner charged that Reno was "playing with fire."[9] *Entertainment Weekly*, under the headline "Reno and Butt-Head," juxtaposed the Attorney General with a moronic adolescent cartoon character, and quoted a television producer complaining that

> the violence debate is old, and the real debate was debated when they wrote the Constitution, goddamit! They want to tell us what we can see. To violate the perfect music of the Constitution to put a f–ing Band-Aid on a problem and divert our attention is a f–ing sin. If Thomas Jefferson were alive, he would walk into Senator Simon's office and kick his ass.[10]

Anyone familiar with Jefferson's musings about the press might come to a different conclusion about where, if consulted on the matter, he might plant his foot. Similarly, anyone familiar with what Jefferson considered his greatest legacy—the founding of the University of Virginia—might think differently about the First Amendment implications of asking broadcasters to air an hour each day of educational programming for children.

But in this day and age, it seems, we can think none of these things. Unwittingly, perhaps, too many Americans acquiesce in the view of the commercial interests who control television and who take the First Amendment to mean that our children are stuck with the strangers whose only desire is to exploit them, and that their parents, teachers, and public officials are forbidden from trying to protect them or even from offering them something better. In 1992, for example, when a Texas dentist, Richard Neill, organized a campaign to draw attention to the fact that *Donahue* and other television talk shows aired in afternoon time slots when many children were watching, he was ridiculed for his effort. According to Neill, about 5 percent of *Donahue*'s audience were children, 400,000 nationwide, and he targeted Phil Donahue because, he said, his was one of the best talk shows, and Donahue was in a position to set an example for the rest. Most talk shows, the dentist accurately noted, were out-and-out freak shows, and he wanted to know why they couldn't air at night, when far fewer children would be likely to see them. In response, Phil Donahue called Neill—who had acknowledged being a religious man—a censor and a zealot. Later, when pressed by CBS News reporter Dan Rather, Donahue asked rhetorically, "What kind of country do we want?"[11]

That *is* the question, all right. The answer, apparently, is a country in which a television set is a device whose only purpose is to sell things, and where anything that impedes that goal—even self-regulation—is said to violate the First Amendment. When Senator Simon urged the television industry to regulate itself by creating an "advisory office on television violence" to report to the public, Geoffrey Cowan, a producer and board member of the National Council for Families and Television, reportedly objected that the proposal was tantamount to censorship.[12]

It used to be that broadcasters told parents to turn their sets off if they didn't like the programs; now even that recourse is suspect, with commerce pushing us to accept the link between money and free speech. In November 1992, when a group of women organized a national Turn Off the TV Day, Peter Chrisanthopoulos, president of the Network Television Association (which represents ABC, CBS, and NBC), said: "Viewers should express their opinions and act accordingly, but participating in national boycotts is an infringement on the network's First Amendment rights."[13] It is richly ironic that the networks, having long insisted that a parent's only constitutional recourse was to turn off the set, now view even that act as unconstitutional. Several months later, Motion Picture Association of America president Jack Valenti objected to the installation of v-chips in television sets: "I'm opposed to a single button that can block out a whole program day or a single program week. That is not parental responsibility."[14] Isn't it? So long as a parent controls the on-off switch, does it really matter where it is? If the v-chip is unconstitutional, so is a remote-control device—and so, too, are parents who control what their children watch.

If we truly believe that the entertainment industry should have unrestricted access to our children, that neither government nor parents themselves have a duty or the right to intercede on their behalf, then we have converted the First Amendment from a sword of freedom into a shackle of bondage. We have used it to abandon our children in a wasteland and to trap them there, without any opportunity to escape; we have used it to make economic opportunities out of human beings. To paraphrase Phil Donahue, is this the kind of country we want?

When the Federal Communications Commission launched into full-force deregulation in the 1980s, even some proponents of the move wondered if its enthusiasm for market forces wasn't a bit overblown. An August 1985 cover of *Business Week*, for example, asked, "Has the FCC Gone Too Far?" Certainly many people thought so when, in 1983, Chairman Mark Fowler dismissed criticism of its policies by declaring that a television set was nothing more than a "toaster with pictures."

The analogy struck virtually everyone with any knowledge about television's role in American society and throughout the world as ill-considered and uncaring. But Fowler had inadvertently put his finger on American television's greatest failing: no thinking adult would leave a small child unattended to play with a plugged-in toaster for hours on end—to do so would be reckless and irresponsible, if not criminal. Yet because we have neglected to take seriously the implications of the Communications Act's "public interest" requirement, leaving an unattended child in the company of a television set is just as dangerous.

Television is the most violent part of a nation that is itself the most violent country in the developed world. Every year in the United States there are more than 1.9 million violent crimes and more than 20,000 homicides. Someone is murdered in the United States every twenty-two minutes. These are the numbers that television executives like to quote when they say that the violence on the screen mirrors the violence in real life. But it doesn't. The simple arithmetic is this: in a country of more than 250 million people, an American's chance of being a victim of violent crime is statistically very small; by comparison, a random walk through prime-time television reveals a world in which almost half the characters are either victims or perpetrators of violent crimes (the percentage comes from research by George Gerbner at the University of Pennsylvania); in children's programs, the percentage rises to 79 percent. Critics complain that these percentages are grossly inflated by narrow definitions of violence that include everything from pie-in-the-face jokes to news programming. But even a generous allowance for such narrowness still leaves the world of television an exaggeratedly brutal place. In one eighteen-hour period in April 1992, for example, the Center for Media and Public Affairs monitored ten broadcast and cable channels in Washington, D.C., and counted 1,846 violent scenes, 175 of which resulted in a fatality.[15] If only half of the latter group—87 or 88 scenes—were homicides, that would give television a murder rate of one every twelve minutes, almost twice the rate of real murder. Most important of all is that this statistical comparison greatly understates the point: television homicides, unlike those on the street, are witnessed by hundreds of millions of people, among them, every weekday night, about 13 million children.[16] Even in a nation where a gun can be found in every other home, television's portrayal of violence is so skewed as to have made a norm out of the extreme, the sensational, and the improbable. Through television, Americans have created a cosmology of terror that overshadows reality itself.

So routinely do Americans accept television's version of their lives that on January 18, 1993, when seventeen-year-old Gary Scott Pennington walked into his high-school English class in Grayson, Kentucky, and fired a .38-caliber bullet into his teacher's forehead, killing her, one of the students who witnessed the murder remembered thinking, "This isn't supposed to happen. This must be MTV."[17] Must be. The average student in Gary's senior class had already seen 18,000 murders on television. The average student in the class had spent between 15,000 and 20,000 hours watching television, compared with 11,000 in school; every year the average American child watches more than a thousand stylized and explicit rapes, murders, armed robberies, and assaults on television.[18]

Small wonder that countless studies and reviews over the past decades have argued that there *is* a link between aggressive behavior and exposure to television violence. Small wonder that the Surgeon General in 1972, the National Institute of Mental Health in 1982, and the American Psychological Association in 1992 have all said such a link exists. Broadcasters like to say that these studies don't prove anything, and in one respect they're right. Social science is not in the proof business, but in the business of identifying relationships and measuring their significance, strength, and direction. Where television violence is concerned, social science relies on several methods of testing the relationships, ranging from simple laboratory experiments to thirty-year studies of people's lives that take into account all the factors—family income, education, family cohesion—that contribute to social violence. Virtually all this research has been done in the studies of television, and all of them consistently show that television violence contributes to real violence, and to a pervasive sense of fear.

The most famous of these studies is the 1972 Surgeon General's report *Television and Growing Up: The Impact of Televised Violence*.[19] The report had its roots in earlier congressional inquiries into social violence, in 1961 and again in 1964, and in the Kerner Commission, convened by President Lyndon B. Johnson to examine the root causes of unrest in a nation that had borne witness to three major political assassinations and disastrous urban riots. As part of its work, the commission established a task force to study media violence. The task force drew the attention of Rhode Island senator John Pastore, then chairman of the Senate Subcommittee on Communications, who wanted a definitive answer to the question of whether violence on television affected behavior. In 1969 Pastore directed the Surgeon General to look into the matter and to report the following year.

Broadcasters immediately saw the project as a threat and moved to cripple whatever results it might present. They did so by challenging the credentials of seven of the distinguished social scientists who were selected to the project's advisory committee, and by eventually installing on the board five additional members to their own liking, some of whom were, or had once been, employed by the networks. The move angered many social scientists, who thought it damaged the project's credibility, but the work went forward anyway. The research included twenty-three different studies based on laboratory experiments, field research, and organizational and institutional studies and surveys; and the final report, completed on December 31, 1971, greatly increased what we then knew about children and television. Despite fears that special interests would compromise the findings, the report stated unequivocally that there was a causal relationship between aggressive behavior and watching violence on television.

That was not, however, what the public learned. In one of his few errors in a distinguished reporting career, *New York Times* television writer Jack Gould, who had obtained a copy of the report's final chapter (which almost certainly came from a source friendly to the networks), overlooked its central conclusion and misinterpreted the rest. Gould reported, in a front-page story, that the "Surgeon General has found that violence in television programming does not have an adverse effect on the majority of the nation's youth, but may influence small groups of youngsters predisposed by many factors to aggressive behavior."[20] Compounding the error, the headline read: "TV Violence Held Unharmful to Youth."

Gould's report caused a furor among many members of the Surgeon General's Advisory Committee, as well as among members of Congress and academia who labeled the report a "whitewash." Despite subsequent news conferences in which Surgeon General Jesse Steinfeld declared that the study showed "for the first time a causal connection between violence shown on television and subsequent behavior by children,"[21] the damage was done. Gould's report set the tone for the majority of media reports around the country, not the least one which appeared in the industry trade magazine *Broadcasting*. "A blue ribbon committee of social scientists has concluded that there is no causal relationship between television programs that depict violence and aggressive behavior by the majority of children," the magazine reported.[22]

So distorted was coverage of the Surgeon General's report, and so acrimonious the ensuing debate about it, that Senator Pastore convened hearings to review the research and the findings. Pastore called to testify virtually all the researchers whose work comprised the report, and eventually established that, indeed, they had found television violence a cause for serious public concern. Ithiel de Sola Pool, a political scientist, summarized the report for Senator Pastore in one sentence: "Twelve scientists of widely different views unanimously agreed that scientific evidence indicates that the viewing of television violence by young people causes them to behave more aggressively."[23] The networks' own researchers concurred, and, pressed by Senator Pastore, the television executives who testified did also.

Nothing happened. In 1974, the communications scholar Douglass Cater reviewed the background of the Surgeon General's report, its findings, and the controversy that swirled around them:

That was the high-water mark. At the time of this writing—two years since those initial hearings—there has been less than persuasive evidence that the commitments given to Pastore have been met with alacrity. Violence on the television screen . . . has continued at a high level. Violent incidents on prime time and Saturday morning programs maintain a rate of more than twice the British rate, which is itself padded with American imports . . . The FCC has not yet dealt with the issue of violence in children's programming. Thus promise *still* lies ahead.[24]

It *still* does. The greatest legacy of the Surgeon General's report has probably been the doubt sown by Jack Gould's report in *The New York Times*. Their admissions before Congress notwithstanding, television executives have challenged every subsequent report with the refrain that the connections between viewing television violence and behavior are tenuous at best and, in any case, prove nothing. Their denials, and even many of their counterarguments, are similar to those made by cigarette-industry executives who refuse to acknowledge the connection between smoking and heart and respiratory diseases.

Where television and entertainment people do admit connections, they simultaneously debunk them. Society's ills cannot be laid at television's door, they say, certainly not in a country where guns are emblematic of freedom, where vast disparities of income exist, as well as of educational and economic opportunity, where divisions of race and ethnicity have caused violence for two hundred years, where more families fall apart than stay together. "TV is not the sole culprit," says Jack Valenti. "You cannot press a button and make your child immune to watching his school kid friends pack a .357 Magnum to school. You can't press a button and keep your child from knowing that there is drug dealing and drugs around the neighborhood. You can't press a button and repair broken homes, . . . and you can't press a button and tell your child not to succumb to peer pressure."[25]

All this is patently true, but arguing that any one action is the key to ending violence makes a mockery of moral responsibility. Here is the communications professor George Gerbner, who has been monitoring television violence for two decades:

> We're dealing with a syndrome to which there are many contributing factors. We happen to be talking about just one of them, but let us not assume it's the only one, or, under all circumstances, the primary one. To make it the only one is, I agree, an evasion of our responsibility for the condition of our cities. Equally harmful is to say that it makes no contribution . . . But the notion that, sure, there is violence in fairy tales, there is violence in Shakespeare, and therefore we shouldn't be concerned about it, is a powerfully misleading notion.[26]

Misleading indeed. Brandon Tartikoff, former president of NBC, says, "I definitely think moving images influence behavior. In television, I had different views than the social scientists my network was hiring from places like Yale to provide data that violence on TV does not lead to acts of violence. TV is basically funded by commercials, and most commercials work through imitative behavior. They show somebody drinking a cup of hot coffee, saying, 'Mmmm.' They expect you to go out and buy Yuban."[27]

The movie producer Lawrence Gordon, whose credits include *Die Hard, 48 Hours,* and *Field of Dreams,* discovered the connection between entertainment and behavior when teenage viewers of his 1979 film about street gangs, *The Warriors*, left theaters and tore into each other; nationwide, three killings were attributed to the film. "I'd be lying if I said that people don't imitate what they see on the screen," Gordon says. "I would be a moron to say they don't, because look how dress styles change. We have people who want to look like Julia Roberts and Michelle Pfeiffer and Madonna. Of course we imitate. It would be impossible for me to think they would imitate our dress, our music, our look, but not imitate any of our violence or our other actions."[28]

Like all media, television is a teacher. But television is a more powerful teacher than most, and its principal pupils are very young children. Today, in most American homes, children aged two to eleven watch television for twenty-two hours a week; teenagers watch about the same, about twenty-three hours a week.[29] This means that most children spend more time each week watching television than doing anything else except sleeping. For black and Hispanic children, regardless of their families' income levels, these numbers are even higher; and for poor children, who typically have few alternative activities, the numbers go higher still.[30]

Over the last two decades the level of violence on broadcast television has been fairly steady, with twenty to twenty-five violent acts per hour in children's programs compared to about five to six violent acts per hour in prime time.[31] What *has* changed, as anyone who watches television knows, is that television violence is far more graphic now, and far more likely to be sexual. A lot of the violence children see occurs in adult programs, but, amazingly, most of it is in material created specifically for them, in cartoons and animated features. The National Institute of Mental Health reported a decade ago that more than 80 percent of children's programs contain some sort of violent act.[32] Researchers typically define an "act of violence" as, for example, "an overt physical action that hurts or kills, or threatens to do so."[33]

Yet television executives go on ridiculing these definitions and their implication that *Road Runner* or the *Teenage Mutant Ninja Turtles* teaches violence. At a 1994 conference, USA Network president Kay Koplovitz said flatly, "I don't believe it." Why not? Anyone who has seen a young child enthralled by *Barney and Friends* or *Mister Rogers' Neighborhood* should know that children perceive television quite differently than adults do. Why is it so hard to believe that children who learn well from simplified, exaggerated presentations can also learn from graphic depictions of violence?* Indeed, it may be that the violent messages which television sends to the very young, however innocuous they may appear to adults, are the most damaging in the long run. As the researcher Brandon Centerwall writes:

> The average American preschooler watches more than 27 hours of television per week. This might not be bad if these young children understood what they were watching, but they don't. Up through ages three and four, most children are unable to distinguish fact from fantasy on TV, and remain unable to do so despite adult coaching. In the minds of young children, television is a source of entirely factual information regarding how the world works. There are no limits to their credulity. To cite one example, an Indiana school board had to issue an advisory to young children that, no, there is no such thing as Teenage Mutant Ninja Turtles. Children had been crawling down storm drains looking for them.
>
> Naturally, as children get older, they come to know better, but their earliest and deepest impressions are laid down at an age when they still see television as a factual source of information about the outside world. In that world, it seems, violence is common and the commission of violence is generally powerful, exciting, charismatic and effective. In later life, serious violence is most likely to erupt at moments of severe stress—and it is precisely at such moments that adolescents and adults are most likely to revert to their earliest, most visceral sense of the role of violence in society and in personal behavior. Much of this sense will have come from television.[34]

Centerwall's comments added spark to the congressional inquiries held during the summer of 1993, for they received enormous press attention, mostly because of the data he had gathered in

---

* Sadly, many adults cannot bring themselves to tolerate, much less appreciate, the one or two quality children's programs on television that are made *only* for children, without adults in mind at all. In the last two years, "Barney," friend to millions of preschoolers, has been the target of hate columns in the national press, including at least one, on *The Wall Street Journal* editorial page, that pictured the purple dinosaur in the crosshairs of a rifle scope. That same day, on the same page, the *Journal* featured an unsigned column on the breakdown of "simple decency" and "civility" in public life.

remote towns in the United States and Canada that, for technical reasons, did not receive television signals until the mid-1970s, long after everyone else. In each of these towns, Centerwall discovered, the introduction of television was followed by an increase in aggressiveness among boys. Was there, he wondered, a connection? He tested the hypothesis by comparing the homicide rates of the United States and Canada with those of South Africa, which did not get television until 1975. After controlling for factors such as economic growth, alcohol consumption, and firearm availability, Centerwall found that the homicide rates in the United States and Canada rose by more than 90 percent between 1945 (about the time television was introduced in those countries) and 1974, while over the same period homicide rates among white South Africans declined by 7 percent.

But even many who admired Centerwall's argument often missed his most compelling point. Responding to research done by NBC that showed screen violence to be only "modestly" related to violent behavior, affecting only about 5 percent of 2,400 children in a three-year study, Centerwall observed that such a seemingly small effect is actually quite significant:

> It is an intrinsic property of such "bell curve" distributions that small changes in the average imply major changes at the extremes. Thus if exposure to television causes 8 percent of the population to shift from below-average aggression to above-average aggression, it follows that the homicide rate will double. The findings of the NBC study and the doubling of the homicide rate are two sides of the same coin.[35]

In other words, the effects of violence can have exponential consequences. The issue is not, as Sam Donaldson once asked, whether people "watch movies, then grab their guns and go out to do mayhem"—the proverbial straw man raised by the industry—but whether the totality of depictions creates a climate that fosters violence in general. It's like dropping a stone into the calm surface of a large pond: suddenly the water is not so still anymore.

The entertainment industry observes, correctly, that the water was never still. Its business—as with journalism, as with literature, as with all art—is to create, to stimulate, if necessary to provoke, to shock, or even to offend. Creators in every age are scorned for their assault on common wisdoms and prevailing sensibilities, and one of their tools has always been violence. From *Medusa* to *Hamlet*, from Herman Melville to Alice Walker, violence has been a major component of dramatic storytelling.

Children's stories are not, nor have they ever been, immune from this. In his classic book *The Uses of Enchantment*, the psychologist Bruno Bettelheim noted that many fairy tales and nursery rhymes we all know from childhood are in fact terrifying, and were meant to be. Primeval stories of murdering witches, cannibalistic giants, and monsters of more common appearance and demeanor have regularly been told to young children to alert them to the many moral and physical dangers that lurk in the world.

What is more, children invent their own macabre tales with which to make sense of reality. When children recite "Ring around the rosey, . . . ashes, ashes, all fall down," they are playing a game that dates from the Middle Ages, when the plague devastated Europe; and when the children fall down, it's because they're supposed to be dead. Today, psychologists know, inner-city children go out on the school blacktop at lunchtime and play drive-by shooting. Children see their world very well and, through acting it out, make sense of it. Why, people ask, should television be held to some higher standard? After all, the charge that television harms children is strikingly reminiscent of the charges made against dime novels and the penny press in the nineteenth century, and in the twentieth against the cinema, comic books—any new medium. They are the same charges leveled against dozens of children's titles on the American Library Association's list of most-censored books.

There are several answers to this question. An obvious point that we shall explore more deeply in Chapters 2 and 3 is that broadcasters are licensed to serve the public interest and have a statutory obligation to do better. But apart from the black-letter requirements of the law, an important answer has to do with the nature of stories—and of television. The tradition of oral and written storytelling embodied in both fairy tales and modern children's literature developed in the service of children's moral education, and its lessons helped to define the boundaries between childhood and adult-hood. In traditional settings, violence was but *one* possible outcome of conflict, not the only one or even the primary one. Moreover, stories that included violence surrounded it with meanings created by adults for instructing children, not by adults for entertaining adults.

In the Middle Ages, before most people could read, there was no clear distinction between childhood and adulthood; such as there was fell at about age seven, when a child's knowledge of the world was deemed to be roughly equal to that of most adults. The invention of the printing press changed people's perceptions of childhood by greatly extending the reach of adult literacy and, simultaneously, the range of knowledge separating children from adults. In fact, widespread adult literacy gave rise to the very concept of childhood, and to the corresponding idea that children are possessed of special rights and protections owing to their innocence and ignorance.[36]

Television changed all that. Unlike the theater and cinema, it comes directly into the home, and unlike printed stories, its tales are not cautionary ones or moral lessons but commercial products whose purposes are hidden from small children. Unlike any print medium, television's stories are accessible to any child, no matter how young, physically and emotionally dependent, or illiterate. In fact, television establishes a new standard of visual literacy, which requires none of the intellectual or reasoning skills necessary to understanding print, but merely eyes to see.[37]

Indeed, what print literacy accomplished over the course of several centuries television obliterated within a decade. Between 1950 and 1960 television dropped the veil from the adult world, making available to children many of the experiences and knowledge theretofore available only to adults. In so doing, television also served to undermine the authority of the adult world—government, schools, church, parents—to lay down the rules of social behavior. Through television, even the smallest children could see men blown apart on a battlefield a world away; they could witness real and fictional murders, riots, wars, and natural disasters. They could watch cartoon characters shoved through keyholes, thrown off cliffs, run over by trucks, ripped through with buckshot. Anything that adults could see, they could see, too. What might once have been judged inappropriate for a thirteen-year-old, television made available to toddlers not yet able to speak. And for most children, whose frame of reference is smaller than an adult's, the statistical and physical aberrations appearing on television became the norm. A television set became, literally, a child's window on the world.

In most democratic countries, television's exceptional power to breach the boundaries of childhood has suggested caution or, at the very least, called for some distinctions to be made about what is appropriate television material for children. Those distinctions do not—and obviously cannot—deter children from watching programs intended for adults. But other nations have taken the precaution of limiting programs with patently adult subject matter to airtimes when children are least likely to see them, such as late at night. Yet in the United States most television and entertainment executives insist that no such distinction can be made. Even if it could, they say, for the government to act on it—or for the entertainment industry itself to act on it—would be unconstitutional.

Their response is not rhetorical. Federal courts have, at various times and in various ways, struck down plans to move adult programs to late night or, more remarkably, to have family-friendly programs air at times when children are known to predominate in the audience. Some of television's most bizarre and grotesque fare now appears in the early morning and late afternoon, when children make up a significant part of the audience.[38] In May 1993, for example, the electronic political newsletter *Hotline* monitored four days of television programs during the morning, afternoon, and early evening hours, time periods during which more than 10 million children ages two to eleven—28 percent of all the nation's children—are watching television. This is what it found:

Donahue: Virtual reality and sex; and a California man who sued his female boss for sexual harassment.

Geraldo: Abusive husbands; parents who run an escort service and their kids who help out; fathers who steal their sons' girlfriends; and child-killing cults, for which a former Branch Davidian member explained "ritual child abuse and brainwashing."

Jenny Jones: A stepmother and stepson who want to get married; friends who fight over the same man; Amy Fisher's alleged jailhouse lesbian lover; Amy's alleged heterosexual lover; and the author of "Lethal Lolita."

Oprah: A mother who was upset that her four children were gay; a couple accused of killing their children; men and women who have been stalked by obsessive ex-mates are joined by a stalker; women whose babies have been stolen and sold.

The Maury Povich Show: Tom Arnold tells "why he repressed memories of sexual abuse by his babysitter"; the alleged mistress of a Dallas minister who was charged with the attempted murder of his wife; people who keep their marriages secret so they can keep their health benefits.

Sally [Jessy Raphael]: Men raising children from their wives' extramarital affairs; a 10-year-old girl with a 38C bust; and an imprisoned man who killed his 2-year-old daughter while trying to convert his brother to his religion.

The Joan Rivers Show: high-profile murderers such as Jeffrey Dahmer and Robert Chambers.

The Jerry Springer Show: Women who have affairs with relatives; a male prison inmate undergoing a sex change operation who wants to be put in a women's jail; parents of missing children; a white woman who confronts the father who tried to kill her husband because he was black.

The Montel Williams Show: The swimsuit edition; parents who take their kids to strip joints; women who steal other women's men; women who pamper and spoil their men.

A Current Affair: A mom who wants to divorce her kids; an update on the killing of a boy after a Little League game; the ex-wife of Houston Oiler quarterback Dan Pastorini, who claims he is a deadbeat dad; a woman who recorded her own death at the hands of a stalker; a sex scandal at Northeast High in Pasadena, California; and a man who used hidden video cameras to look up women's skirts at shopping malls.

Hard Copy: A hidden camera in the dressing room of a New York strip club; following a cab driver through "Hollywood's hidden world of sex and sin"; an interview with Rhonda Spear, the "bimbette" host of USA Network's "Up All Night," about the Hollywood casting couch; Shannen Doherty's boyfriend alleging she beat him; and an aspiring artist who became a stripper and was later murdered.

Inside Edition: A divorce lawyer who bilks clients; Arnold Schwarzenegger's pre-stardom interview on an x-rated cable show; "millionaire athletes on the rampage"; and an update on a high school girl who killed her boyfriend but isn't going to jail.[39]

Small wonder that 80 percent of Americans think television is harmful to society and especially to children.[40] "Where was I," wrote one mother to the *Chicago Tribune*, "when they allowed the kind of language on TV that you now hear all the time? Was 'bitch,' 'slut,' 'bastard,' 'hell,' 'dammit,' 'ass' always allowed on prime-time TV, and I just didn't notice? Or has it just come along in the last few years? I just want to know, when did American standards become so low?"[41]

Some people maintain that television's standards have become not low but different and more varied thanks largely to the growth of cable. And they suggest that with channels like CNN, C-SPAN, A&E, Discovery, Disney, the Learning Channel, and Nickelodeon and with public-minded services like Cable in the Classroom, television is also *better* than it once was, notably for children. But even where these networks offer exemplary original programs for children, as many do, the children who most need their benefit are the least likely to see them: poor families cannot afford cable, and cable companies often do not want to wire poor neighborhoods.[42] Anyone who has cable can quickly see the consequences of that fact by conducting a simple test: watch only broadcast channels for a week. Were it not for public television, children's television would be a vaster wasteland than ever. In 1993, of the twenty children's shows that *TV Guide* ranked as the best for children under twelve, eight were available only on cable, and therefore unseen by as many as half of our children; eight aired on PBS; only four were commercial broadcast offerings.[43] It may be that more cable services will come on-line in the future and that some will serve children, but that is only a hope. The introduction of new cable services has slowed because of still-limited channel capacity on many systems, and also because the services that once ate into broadcast television's audiences are now beginning to compete with one another: many new cable services are either spin-offs of existing ones or are pay-per-view or home-shopping services that give cable operators access to new sources of revenue. The only new service created for children in the past two years was the Turner Network's Cartoon Channel.

Finally, there is a dark side to the explosion of cable and new interactive televisual media. Videotapes, cable television, and video games have not only increased the amount of violence children are exposed to but changed the nature of the violence they see. Sexual violence, for example, long an accepted staple of Hollywood films, is now common in video games, in "slasher films" available at video rental stores, in cable movies and music videos.[44] In response to these new forms of competition, broadcasters have increasingly made sexual violence part of their own repertoire. It is no longer uncommon, for example, to see rape dramatized on prime-time network television—accompanied, of course, with a brief warning to viewers. For many young people these media products will provide their first encounter with sexual material.

There was a very brief time when in its pursuit of profits television treated children quite differently. In what we now think of as television's golden age, high-quality children's programs were among the most distinctive features of the new medium, and a television set was seen as an agent of family unity, a great leap forward over that home-wrecker radio. In the words of one writer in a 1948 issue of *Parents Magazine*: "With practically every room having a radio, it was not uncommon for all to scatter to enjoy particular programs. With the one television set, our family is brought together as a unit for a while after dinner."[45]

It was largely on this theme—television as a uniquely family-friendly medium, of special benefit to children—that the Radio Corporation of America (RCA) and other manufacturers using its patents promoted the purchase of television sets as an essential consumer appliance in the years after World War II. Television would rekindle a world of domestic love and affection, the ads suggested, allowing married couples to spend more time together and keep their kids off the street.[46] In the mid-1950s, the scholar Mary Ann Watson has written, "the function of network programming was not only to deliver audiences to advertisers, but also, perhaps more important, to encourage the sale of TV receivers to the public. Since families with children in the household were more likely to purchase television sets, they were targeted for incentive."[47]

Programmers did their part to promote the new "family" television by offering a range of different children's shows that, whatever else could be said of them, featured an originality and variety that has not been seen since on broadcast television. "In the attempts to establish the new medium and build its audience," writes one historian, "programmers borrowed heavily from all idioms of entertainment, including those established in radio, film and literature to fill the void. Although chronically underfunded, the children's television of the 1950s was therefore diverse in program offerings and experimental in approach."[48] Taking careful note of the advice given to parents by everyone from Dr. Spock to *Reader's Digest*, broadcasters made programs like *Ding Dong School*, *Captain Kangaroo*, *Howdy Doody*, *Lucky Pup*, *Time for Beany*, and *Kukla, Fran and Ollie* children's standards. In 1951 the networks' weekly schedules included twenty-seven hours of such programs, most of them broadcast after school and in the early evening. Local broadcasters developed their own children's shows, many of them designed to promote some activity or another. Popular formats included puppet shows and drawing shows, the latter featuring artists who either drew a story or encouraged young viewers to submit their own.

Some of these programs were unabashedly commercial. For one drawing program, for example, you needed a clear plastic mat that adhered to the television set and on which the child could draw along with the artist. Parents had to buy the mat, of course, and the show's host made it clear that without it one couldn't enjoy the program. But some of the more patently commercial programs were also among the best. Walt Disney Company's *Disneyland*, for example, which debuted in 1954, and its *Mickey Mouse Club* (1955), both served to promote Walt Disney's California theme park and a host of tie-in products. Both are also among the best-known and best-remembered regularly scheduled children's programs of all time. *Disneyland* won both a Peabody Award (for its educational value) and an Emmy Award, and *The Mickey Mouse Club* focused on a complement of prosocial themes.

Yet even then, television's influence on children was a matter of growing concern. In the advice literature of the period, writes the communications scholar Lynn Spigel, "mass media became a central focus of concern as the experts told parents how to control and regulate media in ways that promoted family values." Women's magazines like *Better Homes and Gardens* and *Ladies' Home Journal* warned parents that television could turn their children into passive television "addicts," and that this addiction "would reverse good habits of hygiene, nutrition and decorum, causing physical, mental and social disorders."[49]

Taking heed, the National Association of Broadcasters issued a standards and practices code for television in 1952—a code that would remain more or less intact for thirty years—and included in it an entire section on children's programming:

> Television and all who participate in it are jointly accountable to the American public for respect for the special needs of children, for community responsibility, for the advancement of education and culture, for the acceptability of the program materials chosen, for decency and decorum in production, and for propriety in advertising. This responsibility . . . can be discharged only through the highest standards of respect for the American home, applied to every moment of every program presented by television.

Congress was not dissuaded by the code, however, and in 1954 Tennessee senator Estes Kefauver, chairman of the Subcommittee on Juvenile Delinquency, opened hearings to examine the supposed connection between behavior and the images in all the mass media, from comic books to television. Worried about children's exposure to "crime and horror, sadism and sex," Kefauver raised the issue of television violence to a level of public concern that has never abated. There are two related reasons for this: since 1954 the networks have regularly promised to reduce the level of violence on television and have not; and Congress has repeatedly chosen merely to toy with the issue rather than to act on it. The American "debate" over children and television has thus been something of a traveling circus, reappearing every few years, preceded by grand pronouncements and followed by meaningless gestures.

To most democratic governments—in Britain, Australia, Sweden, and Japan, to name a few—television's exceptional power to affect children has suggested not just caution but possibilities. If television could show the worst of life, it could also show the best. If it could show children death and destruction, it could also show them truth and beauty, art and culture. That realization has led other nations to establish organizations with special responsibilities for children's programs and funding mechanisms with which to pay for them.

In England, for example, the publicly financed British Broadcasting Corporation airs about 840 hours of children's programs every year, slightly more than 12 percent of the BBC's entire television schedule. Only about a quarter of these are reruns, and they include programs to suit children from preschool age to the early teens. American public broadcasting, by contrast, carries fewer than 200 hours of children's programs each year and must rely heavily on reruns;[50] of the American commercial networks, only Fox features regularly scheduled weekday children's programs, and they are mostly cartoons, many of them, like *X-Men*, designed to sell toys.

Sweden also gives about 12 percent of its broadcast time to children, and also features programs for adults *about* children, their nature, and needs. Australia, which for years left children's programs to the marketplace, decided in the 1970s that the market had failed and created the Australian Children's Television Foundation, a nonprofit production center that creates programs and, through the secondary sale of its programs and program-related products, is largely self-supporting. In Japan, the public broadcasting giant NHK invests heavily in children's programs, some of them produced specifically for children who may be watching television alone, and supplies nursery schools with television sets. Throughout Japan's educational system, television is used to supplement what goes on in the classroom.[51]

In the United States, the only consistently educational children's programs are seen on public television, beginning with *Sesame Street*. Through *Sesame Street* and other productions of the Children's Television Workshop, we know that television can be an entertaining, efficient, and extremely cost-effective teacher. Research by the U.S. Department of Education, for example, shows that *Sesame Street* reaches the majority of children in virtually all demographic groups, including minority children and children in poverty; that viewing the program predicts better school performance in the long term; and that low-income children who watch the program are more likely to show literacy and numeracy skills than those who do not. The most watched television program in the *world, Sesame Street* accomplishes its educational mission in the United States for about one penny per child per day. The point is, as *Sesame Street* creator Joan Ganz Cooney says, "Good, compelling, engaging, entertaining educational television can and does make a difference."[52] Television can teach skills and behaviors that are important to intellectual and social development, including academic skills like reading and arithmetic. So the hours that very young children spend watching commercial television represent a tremendous lost opportunity. Research shows that at the age of four children's brains are more than twice as active as adults', stay that way through age ten, and do not taper off to adult activity levels until the age of sixteen. Children can, if properly stimulated, literally soak up information like a sponge. Similarly, deprivation of stimuli can inhibit brain development.[53]

Sometimes television can provide a kind of "safe" learning environment that even the best schools cannot. In the early 1980s, for example, researchers found that a CTW reading program called *The Electric Company* was successful because, by teaching children to read and write in the secure privacy of their homes, it spared many of them the humiliation that is often experienced in the classroom.[54] And television can also develop interests and motivate children to learn, especially when they watch along with parents or older siblings. Today, another CTW reading program for older children, *Ghostwriter*, draws a bigger audience in its age group (seven to ten) than most of the commercial programs with which it competes.[55]

Remarkably, these well-known facts have been all but irrelevant to public policy concerning children's television in the United States. We have never had a serious debate about any aspect of television's performance in our society, and certainly not one about whether our children deserve greater consideration than the market gives them. The golden age of children's television ended almost as soon as the industry succeeded in saturating the populace with television sets. By the mid-1950s, when a majority of American homes had sets, broadcasters had already begun to drop their special programming efforts on behalf of children and to concentrate instead on those that would sell products for advertisers. The early evening prime-time hours became a haven for Westerns and private-eye shows; and local broadcasters, who took over the 4 p.m. to 7 p.m. slot, frequently dumped the networks' good children's programs in favor of low-cost and low-quality cartoons.

As a nation, we let the moment pass without so much as a murmur of protest. By 1960 children's programs were confined to what was known as the Saturday-morning ghetto, about six hours during which broadcasters made children's programs an enormously lucrative business, seeing the children who dominated the viewing audience on Saturday mornings as a small but untapped consumer market. Many shows were nothing more than program-length advertisements, thirty-minute adventures with and about the same toys that appeared in the commercials. The NAB code was revised to permit sixteen minutes of commercials per hour in children's Saturday-morning programs, a limit the FCC agreed was reasonable even though it was almost seven minutes longer than what the code permitted during prime time.

The practice was neither incidental nor unmindful. In 1965 a columnist in *Advertising Age* reminded clients that:

When you sell a woman on a product and she goes into the store and finds your brand isn't in stock, she'll probably forget about it. But when you sell a kid on a product, if he can't get it, he will throw himself on the floor, stamp his feet and cry. You can't get a reaction like that out of an adult.[56]

Readers of *Broadcasting* received similar advice in 1969:

Sooner or later you must look through kids' goggles, see things as they see them, appeal to them through their childish emotions and meet them on their own ground.[57]

Perhaps the most notorious of the sponsors' efforts to seduce children through programming was *Hot Wheels*, produced by the toy maker Mattel and featuring Mattel's little toy cars. No one paid attention to the program until a rival toy company complained in 1969 that it was nothing more than a commercial and therefore violated the FCC's (and the NAB's) generous time restrictions on advertising.[58] *Hot Wheels* was dropped before the FCC ruled on the complaint, but when it finally did, in 1974, it commented only that the show's patent commercial objectives were "disturbing," and cautioned broadcasters against "practices in the body of the program itself which promote products in such a way that they may constitute advertising." It also required broadcasters to make a clear distinction between programs and commercials.

Weak as this ruling was, had it not been for five women in Boston the agency probably would have issued no statement at all. The women—four of them with experience in the television business and all of them mothers who were alarmed by the steady diet of violence and commercials that made up children's programming—had formed Action for Children's Television (ACT) in 1968; in a letter to *The New York Times*, the group's first president, Evelyn Sarson, argued that television needed "some basic rethinking about children as viewers."[59] The industry, however, wasn't interested, nor did it need to be. As two former FCC staff members later recalled,

The Commission didn't have what could be called a policy towards children's programming [then]. In 1960, the FCC had cited programs for children as one of 14 elements "usually necessary to meet the public interest, needs and desires of the community"; but the Commission emphasized that these elements should not be regarded as a "rigid mold or fixed formula." Programming for children was a minor element in a lengthy litany of hollow promises that licensees would recite prior to acceptance of their stewardship of the airwaves. If broadcasters happened to win a prize for a certain children's program, they would boast about it; but if they simply took network offerings or ignored the category altogether, they had no fear of losing their licenses.[60]

Frustrated, the women went to see FCC chairman Dean Burch in February 1970. President Nixon's new chairman was eager to hear what they had to say—he had been at home ill in the days preceding the meeting, and had spent some time watching television with his own children. As a consequence, he found ACT's proposals at once reasonable and radical. The women proposed a code of ethics for children's television that encouraged age-appropriate programs for preschoolers, children six to nine, and children ten to twelve, all to run at designated times; that prohibited performers from promoting or advertising products during programs; and that forced all commercials to run at the beginning and end of the programs. In short, they proposed a system that resembled those found in Britain or Japan. Burch was sympathetic, but observed that the proposals were tantamount to a full-scale assault on the commercial structure of American television.

A week later the FCC made ACT's proposals public and asked for comments. The result was a deluge of legal briefs from broadcasters, toy makers, and other advertisers, all of whom characterized the new ideas as censorious. Burch then went on the offensive, chastising broadcasters at the annual NAB convention for their poor service to children and proposing (as I did during my own tenure at the FCC*) an antitrust exemption whereby the networks could cooperate to plan "outstanding" children's programs each weekday between 4:30 p.m. and 6 p.m. Burch was soon disappointed. When he met with the three network presidents in late 1970, they reportedly told him to "give it your best shot" but not to expect anything from them.[61]

A month later, in January 1971, Burch took his shot. With the arrival of a new commissioner, he had the votes necessary for the FCC to issue a notice of inquiry and a proposed rulemaking on ACT's petition. ACT was disappointed, for a notice of inquiry starts a drawn-out process that allows broadcasters to put their best foot

---

* While this book has two authors, for the sake of narrative clarity we choose to use the first person singular throughout whenever we refer to the senior author.

forward and hide the rest; moreover, ACT had already documented much of what the inquiry was supposed to find out. So, too, Evelyn Sarson commented, did *TV Guide*—every week.

While the inquiry proceeded, broadcasters did exactly what ACT predicted they would: they held well-publicized conferences in which they wrung their hands over their own "moral delinquency," proposed ending the practice of measuring Saturday-morning audiences, and held out the branch of corporate responsibility. In comments filed with the FCC, they argued that television influenced children very little, trumpeted the NAB code's strong language with respect to children's programming and the networks' "significant improvements" in the area, and warned of the dangers of government censorship. CBS complained that the networks were being made scapegoats for the "failings of the multi-billion-dollar educational system in the United States."[62] Meanwhile, they all continued to air sixteen minutes of commercials in each hour of children's programming, kept the program-length commercials, and ignored the practice of program hosts selling sponsors' products.

One of the most significant comments filed in support of ACT's petition came from the American Civil Liberties Union. Known for its unequivocal position on civil-liberties issues, the ACLU warned the commission against interfering in broadcast programming or content, but nonetheless said that where children were at stake the FCC was right to prohibit overcommercialization and, more important, that the commission was within its rights to require service to children as a condition of licensure. In addition to formal comments like this one in support of ACT's petition, the FCC received some 100,000 letters from people around the country.

To try to give the ACT petition further standing, Chairman Burch created a special, permanent children's unit within the commission. He knew well that broadcasters tend to respond to pressure when the heat is on, only to return to business as usual later. Within a few months of Burch's action, the NAB responded by reducing the commercial time its code allowed in Saturday-morning cartoons to twelve minutes per hour; forbade the practice of "host selling," and limited the number of commercial interruptions in any thirty-minute children's program to two, or in sixty-minute programs to four.

ACT, the FCC, and the broadcasters were embroiled in public hearings for the next two years. More and more, discussion of children's television was framed in terms of broadcast practices and finances rather than around the idea ACT had originally proposed—that children's programming should be divorced from the marketplace altogether. By 1974 Dean Burch had left the commission and President Nixon had replaced him with Richard Wiley, who had been the commission's general counsel. Wiley picked up where Burch had left off. In May 1974, he noted in a speech before the Television Academy of Arts and Sciences that children's programs were still more commercialized than adult programs and warned that if the industry did not act to do better he would.

Wiley came under immediate attack from broadcasters, who called his comments "irresponsible" and "ill-advised." But apparently this only steeled the new chairman's resolve. Quickly he made the issue of advertising time the key: he wanted broadcasters to agree to bring advertising minutes in children's weekend programs down to the 9½-minute limit observed in prime time. He succeeded. In June, the NAB agreed to do this within two years and to reduce the ads during weekdays from sixteen minutes to twelve. It also agreed to forbid in its code commercials for vitamins or other drugs during children's programs, to formalize its ban on host selling, to separate more clearly commercials from programs, and to ensure that, so far as the broadcasters knew, the children's products they advertised were safe.

The FCC's own policy on children's television, issued in October 1974, was not scheduled to take effect until 1976—a two-year span intended to allow the industry to appear to be acting voluntarily. Just as important, the policy change came in the form of a statement rather than a rule, which meant that its implementation was up to broadcasters. But as far as ACT was concerned, there was nothing to implement. The FCC statement declared that service to children was an important part of "the broadcaster's public service obligation," and "educational or informational programming of particular importance." But it set no specific time requirements for how much such programming there should be (saying only that there had to be *something*); and as for age-specific programming, one of ACT's key objectives, it made only the vaguest suggestion that "some effort" should be exerted on behalf of preschool and school-age children.

The inadequacy of all this was captured, ironically, in the statement's closing sentence, which urged "profits second, children first." This was a far cry from what ACT had first proposed to Chairman Burch four years earlier. "It is not enough to rely on the sense of commitment of broadcasters," said Peggy Charren, who had succeeded Evelyn Sarson as ACT's president (and who would be the most important and articulate advocate for children's television for the next twenty years). "If it were, ACT would not have had to come into existence."[63] Former FCC general counsel Henry Geller asked the commission to reconsider its policy statement, pointing out that its vague definitions were a disservice to broadcasters and citizen groups alike, and no help to anyone who might want to monitor stations' performance. But all to no avail.

Frustrated at the FCC, ACT in 1977 turned its attention to the Federal Trade Commission, which in those days had the authority to rule on "unfair" advertising practices. ACT had worked with the FTC from the start of its campaign, petitioning the agency in 1972 to adopt rules on toy, food, and drug advertisements. Now, together with the Center for Science in the Public Interest, ACT petitioned the FTC to ban commercials on all children's programs. Not surprisingly, the ensuing FTC Notice of Proposed Rulemaking was attacked not only by broadcasters but by toy, candy, and cereal companies—by anyone whose business relied upon selling goods to children.

While waiting for the FTC's ruling, ACT pushed the FCC in 1978 to ascertain whether broadcasters were in fact following the 1974 policy statement, and asked if the commission planned to do anything about those stations, networks, or other forces who ignored it. The FCC responded by creating the Children's Television Task Force, which reported a year later that educational, age-specific programming for children had not increased significantly and that where it had, it was because of the efforts of independent broadcasters, not the networks.

Still, the networks had to respond to the FCC's pressure somehow. "When the heat was turned on in Washington," says former ABC children's programming executive Squire Rushnell, "you could feel it." ABC began its *ABC Afterschool Specials* in the 1970s, dramatic programs that gave thoughtful treatment to children's problems, and *Kids Are People Too*, a Sunday children's magazine show. On Saturday mornings it aired snappy little commercials for academic subjects under the rubric *Schoolhouse Rock*, and CBS showed one-minute Saturday-morning spots called *In the News* that ran like commercials between cartoons. CBS News also broadcast weekly magazine shows—*Razmatazz* and *30 Minutes*, the latter a kid's version of *60 Minutes*. NBC had after-school specials called *Special Treat* and a program for young teens called *Hot Hero Sandwich*. For their part, many local broadcasters also turned to exemplary children's programs: The Westinghouse Group, for example, created *Call It Macaroni*, which took real kids and sent them on adventures in strange places. Post-Newsweek used old mystery movies to teach reading skills.

Despite these efforts, the FCC issued a Notice of Proposed Rulemaking on children's television in 1979. Among the proposals the commission considered was Henry Geller's suggestion that it establish specific requirements for children's programs. But neither of the rulemakings, at the FTC or the FCC, ever came to pass. In 1980 Congress stripped the FTC of the power to rule on "unfair" advertising practices, and a year later a new administration came to Washington, and with it a new FCC chairman, Mark Fowler. The new chairman came to the job with one objective: to deregulate the communications industries and to expose them to market forces. Children's television had no place in his plan, and almost overnight it disappeared from the list of the FCC's concerns. The FCC even refused to proceed with its 1980 Notice of Proposed Rulemaking until ACT took it to court; when it finally did proceed, in 1983, it refused to act. The marketplace, the FCC reasoned, served children well enough.

In fact, the marketplace quickly drove quality children's programming from the airwaves. As part of its deregulation effort, the FCC repealed the 1974 policy that stations should air "educational and informational" programs, which immediately put children's programs into direct competition with television material, whether for children or adults, that could command bigger audiences and more advertising dollars. The result was predictable: where in 1980 the three major networks were showing more than eleven hours' worth of *Schoolhouse Rock*, *In the News*, and other such programs each week, by 1983 such programming had dropped to four and a half hours a week, and all after-school programs had been eliminated. A year later, CBS withdrew *Captain Kangaroo*, an educational program that had served two generations of children; it was the last weekday-morning network offering for youngsters on commercial television. By 1990 network educational programs for children had dropped to fewer than two hours each week.

Meanwhile, over the same decade, toy-based programs for children boomed, from about thirteen in 1980 to more than seventy —more than half of all children's programs—in 1987. This, too, was the result of the FCC's adjustments: not only had it dropped the requirement for educational programs, but it had repealed its regulations on commercial time limits. In the deregulated marketplace, the economics changed dramatically and, with it, the children's programs.

Before deregulation, a half hour of children's animation cost between $250,000 and $300,000 to make, and a network advertising spot cost about $26,000.[64] (Some spots cost more, especially for popular programs, but even the normal rates were high enough to allow the networks to lumber along, with a minimum of imaginative programming, and still earn a handsome profit.) Once the FCC lifted the time limits, the networks lost their competitive advantage to syndicates—groups of independent stations that, acting as ad hoc networks, collaborated on broadcasting programs whose sponsorship had either been presold or could be sold by the stations themselves. These syndicates bought cheaper children's programs whose costs had been subsidized by toy makers, enabling the syndicates to undercut the networks' advertising rates and deliver a substantial portion of the child audience to national sponsors. By 1984, syndicates controlled 25 percent of children's advertising revenue on television, which forced overall rates for children's advertising down and greatly diminished the networks' incentive to produce any children's programs at all. Today, one network—NBC—produces no Saturday-morning children's programs.

An important contribution to this new, predatory climate was made not by the FCC but by the Justice Department, which with mindless zeal succeeded in killing the NAB code in 1982, claiming that its restraints on commercial time violated antitrust laws. (In fact, of course, they did, but in a manner conducive to the public interest.) In 1979, when the Justice Department initiated its suit, five hundred television stations—65 percent of the nation's total—subscribed to the NAB code.[65] The suit baffled not only the NAB, but Congress as well. Senator Daniel Inouye called it "wrong," and newspaper columnist Art Buchwald quipped, "The beauty of government servants is that they are always willing to help American citizens, even when you don't want them to." The absurdity of the case was noted even by U.S. District Court Judge Harold Greene, who in exasperation during oral arguments asked a Justice Department attorney, "Except for the fact that the Sherman Act is there, like Mount Everest, what did you hope to gain?"[66]

A good question. In March 1982, Greene reluctantly ruled that a portion of the NAB code's commercial limitations was a *per se* violation of the Sherman Anti-Trust Act. Fearful of the treble damages that antitrust actions incur, and on the advice of its lawyers, the NAB voted in 1983 to disband the code in its entirety, thereby abolishing perhaps the only nongovernmental articulation of the "public interest" in broadcasting and ending fifty-five years of self-regulation. Four years later, in 1987, retiring Westinghouse Broadcasting CEO Dan Ritchie paid for space in *Broadcasting* magazine to complain about the proliferation of commercials and to urge the industry to seek an antitrust exemption from Congress—as Judge Greene had himself suggested—so that it might reinstate the code. Without it, he wrote, the only alternative was government regulation. The Justice Department had effectively removed any hope of a middle road.

What *had* Americans gained from this? A television marketplace in which broadcasters were encouraged to exploit children for profit, and where economic considerations compelled them to. The kinds of commercial indiscretion that had prompted ACT to peti-

tion the FCC in 1970 had not only worsened but increased exponentially. Where in the late 1970s children saw about 20,000
commercials on television each year, they saw about double that
in 1987—80 percent of them for toys, cereals, candy, and fast-food
restaurants. Where in 1970 the FCC had concerned itself with
whether *Hot Wheels* existed merely for the purpose of selling toys,
in 1985 the commission gave toy manufacturers and broadcasters
the go-ahead to turn toys into programs. *He-Man and the Masters
of the Universe, GoBots, Thundercats, GI Joe: A Real American
Hero, Transformers*, and others now dominated children's television. In only five years, the time given over to war cartoons grew
from about one and a half hours per week to twenty-seven, and
the sale of war-related toys surged with it.

Of course, many companies and people were making a great deal
of money. *He-Man* generated some $350 million in sales in just
three years. Other shows, such as the Mattel Company's *Captain
Power and the Soldiers of the Future*, were "interactive," but only
if the watching children owned Mattel's forty-dollar XG7 Power
Jet. (When a child fired the Power Jet at the show, the show "fired
back.") When Congressman Edward Markey questioned Mattel in
1987 about *Captain Power*'s designs on America's children, a company vice president for entertainment objected to Markey's insis-
tence that the show was a glorified commercial, though he did
acknowledge that Mattel retained script control and that "action
segments" were specifically included for interactive viewing.[67] Ohio
congressman Dennis Eckart found Mattel's explanation uncon-
vincing. If *Captain Power* was interactive television, he said, "I
can't help feel we've dropped to the lowest common denominator."
Markey added, "Children's television today is not a wasteland but
a waste site, strewn with war toys, insipid cartoons and oversweet-
ened cereals."[68]

The FCC could not have cared less. Toy-based programs were
by definition in the "public interest," the commission had ruled in
1985, on the basis of their phenomenal sales success. But the ob-
literation of educational programming and the overnight success of
toy shows did trouble Congress, which, after two tries, passed the
Children's Television Act in 1990. The new law reflected what Peggy

Charren, Joan Ganz Cooney, and other advocates for children's television had been saying for twenty years—that whatever the successes of the television marketplace, children's programming was not one of them, nor would it ever be.

But the new legislation was hardly a great triumph. For the most part it merely wrote into law the vague and toothless 1974 FCC policy. Henry Geller, who helped to draft it, characterized it as a "stopgap" measure, and acknowledged that it was an insufficient response to the economic forces militating against diverse children's programming. The law requires broadcasters to air an unspecified amount of programming designed to be "educational and informational" for children (implicitly, therefore, designed for children of different ages), and it makes no provision for when such programs should air or how long they should be. Indeed, the requirement can be met piecemeal anywhere in a broadcaster's schedule—if a Ninja Turtle pauses to tell children to drink their orange juice, for example, that can be construed as "educational." And the law lets commercials in children's programs go back up to ten and a half minutes per hour on weekends and twelve on weekdays, though it bans host selling and requires that programs and commercials be clearly distinguishable.*

Even though it gave the force of law to the 1974 children's programming statement, the 1990 act could not and did not dispel the profiteering practices that had sprung up around children's programming in the 1980s. In 1991, for example, the FCC ruled that toy-based shows could only be characterized as program-length commercials if they included paid advertisements for the toy the show was based on. Today, most children's programs on commercial television are parts of marketing efforts to sell already existing toys. One of the most successful of such shows to date has been the *Teenage Mutant Ninja Turtles*, which during its best year earned $450 million on sales of about a thousand licensed products. In 1994 Saban Entertainment's *Mighty Morphin Power Rangers*—featuring the adventures of martial-arts action figures made by Jap-

---

* The commercial time limitations of the Children's Television Act apply not only to broadcasters but to cable programmers as well.

anese toy maker Bandai—ended the Turtles' preeminence with gross merchandising of almost $1 billion.[69] So important are these shows to toy merchandising that toy companies often give them away for *free*. Some television stations have further lined their own pockets by demanding that producers of toy-based children's programs commit to large amounts of additional advertising time on the station, much as radio stations once demanded payola. Manufacturers literally buy the best airtime for their programs.[70]

Today advertisers spend slightly more than $470 million a year on broadcast sponsorship aimed at children.[71] It's money well spent: children are one of the hottest and fastest-growing consumer markets, with preteens spending about $8.6 billion of their own money every year and teenagers $57 billion; together, they influence how their parents spend another $168 billion. Communications companies naturally enough zero in on this market. The cable channel Nickelodeon, for example, regularly solicits its child viewers for opinions on everything from their favorite TV shows to their favorite fashions. It does most of its marketing research on-line, through home computers, which speaks volumes about what kind of customer Nickelodeon is interested in and who its viewers are —mostly well-to-do and white.[72] All the more remarkable, and disturbing, is that Nickelodeon was originally a commercial-free channel. While its programs are among the best at treating children as children rather than as consumers, one has to be concerned with the steady encroachment of advertising and its long-term effects on Nickelodeon's programming.

With all the competition for children's dollars, there are doubtlessly more children's programs on television today than ever before. Only by the most charitable of criteria, however, can many of them be said to meet the spirit of the 1990 Children's Television Act. In mid-1993, at least twenty-five new "FCC-friendly" children's shows came on the air, some of them exemplary, some questionable, and most fated to such impossible time slots as 5 a.m. This made perfect sense to broadcasters, who were convinced that children would not watch the shows anyway. As Judy Price, CBS's executive for children's programming, said, "If broccoli is the only thing on a kid's plate, that doesn't mean he's going to eat it. Who's to say what's appropriate for our young? How can you have rules about something that subjective? And with all respect to Peggy Charren, who elected her to represent the values of the nation's parents?"[73]

The real question here is, who elected Judy Price? The truth is, parents' values are constantly overruled by advertisers' values in deciding what television will offer children. The problem has always been that when the market decides, the children lose. Programs that really *are* educational and informational, and that target narrow age groups, will always have audiences too small to generate the ratings that sponsors want. Speaking before the FCC in 1983, Bob Keeshan—aka Captain Kangaroo—told the commissioners:

> People over the years have said, "Well, the Captain had a very small audience." Well, my God, if I had a large audience, I'd start questioning what I was doing wrong. Fifteen percent of this nation is the total juvenile audience. How can I possibly, by commercial network standards, build a large audience when I start with that small number? So there is no good commercial reason for doing quality-oriented children's programming. The marketplace will not take care of the child audience.

Broadcasters say that even where advertisers do support educational shows, the limits on commercials imposed by the law work against them. "We're also trying to deal with undercounting of metered kid viewers and eroding audience shares to cable," says a Washington, D.C., broadcaster, "so it's really a triple whammy for us. What we have are stations that can barely stay afloat, and if the FCC would like to see more locally produced educational programming, most of the stations would do low-budget, low-quality junk that airs at 5 a.m. That's all we can afford to do."[74] Jonathan Rodgers, president of CBS television stations, told Congress the same thing in 1994: "If you make us do an hour [of children's programming] a day, we're going to spread those dollars much too thinly and we won't be able to do quality shows like 'Beakman's World.' "[75]

How on earth did the American people arrive at such a tragic and unworkable state of affairs?

2 : Whence the Stranger?
The Elusive Public Interest

Human blunders usually do more to shape history than human
wickedness.
                                               —*A.J.P. Taylor*

THE STORY OF CHILDREN'S TELEVISION—OF ACT'S EFFORTS TO END
commercial exploitation, of the failed attempts to curb violence,
and of the wasteland of "low-budget, low-quality junk" that exists
today—is but one chapter in a larger story: the story of the public
interest, and of how and whether broadcasting has served it. In
order to understand the state of children's television today, one
must first understand this larger story and the circumstances in
which American broadcasting was born and came of age. It is a
story of missed opportunities.

    When radio broadcasting began early in the century, most dem-
ocratic countries chose to establish strong, publicly financed broadcasting systems first, commercial systems much later. They did so
in the belief that the airwaves were too valuable a resource—for

education, for culture, for citizenship—to entrust exclusively to private, profit-seeking companies. The United States did just the opposite, choosing not only to give for-profit broadcasters access to the people's airwaves but to make them the foundation of the system. For their privilege, broadcasters were required by law to use the airwaves as trustees of the "public interest." The meaning of that term, along with questions about who should define it and enforce the law, has been a subject of debate ever since. That debate, the opportunities it presented and those it missed, are the subject of this chapter.

Perhaps the most telling feature of this history is that it was begun by a man who in his day was one of the country's most visible, active and articulate advocates for children, Herbert Hoover. It was Hoover who, first as Secretary of Commerce and later as President, oversaw the development of early broadcast regulation and gave meaning, in public and official actions, to the term *public interest*. Yet rarely, if at all, did Hoover make the connection between the power of broadcasting and the children whose lives he worked so hard to improve. Now, as the century draws to a close, the meaning of the public interest is focused here and throughout the world on those whom Hoover forgot: the children. And we must start the story at the end, with what is going on with our kids in a new world of information and entertainment that Hoover never dreamed of.

In 1983, when the FCC denied ACT's request to revisit the issue of children's television programming, Chairman Fowler insisted that the market would serve children well enough. In short, he said, someone would sooner or later figure out how to do what the networks had historically failed to: make a profit while doing quality children's programs.

Today, that someone is Geraldine Laybourne, president of Nickelodeon, a cable television channel that has become a very successful television programmer. By the company's own estimates, Laybourne says, Nickelodeon has 30 percent of the entire child television audience (compared to about 4 percent each for ABC and

CBS), even though the service is available in only the roughly 60 percent of the nation's homes that are wired for cable. Among children six to eleven years old, Nickelodeon is the most popular children's service, with about 20 million viewers each month; in 1993, the channel had revenues estimated at $245 million and profits estimated at $95 million.[1] In addition to earning revenue from the advertisements in its children's programs (about half of what most broadcast channels carry), Nickelodeon publishes a bimonthly magazine for children, licenses about four hundred toys, and, in conjunction with Mattel, works to develop new products. "The name Nickelodeon is now almost synonymous with kids' television," says one advertising executive. "They have created a very successful brand image."[2] So successful, in fact, that in March 1994 Nickelodeon announced it would spend $30 million to develop original programs to compete with public broadcasting for younger viewers, those between the ages of two and six.

Public broadcasting has for years been the only major programmer for very young children, with traditional favorites like *Sesame Street* and *Mister Rogers' Neighborhood*, as well as newer programs like *Barney and Friends*, *Lamb Chop's Play-Along*, and *The Kidsongs*, holding in thrall each day a nationwide preschool audience estimated at 16 million children. However, public broadcasters show no advertising in their children's programs, so as far as advertisers are concerned the preschool market is virgin territory. The only other channel with an equally substantial block of preschool fare is cable's the Learning Channel, whose "Ready, Set, Learn!" block on weekdays from 6 a.m. to noon is also noncommercial.

Geraldine Laybourne's goal is to make that market pay. "By getting kids to watch us at this age, we have them for life," she says. "That's exactly the reason we're doing it."[3] She is not alone. Fox Children's Network has announced its own "aggressive commitment to educational programming aimed at preschoolers," and cable channels like Showtime, Lifetime, and Disney continue to premiere new preschool programs.[4] They are all doing it for the same reason. As Betty Cohen, executive vice president of the Cartoon Network says, "Advertisers are starting to value programs that parents view with their kids. They're seeing children influence purchasing decisions in family life."[5]

To critics, Laybourne responds that service to children and service to advertisers are not incompatible. Nickelodeon, she says, tries to provide a "nurturing, protective environment" for children. "While we are a business, we're responsible as kid advocates to protect them from commercial exploitation . . . That means walking a very distinct, but fine line."[6] Her claim is right in one respect: advertising is not necessarily inimical to good or imaginative service.* Throughout the world, exemplary magazines and newspapers are supported by advertisers, not readers, and it is conceivable that the same might one day be said of video programs.

But even granting the best of intentions, Laybourne's assumption that a "fine line" can be drawn that will protect preschool children from commercial exploitation is highly questionable. In all the research done about children and television, the one finding on which virtually everyone agrees is that very small children do not understand the difference between programs and commercials. That is precisely why advertisers are interested in hooking children while they are young, as Laybourne says. The idea is to build brand recognition and consumer loyalty in an audience too ignorant to discern a sales pitch and too impressionable to resist one. Programming created with that purpose in mind is almost certain to be mere entertainment, with the educational values that public broadcasting emphasizes kept to a minimum, if anything at all. Laybourne herself has said, "The PBS orientation to kids is different from ours. PBS begins by asking: 'How can we improve kids? There's something wrong with them.'" The Nickelodeon approach, she says, is "to celebrate being a kid . . . We don't try to prove kids know their alphabet."[7]

There is nothing wrong with building an audience by entertaining children, of course, particularly if it is done well, as Nickelodeon often does, with the needs of children rather than the needs of advertisers first in mind. But history also suggests that the fine line

---

* In one inspired use of the medium, for example, Nickelodeon aired a twelve-hour "Big Help-a-Thon" in September 1994. Nearly 5 million children called and pledged their time to community-based volunteer organizations around the country. The telethon was part of a larger Nickelodeon effort, "The Big Help," launched in March 1994 and intended to be a "multi-year, national grass-roots effort to encourage and empower kids to participate in community service activities."

Laybourne speaks of has a way of receding, in almost imperceptible increments, into the bottom line, until the two are indistinguishable. Moreover, children's programs that are designed with an ulterior motive—to sell television sets, or to build brand loyalties among children still in diapers—will not outlive their service to that motive. Nickelodeon itself, for example, began life as a noncommercial children's channel in 1979, a shining example of public service from a cable industry eager to be free of federal regulation. After Congress deregulated the industry in 1984, Nickelodeon began to carry advertising. More recently, its parent company, Viacom International, took on an enormous debt when it paid nearly $10 billion to acquire Paramount in the spring of 1994; what is to ensure that Nickelodeon, along with Viacom's other properties, will not come under increasing pressure to deliver higher revenues? What is to ensure that Nickelodeon will not, if so pressured, increase its advertising in preschool programs from four minutes per hour to eight, or perhaps to the permissible new maximum of ten and a half? What is to ensure that its original programs don't vanish into an array of reruns and cheaply produced cartoons? Nickelodeon, after all, is a product of market forces, not of regulation.

Even if the company were to boost advertising time significantly, it might still do so in the service of exemplary programs. The great children's shows from television's golden age were also products of marketing decisions, not regulation. But they passed into history as soon as broadcasters learned that other types of programs would better serve their profit-and-loss statements. Given the size of Nickelodeon's audience and its specialty niche, perhaps it will continue to be a quality service. But it is still a pay service, available only to those children who have cable, unavailable to tens of millions of others. If, as many experts think, television becomes more consumer-supported in the future and advertising becomes *less* important, that disparity will become even sharper, with good television available only to children whose parents can foot the bill for it. For now, however, the future of all children's television programming apparently depends on what advertisers see fit to provide, if anything. In this respect the future of children's television, however fantastic its promises or golden its potential, is likely to be merely a repeat of its past.

This is true even when the television of the future is not a "television" at all, but a "SuperTube," a computer-driven video server that, by converting all information into the 1's and 0's of digital language, will expand exponentially the power of individual viewers to manipulate information—to create it, transmit it, store it. Digitization makes possible innovations in America's economic and civic life that were once only the stuff of dreams, as broadcasting did in the 1920s and 1930s. Unlike broadcasting, however, digitization's great potential is not in mass communication but in highly personalized work initiated and controlled by people themselves, whether as participants in an on-line computer forum, shoppers using their televisions' remote-control units to browse through department stores, or children wandering in the archives of the Smithsonian. In a sense, communications technology has come full circle, back to the point-to-point exchanges for which radio was first used a hundred years ago.

The rubric under which this future goes most often is the "information superhighway," and of all its promises none are more glowing than those held out for children. Public education especially, which has always straggled behind technological change and has distrusted television, has been the subject of some of the most fervent revolutionary dreams. According to Lewis J. Perelman, an advocate of what he calls "hyperlearning," SuperTube will allow students to learn twice as much for each dollar spent on their education: "Multimedia technology can give every individual learner even more choices of 'schools' than of cable TV channels, as long as 'school' stops referring to buildings and classrooms. Multimedia distance-learning technology can enable virtually anyone to learn anything, anywhere, anytime, any way, with grade A results."[8]

If a bit hyperbolic, Perelman is not merely wishful. In Milwaukee, sixth-grade students can use a computer joystick to control a camera on a submersible robot named JASON, sixteen hundred miles away in the Sea of Cortés below California. The underwater camera relays its pictures to a ship that beams them to a satellite, which relays the signal to EDS Corporation in Plano, Texas, and to Turner Broadcasting in Atlanta, each of which adds computer graphics and sends the signal on to watching students in twenty-eight schools in the United States, Mexico, Canada, Bermuda, and Great Britain—750,000 students in all. (The corporate backers of this project include Turner Broadcasting, AT&T, and the computer-maker Cray Research.)

The JASON project is spectacular—and spectacularly expensive. Other, more proven applications of communications technology are gaining new acceptance in schools all over the United States. "Distance learning," for example—expanding education's reach by moving information around instead of people—was available in fewer than ten states in 1987 and today is found, in varying degrees of completion and complexity, in all fifty states.[9] One of the most successful distance-learning projects is the Annenberg/CPB project, which develops telecourses that students can take for college credit; it has served more than 400,000 people since its creation in 1981. One of the most ambitious of the new technology projects is in Iowa, where over a decade ago the state invested $3.5 million in a project at tiny Kirkwood Community College, in Cedar Rapids; Iowa is now investing $100 million in a fiber-optic network that will reach every county in the state.[10] In North Carolina, sixteen public schools began sharing facilities over a fiber-optic network in 1993; today more than one hundred schools use the system, which reaches from the islands of the Outer Banks to the hollows of Appalachia and enables students in remote rural districts to study subjects like Latin, Japanese, and oceanography.[11]

Many of these efforts are joint ones between public-school districts and private companies. The Chicago-based Ameritech Corporation, a regional telephone company, operates distance-learning projects for several mostly remote and rural school districts around the Great Lakes, which allows them to share teachers, curriculum materials, and expertise. AT&T itself operates the Learning Network, an interactive science-curriculum service available in two hundred schools in twenty-nine states and nine countries. Northern Telecom, IBM, and South Central Bell have teamed together with Mississippi educators to build an interactive distance-education network that will allow the state to implement new high-school graduation requirements. In Ohio and Kentucky, Cincinnati Bell and Apple Computer are building an interactive education system with which students can hook up with college campuses on ordinary phone lines. The National Geographic Society and the National Science Foundation have developed National Geographic Kids Network, a service in which elementary-school students can collect data on a subject such as acid rain, then share it via modem with other student researchers all over the world.

As inspiring as these projects are, in the absence of a public policy commitment to them their continued existence—and certainly their expansion—depends entirely on the good will of the companies now funding them. As we shall see, the great hopes for broadcasting service to children were also left to the good will of private industry, with disastrous results. SuperTube, which thus far has none of the traditional public-interest obligations once expected of broadcasters, is likely to neglect children except when they can be construed as marketing opportunities. Bell Atlantic has given some indication of how children fit in the world of new communications technologies: the five applications that will make SuperTube profitable, it announced in 1993, are home shopping, direct-response advertising, video on demand, entertainment programming, and—the biggest by far—gambling.[12]

Other nations look at these proclamations with mixed amazement and horror. Masahi Kojima, president of Nippon Telephone in Japan, when asked about American plans for new technologies, responded, "Perhaps this is inappropriate for the head of a telecommunications company to say, but I will go ahead anyway. I wonder if this flood of information really makes our life richer."[13]

A fitting question, but it has not received much of an answer in the United States, let alone a public hearing. It is not just that so many Americans assert that technology and market forces are, together, the best arbiters of the public interest. It is also a presumption that these technologies will yield the same kinds of benefits once expected of broadcasting. Will the promises of an "information age" come true for our children and grandchildren, or will they be forgotten? The answer is in the past: we've been here before.

In many ways the race to the information age is simply a repeat of the race that made broadcasting the dominant communications medium of the twentieth century. First with radio and later with television, broadcasting grew in ways unforeseen by its inventors, the course and purposes of its development left almost entirely to industry by legislators who barely understood—and sometimes had no idea—what it was they were supposed to be regulating. The result was a perfunctory version of the "public interest" that enshrined the habits of consumerism—not citizenship or any of its requirements, such as education or the development of children into young adults—as the arbiter of the good and the true, and, in turn, made corporate success the benchmark of consumer satisfaction.

The Federal Radio Commission, created by Congress in 1927 (and later, after the FRC was disbanded, the Federal Communications Commission, created in 1934), was charged with overseeing the broadcast industry in the "public interest, convenience and necessity." Broadcasting had to be regulated in the first place because of its technical characteristics: not everyone can have access to the airwaves. Just what public interest is to be served is another matter. In the United States, there are two schools of thought about this. The first is egalitarian: broadcasters are public trustees whose use of the airwaves—a limited, publicly owned resource—is contingent on their honoring the interests of their communities in addition to their own. Under some conditions, they must even permit others access to the airwaves assigned to them. The second school of thought is libertarian: the term *public interest* is so ill-defined, not only in law but also in practice, as to be meaningless; worse, statutory definitions of the public interest are in fact antithetical to the public interest, since by trying to serve the entire community broadcasters serve no one well; worse still, trusteeship is a patent violation of broadcasters' right of free speech.

These are the broad strokes that have shaped debate over broadcasting in America for much of the century. They are at the crux of almost any controversy having to do with television, whether about political campaign ads or children's programs. Though the particulars are different, these two schools of thought also dominate the debate over SuperTube and the rules of the road for the information superhighway.

The very possibility of SuperTube, however, has dramatically changed the terms of the debate. Cable television has made channel scarcity almost a quaint notion, but SuperTube promises to make it obsolete. A television system with hundreds or thousands of channels—especially channels that people pay to watch—not only destroys the notion of channel scarcity upon which the public-trustee theory rests but simultaneously breathes life and logic into the libertarian model. Relieved of the burdens of trusteeship, programmers can show what they wish and say what they want, the only limitation on their freedom being their success or failure in the marketplace.

It was precisely this theory that led the FCC to tear at the fabric of trusteeship a decade ago. For all the criticism of its policies, it was merely trying to accomplish through administrative decree what Congress had tried and failed to do legislatively only a few years before when it had considered rewriting the 1934 Communications Act in the late 1970s. More important, the FCC did not so much launch a revolution as turn back the clock, recasting for the age of SuperTube many of the assumptions about technology and economics that had animated the drafters of the Radio and Communications Acts in their own effort to codify the "public interest."

When, for example, Senator Clarence Dill told me in 1961 that his purpose in using the phrase "public interest, convenience and necessity" in the 1927 Radio Act was to establish a standard for licensure while simultaneously encouraging investors to put their money in radio, he summed up perfectly what regulators and regulated alike had taken the phrase to mean. Indeed, by the time Congress wrote it into the Radio Act, the phrase had been in use for nearly a century, a vestige of the nation's first great advance in communications technology—the train—whose development in the early nineteenth century had linked America's towns and cities into a truly *national* economy. The railroads were for the most part privately owned, though state governments, which considered them "a vital element in the broad program of public improvements which was to bind the country together and increase its prosperity,"[14] functioned as their de facto partner, establishing monopoly rights-of-way, ensuring financial support, and handing over huge tracts of public land. For their trouble, many states found themselves rewarded with poor, discriminatory, or unsafe rail service, and so began to establish informal commissions to monitor it. Those commissions were charged with regulating railroads in the "public interest," and whenever licenses were required, "convenience and necessity" became the standard for awarding them.

The problem with these state commissions was that they had no legal basis on which to operate, much less to regulate. In 1837 and again in 1877 the Supreme Court upheld the states' authority to act in the public interest, but the commissions remained constitutionally suspect and, as a practical matter, weak.[15] Stronger commissions were created in states where railroad competition was so fierce that the industry itself asked the states to intervene. Ostensibly the rationale was to ensure service for the public, but in fact the railroad companies, often overbuilt and underused, had to be saved from themselves. The genius of the public-interest standard in this situation, as the communications scholar Willard Rowland, Jr., has written, "was its ability to mask distinct differences of view about the obligations of the regulated industries and the authority of the administrative agency."[16] Implicit in the ambiguity, however, was an expectation that, in addition to public service, the financial health of the regulated private industry (and profit for its owners) was a legitimate measure of the public interest.

If today this understanding of the public interest seems beset by contradiction, it is because the history of broadcast regulation is a history of conflict between the public's interest and the industry's. But that history is also full of evidence—in congressional debates, industry statements and practices, court decisions, Federal Communications Commission rulings, and, most important, television programs—that until very recently the workings of the marketplace were not believed to be, by themselves, the sole determinant of the public interest. Equally important, sometimes more so, were ideas about civic responsibility and leadership. Though the congressmen who created the legal framework for broadcast regulation believed fervently in the power of the marketplace to create and sustain the good life, their enthusiasm was tempered by the bitter and often bloody lessons of the industrial revolution and infused with the spirit of Progressivism. They believed that capitalism's rough edges could be smoothed, its strengths magnified, through a new class of leaders schooled not only in the ways of production but also in the social and natural sciences. In other words, the market was but one tool in the making of the good society; the other was education in civic arts. In 1914, President Woodrow Wilson put the matter this way:

> The antagonism between business and government is over. We are now to give expression to the best business judgment of America, to what we know to be the business conscience and honor of the land. The government and business men are ready to meet each other halfway in a common effort to square business methods with both public opinion and the law.[17]

Among those who both preached this doctrine and personified it was Herbert Hoover, who, first as Commerce Secretary under Presidents Warren Harding and Calvin Coolidge and later as the thirty-first President of the United States, worked to turn what he called "progressive individualism" into public policy. In his public life, Hoover presided over one of the greatest periods of growth in American industrial history and, with it, the creation of a consumer economy that offered goods and services never before imagined. Hoover was in many ways both an architect of that economy and its conscience. As Commerce Secretary, he convened hundreds of conferences in which he brought together representatives of various industries to urge them to adopt codes of good practice and, in essence, to regulate themselves. He also staged conferences to examine what the benefits of economic growth should be. Certainly one of its beneficiaries, he believed, should be children. Hoover was a prominent and longtime supporter of the housing and medical reform proposals of the child-welfare movement; in 1929, as President, one of his first official acts was to convene a national conference, entitled Child Health and Protection, at the White House. Hoover also believed that children should be brought more fully into the consumer economy. As Commerce Secretary, he urged manufacturers to create more goods for children, and parents to supply them with their own rooms, furniture, toys, and shopping experiences.[18] These impulses to raise children's "standard of living"—one reformist, the other consumerist—may seem contradictory today, but they did not strike Hoover that way. Most reformers in the child-welfare movement shared them.

In this spirit Hoover and the nation approached the business of radio regulation in 1925. Only a decade before, in 1912, Congress had passed a law that gave the Commerce Department the authority to grant radio licenses and set safety standards. But because the market for radios was at first thought to be in point-to-point communication, as between ships at sea, Congress assumed that the demand for licenses would be small and included no discretionary standard with which to award them. In essence, whoever asked for a license got one.

The act was a failure. Thousands of Americans began transmitting from homes and garages, creating a conflicting jumble of signals that ended only when the War Department ordered amateurs off the air during World War I. After the war, the federal government was reluctant simply to return to chaos. The U.S. Navy, in particular, under whose direction radio had achieved many of its most significant technological advances, wanted some form of friendly monopoly in radio, and together with General Electric it created the Radio Corporation of America—RCA—in 1919. In short order, American Telephone and Telegraph Company, the Westinghouse Corporation, and the United Fruit Company became partners in the RCA venture, which quickly became the dominant radio power in the world.

Despite that power, as the historian Erik Barnouw notes, "events did not quite follow expectation." Then as now, "developments came so fast that the arrangements of the allies were soon obsolete. As unanticipated conflicts arose, the allies quarreled bitterly over their division of the world. At the same time, their very power made the alliance a target—for would-be competitors and government trust-busters."[19]

Of all the unforeseen developments in radio, it seems odd now to realize that broadcasting was one of them. RCA was created largely to give the United States preeminence in the business of international message service. Not until Westinghouse struck upon the idea of selling receivers and sending radio transmissions out to many people at once—broadcasting—did radio become a technology of the common man. In November 1920, Westinghouse launched the nation's first broadcast radio station, KDKA in Pittsburgh, and almost overnight other stations sprang up around the country. The industry's sudden change of direction so confused RCA president Edward Nally that he stepped down in 1922, making way for a new president and also a new general manager, a young man who only a few years before had been rebuffed when he urged RCA to manufacture radio receiver sets, David Sarnoff.

The transformation of radio into an entrepreneurial instrument of mass communication created tension among the corporate giants who controlled RCA. The radio patents that had seemed to guarantee each of them a fortune were suddenly under assault by thousands of enterprising Americans who were busily building and selling both radio transmitters and receivers. But, as with SuperTube today, a greater problem soon loomed: how to find and sustain a satisfactory supply of decent programming.

In 1922 the trade magazine *Radio Broadcast* offered three solutions to this problem. The first was for large private philanthropies to create public stations, in much the same way that Andrew Carnegie had created the nation's public libraries. The second was to finance radio through the public purse, in the same way that most of our schools and museums were. The third, supported by RCA's David Sarnoff, was to pay for radio programming through a tax on radio receivers, essentially the financing mechanism that the British had adopted for the BBC. Independently, AT&T devised a fourth scheme, what it called toll broadcasting. The idea was that, as with telephone service, the company would make no programs but merely supply a service whereby anyone who wished could pay a toll and broadcast his or her message to the world. AT&T, in essence, wanted to introduce advertising to the airwaves on a non-discriminatory, common-carrier basis, and it claimed exclusive province over this scheme, denying it to its partners in RCA; few people thought the idea practical or even tasteful.

Nonetheless AT&T's idea had important consequences. Commerce Secretary Hoover, trying to clear the chaos on the airwaves, had no discretionary standard in the 1912 Radio Act to guide him in his licensing decisions, and in the absence of such a standard, AT&T's claim that its toll stations were open to all comers persuaded Hoover that, indeed, they served a special public purpose. By contrast, he came to regard the many stations operated by schools, churches, labor unions, and the like as—what AT&T called them—"propaganda" stations.[20]

Still, the reallocation process was by any measure exceedingly arbitrary. In April 1926, a U.S. district court ruled that the Commerce Department had exceeded its authority under the 1912 Radio Act and that the act itself was unconstitutional.[21] The ruling left Hoover virtually powerless and let loose a free-for-all on the airwaves, with hundreds of broadcasters signing on, jumping to whatever frequencies they desired, and boosting their power. Congress, called on to restore order, responded with the Radio Act of 1927, which established the airwaves as public property and established as the standard of licensure that broadcasters serve the "public interest, convenience and necessity."

Historians sometimes characterize the Radio Act of 1927 as a piece of emergency legislation, drafted with necessity in mind and its constitutionality in doubt. Parts of its legislative history support that view. But if radio's regulatory apparatus was in doubt, the industry's future had nonetheless received ample attention from Secretary Hoover. Both Congress and the administration had been thinking about an alternative to the 1912 act for some time before the 1926 district court ruling. Between 1922 and 1925, Hoover had convened four national conferences on the issue, bringing to Washington not only the nation's leading electronics executives but also broadcasters themselves (many of these were not really "broadcasters" in the sense in which we understand the term today but, rather, department stores, utility companies, and other private companies, whose main concern was to generate publicity for their primary businesses, not for programming or, even, radio profits).[22] The true pioneers of radio technology were educators, and they, along with other noncommercial broadcasters—city governments, churches, and labor unions—argued for a very different vision of broadcasting. At Secretary Hoover's conferences these broadcasters affirmed the "educational and informational character" of their programming and asked that the Commerce Department recognize its value and make "adequate, definite and specific provision" for it in any future regulatory scheme.[23] To further support their case, they noted that Great Britain and Canada were both forming national, noncommercial services.

Their pleas fell on deaf ears. In the congressional debates leading up to the 1927 Radio Act, advocates of noncommercial radio were ignored, not least because Congress and the general public barely understood what radio was. Even though by 1925 commercial radio was well established, misperceptions about the technology abounded. The most common, and one offered by Secretary Hoover himself, was the notion that radio was a use of the air itself, or the "ether," and not of the electromagnetic spectrum. Some congressmen, for example, thought that radio was a form of electrical energy that rivaled power lines, others that its primary application was in medical therapy. To read the record of their confusion and see their inability to look beyond the technical characteristics of the medium is to be reminded of the current debates, in Congress and elsewhere, over the information superhighway.

Then as now, the language of policy debate came from the vocabulary of technicians and accountants. The focus of concern was not with programming or even with audiences. To the extent these were mentioned at all, they were mentioned in terms of industry needs. Secretary Hoover, speaking at the fourth of his radio conferences in November 1925, said:

> The ether is a public medium, and its use must be for public benefit. The use of a radio channel is justified only if there is public benefit. The dominant element for consideration in the radio field is and always will be the great body of the listening public, millions in number, countrywide in distribution. There is no proper line of conflict between the broadcaster and listener, nor would I attempt to array one against the other. Their interests are mutual, for without the one the other could not exist.[24]

It is remarkable that Hoover did not indicate what the public benefit might be, except to suggest that it was linked to the interests of broadcasters themselves. Not even children, to whom Hoover had devoted so much of his private and public life, merited mention. Certainly other possible benefits had been suggested to him by the educational and religious broadcasters who had attended his conferences, but clearly those arguments, too, had failed to convince him. In merely linking the public interest to the wishes of the "millions" and identifying the interests of broadcaster and listener as one and the same, Hoover had inadvertently made ratings and market success the most important measure of the public interest.

For its part, Congress thought very much the same way. It entertained some thirty radio bills between 1923 and 1927 before finally passing the Radio Act in February 1927, which accepted virtually all the recommendations of Hoover's corporate conferees, requiring licenses of individual stations but imposing no specific obligations on them. In short, the Radio Act understood broadcasting "in the simplest mass audience entertainment terms," as one historian has put it. "It was as if simply stating the fiduciary principle was enough, that by merely declaring the airwaves to be public property and asserting that regulation therefore had to be in the public interest, somehow appropriately diverse program service results would ensue."[25]

The concept of the public interest that developed with railroads, then with the telegraph and the telephone, was thus transplanted into broadcasting—with a critical new twist: many of the traditional public-interest standards and practices that had developed in these other industries were explicitly omitted from radio regulation. Telegraph and telephone services, for example, were treated as public utilities and thus subject to rate and service regulation. Not so with broadcasting, Hoover said: "Those engaged in radio broadcasting shall not be required to devote property to public use and their properties are therefore not public utilities in fact or in law."[26]

In other words, as Willard Rowland has written, "the industry would have it both ways. It would be authorized to operate within a profoundly favorable tradition of public interest interpretation associated with utility monopolies, but would also be exempt from the more onerous rate and service restrictions of such regulations. In a word, it would have the *quid* without the *quo*."[27]

To administer the new law, Congress created the Federal Radio Commission (FRC), whose first order of business was to bring order to the antiquated and chaotic system of spectrum allocations—in short, to knock many stations off the air. To do that, the commission shortened all licenses to three-month terms, after which those broadcasters competing for a particular frequency had to share it. By this process the commission simply starved many stations to death, since those with the fewest hours (or the least desirable ones) were likely to go broke. The big losers in this process were the educational and not-for-profit stations—which the FRC regarded as "propaganda" or "special-interest" stations and which lacked financial and technological strength. Between 1927 and 1930, more than half of the stations affiliated with colleges and universities went off the air; nonprofit broadcasters, who numbered more than two hundred in 1927, were fewer than seventy by 1934.[28] Their frequencies were often reassigned to commercial stations, many of them, in turn, affiliated with the large and growing networks—and almost all, by the FRC's standards, of greater "public interest" than educational or religious stations. Even while this was going on, the FRC asked the commercial stations to provide "well-rounded" programs that included "religion, education and instruction, important public events, discussions of public questions, weather, market reports and news, and matters of interest to all members of the family."[29]

Increasingly desperate, the remaining educational and nonprofit stations asked Congress to reserve for their use a specified portion of the spectrum. Congress considered the matter as early as 1931 but, in the face of opposition from commercial broadcasters, declined to act; these last assured the FRC that their studios were open to educators and that the kinds of educational programs the commission wanted would soon be created.

Their assurances were not baseless. Under the FRC, NBC and CBS had grown at a fantastic rate, such that by 1931 they accounted for 70 percent of all U.S. broadcasting and controlled all but three of the nation's forty most powerful stations.[30] And by contemporary standards—certainly by modern ones—early commercial broadcasting had its share of public-service visionaries. NBC, for example, owned by David Sarnoff's RCA, then considered itself less a for-profit enterprise than a public-service corporation. It had two net-works, a "Red" and a "Blue," and both sold only enough adver-tising to support, as one NBC president put it, "the finer things that are not sponsored commercially."[31] The broadcast historian Erik Barnouw characterizes NBC's broadcasts in those days as "dec-orous," a mix of high and popular culture supported by the "ar-istocracy of American business." Among the offerings on NBC Red was "The University of Chicago Roundtable," and NBC Blue ex-perimented with a weekly program called "America's Town Meet-ing of the Air." During the same period, CBS launched a program called "American School of the Air." Commercials on both net-works were discreet, and the "mention of prices was forbidden, as too crass for network radio."[32]

Nonetheless, millions of Americans quickly became disillusioned with commercial radio. Many programs were created, packaged, staffed, and cast not by broadcasters but by advertisers. In 1922, Hoover had warned that "so great a possibility" as radio should not be allowed "to be drowned in advertising chatter," but a decade later, in 1932, his worst fears had come to pass. To many Ameri-cans, including many in Congress, the Radio Act had been a failure. Advertising had taken over the airwaves, and the industry was increasingly monopolized by the networks, whose power grew in direct proportion to the loss of educational and nonprofit stations.

So it was that when Franklin Delano Roosevelt came to the White House in 1933, hopes for radio reform were high. In the heady days of the New Deal, educators in particular hoped that their vision of broadcasting, which enjoyed growing support in Congress, might yet become law. Roosevelt's cabinet included several prominent and powerful opponents of the commercial network system, and the President himself had urged Congress to draft new communications legislation.

The educators were prepared. In 1930, nine major educational organizations had banded together to create the National Com-mittee on Education by Radio (NCER) in order to lobby for a portion of the broadcast spectrum being set aside for educational use. Other educational groups called for more radical reform—on the order of nationalizing the broadcast system, as was the case in

Canada and Great Britain—while labor and religious organizations developed reform proposals of their own. (Early on, American newspaper publishers had also called for nationalization—largely, as it turned out, for fear of competition for advertising; but by late 1932 they had amassed a significant ownership stake in radio stations, so that they soon became ardent opponents of reform.) From John Dewey to Alexander Meiklejohn to H. L. Mencken, leading public intellectuals argued that commercial broadcasting was inherently averse to controversy and dissenting opinion and that it became intractably so by the nature of advertiser-supported programming. The only solution, they believed, was for Congress to reestablish the airwaves as public property and to regulate them as a public utility.

When President Roosevelt recommended new communications legislation, reform therefore seemed certain. The only questions were, what kind and how much? Two champions of the reform movement emerged in Congress—New York senator Robert Wagner and West Virginia senator Henry Hatfield, both Democrats—and together they introduced an amendment to require the FRC to reserve 25 percent of the broadcast frequencies for educational and nonprofit use. But the Wagner-Hatfield amendment failed, owing largely to the skillful maneuvering of another Democrat, Senator Clarence Dill, who by 1934 had allied himself with the commercial broadcasters, who strongly opposed reform. The final legislation, the 1934 Communications Act, turned out to be a near-verbatim reproduction of the Radio Act. The historian Erik Barnouw has called it "an almost total victory for the status quo."[33] The major difference between the old law and the new was that Congress had put all telecommunications, including telephony, which had been under the jurisdiction of the Interstate Commerce Commission, under one regulatory roof. The FRC was abolished, succeeded by a new Federal Communications Commission.[34]

The defeat of the Wagner-Hatfield amendment had important consequences for American broadcasting, particularly for television. So it is worth examining in some detail the arguments with which commercial broadcasters succeeded in killing it, as well as the reformers' inability to respond with a clear counterargument.

To the spectrum set-aside proposed in the Wagner-Hatfield

amendment, commercial broadcasters answered simply that no such action was necessary, that the FRC already had the power to insist that broadcasters render public service, including the airing of programs devoted to education, religion, labor, agriculture, and similar activities concerned with human betterment. Significantly, no one suggested that such powers conflicted with the First Amendment. This was at least partly because by 1934 the Supreme Court had only recently begun to examine the meaning of the First Amendment; almost all free-speech case law at the time was *state* law, and the great bulk of it explicitly suggested that the right of expression included an obligation to use the right responsibly.[35] Whatever else the First Amendment was thought to bear on at the time, it was not the broad range of issues that it does today. All the more remarkable, then, is that Congress included in the Communications Act an explicit proscription against censorship. That this proscription existed alongside a vague decree that the government had a legitimate role to play in safeguarding the public's interest in private companies' use of the airwaves suggests that Congress didn't see any contradiction in the juxtaposition.

Neither did the American Bar Association. The ABA was a strong opponent of broadcast reform and in the effort to defeat Wagner-Hatfield had gone so far as to argue that the government should have censorship powers over the airwaves. The ABA had formed its Standing Committee on Communications in the late 1920s under the leadership of Louis G. Caldwell, at the time the most influential commercial broadcast attorney in the United States. In urging Congress to reject the reformers' set-aside proposals, Caldwell argued that regulators should have life-and-death discretion over the airwaves. "If all this be censorship," said the 1929 *ABA Report*, "it seems unavoidable and in the best interests of the public."

This argument raised no objection from broadcasters, though they were eager to show Congress that such stern measures would be unnecessary. CBS chairman William Paley, for example, promised the Senate Commerce Committee in 1930 that no more than 30 percent of his network's programming would ever be sold, that the balance would be available for unsponsored educational and noncommercial programs. He reiterated this pledge in 1934, and tried to distinguish his efforts from those of reformers by giving the term *educational* a distinctly populist twist: "We cannot hand the critical and often restive American audience some brand of bright encyclopedic facts and expect it to listen enthralled as might an astonished European peasant who had grown up without benefit of school or newspaper," he said. "If in the American audience we have perhaps the highest common denominator of cultural appreciation in the world—thanks to our democratic school system—we also have perhaps the most critical audience, and one of the most independent in establishing its own standards of appreciation and judgment."[36]

If the arguments from Paley, Caldwell, and other opponents of reform were less than convincing, they did not have to be. Commercial broadcasters commanded tremendous financial resources, and they united behind a common front, which the reformers failed to do. Many of them, in fact, argued that it would be better to work *with* the commercial broadcasters rather than establish an alternative system, as the NCER proposed. The principal advocate of that view was the National Advisory Council on Radio in Education (NACRE), established in 1930 with funding from the Carnegie Corporation and led by University of Chicago president Robert Hutchins. NACRE proclaimed itself to be an "organization to which [commercial broadcasting] can turn for advice and counsel in educational matters." So clearly antithetical was this position to the more radical reform advocated by the NCER that there resulted, as Barnouw has characterized it, a "glorious confusion" about the reform movement's goals, and even who its representatives were.

Various factions quarreled over how best to pay for the kinds of programming they proposed. The American Civil Liberties Union, for example, did not want government underwriting to the extent known in Canada or Great Britain; many educators proposed limited advertising as a solution, while others abhorred the very idea. "Every son-of-a-gun and his brother has a definite idea about the way it should be handled," complained one reformer.[37] In the long run, all these arguments made it impossible for the reformers to reduce their theoretical agreements to specific policy recommendations, and the dissension opened the way for the commercial broadcasters' counterattack. Indeed, it was on the divisive question of limited advertising that Senator Dill eventually succeeded in derailing the Wagner-Hatfield amendment. There was too much advertising on the air already, he said. "That is not what the people of this country are asking for!"[38]

The failure of reformers to unite behind an articulate statement of the public interest in the 1930s should serve as a caution to those who today are trying to give children greater standing in information-highway policy. Equally instructive are some of the other reasons for the failure of the Wagner-Hatfield amendment. Most important was that the Roosevelt administration, for all its reformist fervor, was not much interested in reforming broadcasting. Awarding 25 percent of the spectrum to nonprofit broadcasters would have meant canceling many existing allocations, and Roosevelt, almost universally hated by the nation's (mostly Republican) newspapers, did not want to alienate the owners of this new and powerful medium. Neither did many congressmen, of course, for they quickly found that a local broadcaster was the best kind of friend and the worst kind of enemy. Just as important, broadcasting was one of the very few genuine success stories of the Great Depression, and its success was a much-needed palliative not only for the Roosevelt administration but for millions of struggling Americans.

With the defeat of the Wagner-Hatfield amendment, the possibility of an alternative broadcast system was put to rest. For two more years, NACRE tried to work with CBS and NBC in support of educational programming, but in 1936 it gave up in frustration. "Our experience," a NACRE report said, "has demonstrated a conflict between the commercial interests of the broadcasting company and the educational uses of radio which threatens to become almost fatal to the latter . . . It is useless at this time to attempt systematic education by national network broadcasting at hours when it will be available to large adult audiences."[39]

By then, however, few people cared—or dared to. In 1937 William Paley summed up the industry's viewpoint when he said, "He who attacks the fundamentals of the American system attacks democracy itself."[40] Its position secured, broadcasting ceased to be a matter of public concern. A decade later, on the eve of the age of television, the sociologist Paul Lazarsfeld reported that most Americans knew little or nothing about their system of broadcasting. "They have obviously given it little thought," he wrote.[41]

Such was the world when RCA president David Sarnoff officially announced the dawn of the Age of Television at the 1939 World's Fair in Queens, New York. "Now," he said to a group of reporters, lifting the veil from the small set sitting on a podium, "we add sight to sound." The description was a monumental understatement even in Sarnoff's day. Not only was television the crowning achievement of a century's worth of technological advance in photography, electricity, and telegraphy, but it brought together in one device the news and information functions of the press, the personal and family delights of the phonograph, the entertainment grandeur of the motion picture, and the immediacy of radio. Television was as revolutionary in its day as SuperTube is in ours.

Indeed, broadcasters themselves were most surprised by television; many of them thought the idea nonsense. "While theoretically and technically television may be feasible," said the American inventor Lee De Forest, "commercially and financially I consider it an impossibility, a development of which we need waste little time dreaming."[42] Many dreamed anyway. The idea of sending pictures through the air had been with radio from its earliest inception and had been the object of experiments since the days of the telegraph. The idea of transmitting *moving* pictures—television—was conceived as a technological goal as early as 1875, and in 1884 the German inventor Paul Nipkow had invented a mechanical rotating disc that became the standard for sending images over wires.

Scientific American, reviewing the many experiments under way in the "visual radio" business, dubbed this new technology "television" as early as 1907. Led by Westinghouse, virtually all the companies in the RCA consortium were conducting television experiments by the early 1920s.[43] In 1923 a young Westinghouse researcher named Vladimir Zworykin invented an electronic television camera tube—a dramatic advance over Nipkow's mechanical wheel—and two years later independent inventors in both the

United States and England performed public demonstrations of flickering video technologies. Herbert Hoover, contending for the Republican presidential nomination, appeared in a 1927 test telecast by AT&T, and soon General Electric, having developed a tiny television set, began experimenting with programs. As had happened with radio, amateurs scattered across the country were busy building their own sets, and in 1928 one such home operator, in Pittsburgh, reported picking up the experimental General Electric broadcasts emanating from Schenectady, New York. This flurry of activity sent stock prices of RCA and other communications companies soaring, and led David Sarnoff to proclaim that by 1935 television would be "as much a part of our life" as radio.[44]

He was wrong. The stock market crash of 1929 sent RCA's stock tumbling. It had climbed as high as 500 points a share in midsummer, prompting the company to make a five-for-one stock split, with each share worth well over $100. By January 1930, those shares had dropped to $20. Sarnoff became RCA's president that same year, but he had to wait almost a decade before introducing television to American homes. When he did, the reaction was mixed. Only a few experimental television stations were in operation in the United States in 1939, all of them owned by the networks, all of them broadcasting sporadically for only a few hours at a time. Commercial television was unknown, and the FCC kept it that way until 1941. Few people expected television ever to rival radio. Government restrictions on the manufacture of sets during World War II ensured that it would not, for a time, and some commentators believed that the new device would never be much more than a toy. "The problem with television," a *New York Times* columnist said dismissively in March 1939, "is that people must sit and keep their eyes glued to a screen. The average American family hasn't time for it . . . Television is too confining; the novelty would not hold up for more than an hour."[45] Though Sarnoff announced in 1940 the results of research that showed television would be an effective sales tool, NBC president Merlin Aylesworth dismissed it altogether, saying that it would never make any money. Those who gave television a better chance at success offered only a qualified endorsement. When E. B. White saw a demonstration of the new medium in 1938, he marveled at its potential but feared for its future. With television, he said, "we shall discover either a new and unbearable disturbance of the general peace or a saving radiance in the sky."[46]

White's hope for a "saving radiance" was not merely the hope of liberals and intellectuals. The most enthusiastic champion of television's redeeming social value was none other than David Sarnoff. To be sure, RCA's president had a huge stake in television's future, but he was also a devotee of classical music who had little use for many of the more popular entertainments that had flourished on radio. With television, Sarnoff believed, high culture would flourish on the airwaves as never before. "It is probable," he said in 1939, "that television drama of high caliber and produced by first-rate artists will materially raise the level of dramatic taste of the nation."[47] A few years later he spoke of a "new age of electrical entertainment, which will bring the artist to the public, the lecturer to his audience, and the educator to his student body." Television, he said, would be part of a new age of American democracy in which "the East will see the West and the West will see the East. Television will project pictures across the prairies, over the mountains and into the valleys."[48]

Sarnoff was not alone in this expectation. Speaking in 1945, shortly before the end of the war, FCC chairman Paul Porter predicted that "television's illuminating light will go far, we hope, to drive out the ghosts that haunt the dark corners of our minds—ignorance, bigotry, fear. It will be able to inform, educate and entertain an entire nation with a magical speed and vividness . . . It can be democracy's handmaiden by bringing the whole picture of our political, social, economic, and cultural life to the eyes as well as the ears."[49] A few years later the talent agent William Morris vividly, if weirdly, summed up this aspiration: "Television has the impact of an atomic bomb. It is increasing the people's intellect in proportion to a bomb's destructive power for blowing them to pieces."[50]

The terms used to assess television's future are familiar to anyone acquainted with the breathless predictions made about SuperTube today. In 1949 an industry trade journal offered its prediction that "with the combination of motion picture film and the television camera, coupled with the television receiver in the American home, John Q. America is about to receive the greatest treasury of enlightenment and education that has ever before been given to a free man."[51] A few years later NBC president Pat Weaver—a former advertising executive—said:

> We can create a new stature in our citizens. The miracles of attending every event of importance, meeting every personality of importance in your world, getting to observe members of every group, racial, national, sectional, cultural, religious; recognizing every city, every country, every river and mountain on sight; having full contact with the explanations of every mystery of physics, mechanics and the sciences; sitting at the feet of the most brilliant teachers, and being exposed to the whole range of diversity of mankind's past, present and the aspirations for mankind's future—these and many other miracles are not assessed yet. But I believe that we vastly underestimate what will happen.[52]

Just how these "miracles" would come to pass no one knew. Broadcasting had survived and grown during the New Deal as one of the few industries conspicuously untouched by its reforms, and the defeat of the Wagner-Hatfield amendment meant that the responsibility for fulfilling television's promise was left almost entirely to commercial broadcasters. Congress did not choose to revisit the issue when television was introduced in 1939, and the FCC gave the new medium only slightly more attention; concerned about RCA's potential to dominate the new medium, it did not allow stations to make profits from commercials until 1941. On July 1 of that year, the nation's first for-profit commercial television station, NBC-owned WNBT, went on the air in New York City.

Short of programming and eager to attract viewers, early television stations did what radio had once done: they experimented with as many types of programs as possible and relied heavily on advertisers to supply the rest. The result was an eclectic mix of programs, from tawdry to brilliant. Many were simply imports from radio—sports, comedies, and variety-vaudeville shows—but early television was also the fountainhead of creative talent and storytelling for Broadway and Hollywood. Shows like *Studio One, Philco Television Playhouse, Kraft Television Theatre, Armstrong Circle Theater, The Alcoa Hour,* and *The U.S. Steel Hour* produced distinguished original material and gave voice to a new generation of American artists.

But this period of excellence did not last. Its most inventive and thoughtful programs succeeded precisely because television itself had not. The medium's future was still uncertain, its financing still derived largely from radio revenues, and its audiences were small. Indeed, until the mid-1950s television was not really a mass medium—certainly not in the way that radio was—but, rather, the exclusive dominion of the few who could afford to buy a set and lived within range of a signal. Television sets had been sold in New York City as early as 1938, but few people could afford to buy them. With the resumption of normal manufacturing after the war, new RCA sets cost $385, the equivalent today of almost $2,500. In 1946 the company sold 10,000 of them in a country with only eighteen television stations in twelve cities. Three years later, in 1949, Americans bought more than 2 million sets, and the number of television stations in the nation had grown to forty-eight. Still, by 1950 only about 7 percent of American homes had a TV set, and only large urban areas received television signals.

Television remained an exclusive medium longer, perhaps, than it might have otherwise because of an FCC freeze on new spectrum assignments between late 1948 and mid-1952. But by virtue of that exclusivity, early television audiences tended to be not only well-to-do but well educated and, by modern standards, critical. Women's magazines of the period, for example, were full of advice on how to teach children to be discerning viewers, offering nuanced criticisms of the new medium that understood, in ways that seem even more prescient today, television's visceral power to teach values and influence behavior.

In 1952, when the FCC lifted the freeze, the television industry boomed. That year the commission approved 280 applications for television licenses, and seventy new stations went on the air. By 1956 there were 459 stations operating around the country, a nearly fivefold increase over the number operating in 1950; television sets were in 73 percent of American homes; and almost anyone anywhere in the country could receive a television signal.[53]

With mass audiences, television changed. The economic logic of the Communications Act began to assert itself, and television, like radio before it, turned increasingly to the business of selling the largest possible audiences to advertisers. In truth, it was an easy transition. From the start, television programs had been produced, for the most part, by advertising agencies. To them, dramatic series like *Playhouse 90* were too demanding and often too depressing. In one episode of *Playhouse 90*, for example—"Judgment at Nuremberg"—viewers noticed that a character's speech about the murder of concentration-camp victims with cyanide gas was abruptly interrupted by a deletion of words. The deleted words were "gas chamber," which a CBS engineer had removed at the behest of the sponsor, a natural-gas company. As one CBS executive explained, "We felt that a lot of people could not differentiate between the kind of gas you put in the death chambers and the kind you cook with."[54] Advertisers soon abandoned television drama altogether, preferring game shows; lighter, shorter half-hour dramas; and a new and conspicuously successful television genre, the Western. Years later, an ABC president summed up the change: "When Pat Weaver was president of NBC, he was programming for people who shopped at Saks Fifth Avenue. I was programming for the people at Sears, Roebuck. There are more of them."[55]

By the early 1950s, many public officials were wondering aloud about the value of such programs. Prominent among them were Connecticut senator William Benton, who publicly declared commercial television a lost opportunity,[56] and Eleanor Roosevelt, who hosted a regular Saturday-afternoon discussion program on NBC, *Mrs. Roosevelt Meets the Public*. During one show in 1951 the former First Lady played host to FCC Commissioner Frieda Hennock, and the two women talked about television's neglected potential as an educational tool.

Hennock, who had been appointed by President Harry Truman in 1948, was a successful corporate lawyer who had arrived at the commission determined to revive the spirit, if not the letter, of the Wagner-Hatfield campaign. In 1949, shortly after the FCC instituted its freeze on licenses, she proposed that it consider devoting a full 25 percent of the spectrum to educational, noncommercial broadcasting. "Education now faces its last chance on TV," she said. "In order to realize the full educational potentialities of TV, educators must be provided with their own stations, their own homes in the spectrum. Seventy-five percent of the available channels is more than adequate for mere commercial needs."[57]

As they had in 1934, commercial broadcasters fiercely resisted, and with good reason. By 1949, the Commerce Department was predicting that television would soon become the nation's most important sales tool; television advertising revenues, about $12 million in 1949, were to grow to more than $300 million by 1952. The spectrum was simply too valuable to hand over to educators. Reviving the argument Paley had made in 1934, commercial broadcasters argued that they could best provide cultural and educational programs in the commercial-free "sustaining" time on their own stations. Educators themselves were either indifferent to Hennock's campaign or slow to rally behind her, and those who did support her quarreled, as they had in 1934, over how to find financial support for educational television and whether it should be strictly noncommercial. Nonetheless, Hennock persisted, and in 1952 she somewhat succeeded: that year, when the FCC's 6th Report and Order lifted the freeze, the order also reserved approximately 12 percent of the total number of channels for noncommercial television.[58]

Unfortunately, most of those channels—162 out of 242—were in the ultrahigh-frequency part of the broadcast spectrum. Most television sets in American homes did not even receive UHF signals, nor would Congress and the FCC require them to until 1963.

The UHF band, in fact, had been a casualty of an earlier struggle over technological standards for television, specifically about whether sets would be black-and-white or color, mechanical or electronic. That battle, which was waged between RCA and an upstart CBS, was fought in the name of the "public interest," but it revolved, as such debates traditionally had, around questions of economics and technology. This blinkered approach had the unintended effect of rendering stillborn the many high hopes Americans would have for the new medium.

The color-television battle, together with what came to be known as the "network case," also illustrates the FCC's difficulty in reconciling industry and public interests. The network case, *NBC v. United States*,[59] was the result of an FCC inquiry that began in 1938 and ended three years later with the commission's "chain broadcasting" regulations, which gave the radio and network affiliates greater discretion in their local program schedules and, the commission believed, would foster more local service and make American broadcasting more competitive. The FCC's rulemaking took special aim at RCA and its two NBC networks, the Red and the Blue, which had counterprogrammed each other to the distinct disadvantage of the other networks, at that time CBS and the Mutual Broadcasting System. With the ruling, RCA was forced to sell its Blue network—which it did, in 1943, but not without a fight. In the first test of the constitutionality of the Communications Act, Sarnoff took NBC's case to the Supreme Court, which upheld the FCC's legal authority to foster competition in its selection of licensees.

Justice Felix Frankfurter, who wrote the Court's opinion in the case, had a few words to say about the meaning of the "public interest, convenience and necessity" and its relation to freedom of speech in broadcasting. Clearly, he wrote, if the FCC had the responsibility to supervise its licensees, it also had the responsibility to select them, a discretionary task that could only be carried out according to the commission's interpretation of the public interest—in this case its interpretation that promoting competition served that interest. "Unlike other modes of expression," Frankfurter said, "radio inherently is not available to all. That is its unique characteristic, and that is why, unlike other modes of expression, it is subject to governmental regulation. Because it cannot be used by all, some who wish to use it must be denied."[60] In short, he said, the FCC's rulemaking did not violate the networks' First Amendment rights.

Frankfurter's opinion has stood ever since as a pillar of the principle that the public owns the airwaves, as the legal basis for the FCC's regulation of broadcasters, and as the basis for later Supreme Court decisions on the First Amendment rights of broadcasters. But it may have done more to damage public-interest broadcasting than to further it, for the opinion said nothing about the obligations of broadcasters but merely placed their rights in the context of the economic and technological limitations of the broadcast spectrum.[61] Moreover, for all the acclaim accorded the network case, it did almost nothing to promote competition or its presumed benefit, more diverse programming. On the contrary: in forcing the sale of NBC Blue, the FCC ended Sarnoff's practice of devoting one of his networks to high culture. Sold to WMCA in New York City, NBC Blue became the fledgling American Broadcasting Company (ABC), which, strapped for capital, became another commercial network with decidedly uninspired programming.

The network case had no substantial effect on the growing dominance of the networks either, in part because the FCC, trying to resolve the dispute over color television, spent the late 1940s undoing with its left hand what it had tried to do with its right in the network case. The color battle began in earnest in 1940, when CBS unveiled a color technology with which, it announced, it would seek to unseat RCA as the standard-bearer in television manufacturing. But there were problems. One was that the CBS color system was based on the mechanical rotating wheel that the all-electronic system—with which RCA had built its black-and-white sets—had made obsolete; another was that it was designed for transmission on the UHF band, and RCA's sets received signals only on the VHF (very high frequency) part of the spectrum. UHF broadcasting had several distinct advantages over VHF—it could carry as many as seventy channels, with better picture and sound quality—and in challenging RCA's system, CBS threatened to make RCA's patents worthless.

For the next thirteen years, RCA and CBS struggled to win FCC approval of their competing technological standards. But in determining what kind of television system Americans would have, the crucial years were 1944 through 1946. During that time Sarnoff campaigned relentlessly against the CBS color wheel, lobbying both the electronics industry and the FCC. Despite later accusations that RCA acted improperly, especially in its dealings with the commission, it was not hard for Sarnoff to win sympathy for his case. To manufacturers, their wartime defense contracts gone, RCA's patents represented an opportunity to retool their factories to the demands of a consumer economy. And to the FCC, CBS's gambit was simply a stumbling block in delivering television to a public long promised it.

Under enormous pressure, and despite its own belief that television belonged in the UHF spectrum, the commission concurred with RCA that to delay television further would be detrimental to both the electronics industry and the public: in 1946 it rejected CBS's color disk and, with it, the company's UHF proposal.* Thus it was decided that color television would be electronic rather than mechanical, and that set manufacturers would proceed as planned with RCA's patents. More important, limiting American television to VHF transmission ensured that it would be dominated by the networks and even less competitive than radio.

The concentration of broadcasting power in the hands of a few private companies alarmed many people, not the least of them a small group of public intellectuals and scholars who, led by Robert Hutchins and funded by Time and Encyclopaedia Britannica, had begun meeting in 1943 to discuss that problem and many others which, they believed, seriously threatened the public interest and the press itself. In 1947 the so-called Hutchins Commission published a short report on the state of mass communication in America.[62] *A Free and Responsible Press* opened with a simple question—"Is the freedom of the press in danger?"—which it answered quickly in the affirmative. In its study of the "instruments of mass communication"—newspapers, movies, magazines, books, and radio—the commission made several criticisms that are as trenchant today as they were then. It voiced special concern, for

---

* In 1949 CBS came back with another color system, this one requiring an expensive and clumsy adapter designed to work with existing VHF-only receivers, and the FCC approved it. Likening the CBS color system to a "horse-and-buggy" in the age of motorcars, Sarnoff took the FCC to court, only to have the Supreme Court uphold the FCC's ruling in 1951.

As it turned out, CBS's legal victory was Pyrrhic. When the network aired its first commercial colorcast in June 1951, only twenty-five television sets in the country —out of 10 million—were equipped to see it. A month later RCA demonstrated its own all-electronic color system to great acclaim, and in December 1953 the RCA color standard became the FCC standard.

example, about the growing concentration of power in all the news and entertainment media, not just broadcasting, and about the increasing volume of "sales talk" that passed as "public discussion."

Complicating these difficulties, it wrote, was the advent of a "communications revolution" that had greatly, perhaps dangerously, extended the power of the press in public and private life to the near-exclusive benefit of advertisers. Within a generation, "the development of moving—then moving and talking—pictures; of wireless transmission used for telegraph, telephone and voice broadcasting; of airplane transport; of offset color printing" had brought "the remote corners of the world within a few hours of one another." Television would soon permit people anywhere on the globe "the same face-to-face observation of each other that is now limited to citizens of small communities."[63]

The commission examined the history and rationale of government intervention in curbing the many shortcomings and outright abuses of power in the communications industries and suggested that further intervention might someday become inevitable, but it urged the industries to make self-regulation meaningful and effective. The NAB code was a collection of "innocuous declarations," it said, far less important "than the regulation of content by the advertisers . . . The great consumer industries—food, tobacco, drugs, cosmetics, soap, confectionery and soft drinks—determine what the American people shall hear on the air."[64]

The commission thought the government should promote noncommercial broadcasting with every means "short of subsidy" to offset this commercial stranglehold. If its members knew that only a decade earlier the drafters of the Communications Act had explicitly rejected this idea, they made no mention of it. Neither did they note the even greater concentrations of corporate power in television that the FCC, through its deliberations over color television and the UHF spectrum, had allowed to develop.

But the commission did make several detailed, practical recommendations, all of which were ignored at the time and none of which either the commission or its funders did anything to promote. Some of them—a public debate on national communications policy; independent and well-publicized reviews of the media and their performance; a common-carrier, backbone service to allow Americans to participate more fully in public life—are as urgent today as they were then, possibly more so. But the commission's reluctance to pursue them may have been due to the uniformly hostile reception its report received from the press, which ridiculed it and characterized the authors as a bunch of ivory-tower social planners.

One exception to this hostility could be found at, of all places, the FCC. Inspired by both the Hutchins group and Justice Frankfurter's opinion in the network case, and led by two New Dealers—Commissioner Clifford Durr and Chairman Paul Porter—the FCC issued a statement on the Public Service Responsibility of Broadcasters in 1946, dubbed the Blue Book by broadcasters (according to some, for the blue covers it was wrapped in; to others, for the blue pencil used by network censors).[65] The statement was the most ambitious and articulate effort the FCC ever made to reach beyond the usual economic and technical formulations of the public interest and meet head-on the question of programming. Like the Hutchins Report, the Blue Book examined the problem of balancing principles of free expression with those of social responsibility, the rights of the audience versus the rights of the broadcaster. It was also the FCC's first direct attempt to limit advertising on the airwaves.

The Blue Book's persuasiveness was built most powerfully on a careful case-by-case examination of the casual disregard that so many broadcasters gave to their public-service obligations. Reviewing the records of five sample radio stations, it compared the programming promises they had made in their license applications with their actual performance. In each case, the FCC found, the stations opted wherever possible for recorded music, network programs, and commercials. Armed with this evidence, and citing the FCC's earlier record on license grants, renewals, and suspensions, the commission now asserted that it had not only the authority but the "affirmative duty, in its public interest determinations, to give full consideration to program service."[66]

From there the Blue Book went on to specify the elements that were essential to public service in broadcasting, giving special emphasis to four. The first was programs carried noncommercially, what William Paley had called "sustaining programs"; the second was live, local programs; the third was programs featuring discussion of public affairs; the fourth was limited commercials. All these could be incorporated in a station's programming without harming broadcasters' financial health or profitability, the Blue Book's authors argued, and they proposed giving them new weight in licensing decisions.

But it did not happen. The Blue Book's research and analysis succeeded in exposing the industry's disregard of its public-interest obligations and the FCC's willful neglect of them, but it was never formally adopted, and all five stations it singled out for review had their licenses renewed. Like the Hutchins Report, the Blue Book seemed to many people a stuffy intellectual exercise, especially so in 1946, with the war finally over and the promise of television and all its entertainment wonders so tantalizingly near. It did not help matters that the Blue Book's author was widely known to be Charles Siepmann, a former officer of the British Broadcasting Corporation. His proposals were in fact elegantly written, clear in their reasoning, and generous in spirit, but industry critics nonetheless succeeded in characterizing them as the work of a "socialist," making it very unlikely that a majority of the commissioners would ever support them. Like the Hutchins Report, the Blue Book was scorned by those it took to task; broadcasters complained loudly of censorship and, more discreetly, of the harm its program proposals might do to their profit margins. Congress took no interest, and the FCC, seeing that its effort to give meaning to the law's public-interest requirement had been rebuffed, quietly let it die.

The Blue Book resembled the Hutchins Report in yet another way: it was remembered more for what it did not do or say than for what it did. It did not have any effect whatsoever on broadcaster performance, for example, even though its analysis quickly became symbolic of all that was wrong with American broadcasting. But it was a symbol only, for like the Hutchins Report it said nothing about the structural inadequacies that gave rise to its criticism. Indeed, it took the commercial structure of broadcasting for granted and, in essence, championed the idea of giving the FCC powers of oversight, standard-setting, and correction commensurate with those that other federal agencies exercised. But where those powers seemed natural and reasonable in the regulation of financial markets or interstate commerce, for example, they seemed much less so, for constitutional reasons, in the marketplace of ideas.

The Blue Book's failure made two conclusions clear. The first was that the FCC's power to suspend or revoke broadcast licenses was extremely limited—too great ever to be invoked and too weak to survive a legal challenge.* In the absence of meaningful authority, broadcasters would have to fulfill their public-service requirements, if at all, by somehow heroically disregarding the fact that locally originated public-service programming was expensive and time-consuming to produce, and that the easier course—reliance on the networks—was also more lucrative. The second was that, as one broadcast executive put it, a broadcast license had become "a license to print your own money."[67]

Thus it was that when Americans first started buying television sets in large numbers in the 1950s, the great hopes that had been held out for the new medium were already strangled in their crib. The ensuing scramble to acquire television licenses when the FCC lifted its freeze in 1952 was the greatest grab of public property since westward expansion. Without paying so much as a dime for the privilege, broadcasters could turn a spectrum allotment into a fortune. The FCC for the most part made no effort to revisit the subject but instead joined the party. Porter had left the commission shortly after the Blue Book's issuance, and following him came a succession of chairmen who not only ignored the law but flouted it, accepting extraordinary perquisites from the very people they were supposed to be regulating. During the 1950s, which the broadcast historian

---

* Anyone familiar with American broadcasting history will quickly point out that, in fact, the FCC has revoked licenses, indeed had already done so when the Blue Book was issued. But as Rowland points out, the revoked licenses involved broadcasters who "were obviously outrageous and in many ways unpalatable characters with programming bordering on the fraudulent or slanderous." Some hawked patent medicines, others were hatemongers or had lied to the commission about the ownership of the station. None of the commission's attacks were mounted against any major commercial station.

James Baughman calls the FCC's "whorehouse era," the industry and the agency were stung by several scandals, and one chairman was forced to resign in disgrace.[68]

Those who had hoped, with E. B. White, that television would be a "saving radiance" were bitterly disappointed. Edward R. Murrow said that "television in the main is being used to distract, delude, amuse and insulate us."[69] Allen DuMont, the creator of a faltering fourth network said, "My reaction has been that of the creator of a Frankenstein. Rather than honored, perhaps I should be censured."[70] Even advertising executives professed horror. Said one, "We must never forget that the airwaves do not belong to the advertisers, nor to the networks, nor to the FCC, nor to the federal government. They belong to the people."[71] The historian Arthur Schlesinger, Jr., reflecting in 1957 on the many glorious promises that had accompanied the new medium's introduction only a few years before, called television "a bust,"[72] and in 1961, Robert Hutchins, then retired from the University of Chicago, considered that television had more completely abdicated its civic and moral responsibility than he or his colleagues might earlier have imagined possible:

> We have triumphantly invented, perfected, and distributed to the humblest cottage throughout the land one of the greatest technical marvels in history, television, and have used it for what? To bring Coney Island into every home. It is as though movable type had been devoted exclusively since Gutenberg's time to the publication of comic books.[73]

In May 1961, I told the nation that the years of FCC neglect of the public interest were over. In a speech before the National Association of Broadcasters, I asked them to "sit down in front of your television set when your station goes on the air and stay there without a book, magazine, newspaper, profit-and-loss sheet, or rating book to distract you—and keep your eyes glued to that set until the station signs off. I can assure you that you will observe a vast wasteland . . . Is there one person in this room who claims that broadcasting can't do better? . . . Your trust accounting with your beneficiaries is overdue."*

My speech accomplished two things: it provoked the wrath of the broadcasters, many of whom immediately characterized it as the thin edge of the ax of government censorship; and it helped wake up the American people to the fact that television had fallen far short of its creators' goals. The FCC had no interest in censorship, only in promoting a more reasonable balance between profits and public service. And if television were ever to begin to fulfill its promise, the choices available to viewers would have to increase; to do that, the industry would have to overcome the structural problems and poor habits of mind that had attended its explosive but misguided growth. Thus the commission worked to promote cable and other new technologies, to increase the number of educational stations, and, in 1962, to retrieve them from the twilight zone of UHF by requiring all set manufacturers to make their sets capable of receiving UHF signals.[74] Aware that earlier commissions had failed to enact public-service requirements, the FCC nonetheless made it known that it would not tolerate the egregious abuses of public trust that had been common in previous administrations, and it gave the strictest possible scrutiny to the shadowland between licensees' promises and their performance.

The process of restoring educational television to its rightful place took a significant step forward in 1963 with the creation of National Educational Television (NET). Four years later, under the leadership of the Carnegie Corporation and President Lyndon B. Johnson, Congress created the Corporation for Public Broadcasting (CPB), a noncommercial alternative to network television, though not a strictly educational one.

By that time, however, the "public interest" already had a new meaning, thanks first to the FCC's 1965 statement about comparative hearings for broadcast license applications, and second to a 1966 federal court decision that established the idea of "citizen standing" in challenging existing licensees.

For years the FCC had awarded broadcast licenses arbitrarily,

---

* For the complete text of this speech, see Appendix 2, pp. 187–000.

without any written standards for deciding between two or more applicants. Because most applicants were likely to promise the moon and few to deliver it, the commission's statement on comparative hearings, a formal and innocuous document, had no immediate effect on the assignment of licenses. Within a few years, though, its comparative criteria were applied to license renewals as well, and then it became possible for outsiders to challenge a broadcaster on the record of his promises and his performance. In 1969, a group of Boston citizens did just that, successfully challenging the renewal application of WHDH, a local television station, which in the end had to surrender its license.

The challenge to WHDH was made possible in the first place because of a 1966 suit brought by the United Church of Christ against the FCC. The suit alleged that two broadcasters in Jackson, Mississippi—WLBT (an affiliate of both NBC and ABC) and WJTV (the CBS affiliate)—not only had ignored news of local desegregation efforts but had also censored network news reports about them—this in a city where 45 percent of the viewing audience was black. When the stations wanted to renew their licenses, the United Church of Christ raised the issue with the FCC, which ruled that the church had no rights in the application and voted, 4 to 2, to renew the stations' licenses for one-year terms. The church challenged the FCC's position in court and won.[75]

The case injected a dramatic new element into the formula by which the FCC defined the public interest: the public itself. Ordinary citizens had complained about broadcasters since the earliest days of radio, but, absent a change in the law, their complaints were for the most part simply filed away. Though licensees were supposed actively to seek out public commentary on their programs, few did, and neither did the FCC. With the United Church of Christ case, the court affirmed that citizens had the right (though it was not unlimited) to testify in licensing proceedings at the commission. "Prior to this historic decision," writes one historian, "only other broadcasters alleging economic injury or electrical interference were granted standing to intervene. *United Church of Christ* is the Magna Carta for active public participation in broadcast regulation."[76]

Amazingly, when the appellate court remanded the case to the

FCC for review, the FCC renewed the stations' licenses again! So in 1969 the case went back to the court of appeals, which, disgusted, ordered the FCC to consider alternative applicants for the licenses. Eventually, WLBT lost its license, an outcome that, with the successful challenge against WHDH in Boston, stirred a riffle of concern among commercial broadcasters.*

Worse, from the broadcasters' perspective, was a Supreme Court ruling in 1969 that upheld and extended the notion first advanced by Justice Frankfurter in the network case: that broadcasters' privileged use of a limited public resource—the spectrum—required them to operate as something of a public forum. Broadcasters, in the Court's opinion, could not behave with the same kind of First Amendment discretion and impunity that the print press did. *Red Lion Broadcasting v. the FCC*[77] centered on a Pennsylvania radio station that aired a regular "Christian Crusade" series which on one occasion attacked the author of a book critical of Arizona senator Barry Goldwater; the program called the book's author a shirker, a liar, and a Communist. Not surprisingly the author took offense and, under the FCC's Fairness Doctrine and personal-attack rules, asked the station for free airtime with which to respond to the program's accusations.[78] The station refused, the author appealed to the FCC, and the FCC found in his favor. The station then appealed the ruling all the way to the Supreme Court, which upheld the FCC's position. Writing for the unanimous Court, Justice Byron White reviewed the history of the Radio and Communications Acts and concluded that "as far as the First Amendment is concerned," the technological limitations of broadcasting carried with them a special obligation:

> A license permits broadcasting, but the licensee has no constitutional right to be the one who holds the license or to monopolize a radio frequency to the exclusion of his fellow citizens. There is nothing in the First Amendment which prevents the government from requiring a licensee to share his frequency with others and

---

* While the WHDH case was important, it remains an anomaly. The FCC has almost always renewed licenses, regardless of claims about a licensee's service. The WLBT case was also unique, sending a clear message to Southern broadcasters that they could not discriminate against their black audiences; it did not change fundamentally the process by which licenses were renewed.

to conduct himself as a proxy or fiduciary with obligations to present those views and voices which are representative of his community and which would otherwise, by necessity, be barred from the airwaves . . . It is the right of the viewers and listeners, not the right of the broadcasters, which is paramount.[79]

Taken together, these challenges to the commercial interests that dominated American broadcasting in the 1960s were the most profound they had faced since the New Deal. Soon, public challenges to television licensees became so commonplace that the FCC had to publish standards governing negotiations between citizens groups and broadcasters.[80] The 1970s marked a high point of Americans' disaffection with television and the beginning of orchestrated campaigns to improve it.[81]

The 1970s were also the first decade in which special note was taken of *children* and television. Only twice before, in its 1960 programming policy statement[82] and during my tenure as chairman, had the FCC specifically listed service to children as part of a broadcaster's public service obligations. In 1968, Action for Children's Television picked up this torch, and the attention ACT drew to the exploitative practices in children's programming was given further standing in 1972, with the Surgeon General's announcement that a clear link existed between televised violence and aggressive behavior in children. FCC Chairman Richard Wiley in 1975 prodded the networks to set aside the first two hours of prime time for "family-viewing time."

The purpose of family-viewing time was of course to create a safe haven for young viewers. But the policy resulted in many programs, including some exemplary ones like *M*A*S*H* and *All in the Family*, being pushed to the fringes of prime time; writers and producers therefore complained that family-viewing time violated their rights of free expression. In 1976 the Writers Guild sued the FCC and won; a federal district court judge in California forced the FCC to drop the policy.[83]

The conflict over family-viewing time was just one of many conflicts that made it clear that the reforms of the 1960s, however just or well intentioned, had done very little to clarify the meaning and application of the public-interest standard in the Communications

Act. In some respects they had made matters worse. The broadcast industry's basic structure was essentially untouched, and a thin veneer of public participation served almost no one well—it was simply a source of great expense and growing irritation to broadcasters, who began to lobby Congress for regulatory relief.

What Congress answered with, neither broadcasters nor public-interest groups liked. In 1976, a Democratic congressman from California, Lionel Van Deerlin, was elected chairman of the House Subcommittee on Communications. Van Deerlin, a former newspaper reporter and television-news anchorman, took a strong interest in communications issues, not least the potential of new technologies to increase the volume and variety of televised programs. Soon, Van Deerlin recommended that Congress should consider a "basement-to-penthouse revamping of the Communications Act."[84] It was past time, he said, to bring it into the television age.

Many of Van Deerlin's colleagues in the House and Senate balked, calling his proposal everything from impractical to loony, but the congressman persisted, outlining four broad goals of what came to be known as his "rewrite" project. The first was to repeal those regulations (such as the Fairness Doctrine) and parts of the act (such as the equal-time provision for politicians) that, in his view, offended the First Amendment. The second was to expand the common-carrier industry, both to break the monopoly hold of giants like AT&T and to promote competition, which, he believed, would further First Amendment goals. His belief in the virtues of competition also led him to recommend the deregulation of cable, then under the boot of broadcasters, and the economic deregulation of broadcasting itself. In June 1978, Van Deerlin introduced a huge bill, H.R. 13015,[85] which proposed to abolish the FCC and establish in its place a "Communications Regulatory Commission." The new CRC, made up of five commissioners appointed to ten-year terms and subject to strict conflict-of-interest rules, would be allowed to intervene in the working of the communications industries only "to the extent marketplace forces are deficient."*

---

* At the time, the FCC consisted of seven commissioners, all but the chairman appointed to seven-year terms.

As radical as Van Deerlin's proposals were at the time, broadcasters disliked them for the spectacularly shortsighted reason that the bill did not confirm the kind of carte blanche they had come to think of as their birthright. Broadcasters were in fact much less interested in promoting an open marketplace of ideas than they were in protecting their very valuable privileges under the status quo. And though Van Deerlin had proposed to loosen or eliminate most existing restrictions on their use of the airwaves, he did not propose giving broadcasters de facto property rights in the spectrum. Far from it. The spectrum was still scarce and it was still public property, he said, and in return for deregulation broadcasters would have to be willing to give as well as get. If the Fairness Doctrine and equal-time provisions were repealed, broadcasters would most likely have to accept some kind of mandated public access. In addition, they would have to pay a percentage of their annual revenues to support public broadcasting—this in return for longer license terms. The broadcasters weren't interested. "The Committee kept asking what we'd be willing to give up," said one. "We didn't propose giving up anything."[86]

Broadcasters were cool to Van Deerlin's bill, but public-interest groups were openly hostile. The United Church of Christ called it "a disgrace, a bigger giveaway of public rights and property than Teapot Dome."[87] Other groups complained that nowhere did the words *public interest* appear, even though the bill featured several obvious public-interest measures: it required broadcasters to air regular and locally produced programming; it cut the number of television and radio stations a broadcaster could own from seven to five; and it levied a spectrum fee on commercial broadcasters with which to support a new and independent Public Telecommunications Programming Endowment, free of the many government and industry constraints that hobbled public broadcasting. If the bill was otherwise silent on the meaning of the public interest, Van Deerlin said, it was for a good reason:

We thought the phrase never really meant anything to users of the airwaves and to those who regulate the industry . . . A lot of games have been played with it, and there have been a lot of empty promises made to serve the public interest. But stations automatically received license renewals no matter what they promised, and no matter what the quality of the product.[88]

Many people agreed with Van Deerlin's assessment. In the end, however, it did not matter. Erik Barnouw offered what was the most prescient prediction of the bill's fate: "The commercial broadcasters will attack the notion of the fee to support public broadcasting," he said, "and the media-access people will attack everything else. They'll probably both succeed in chipping away at it."[89]

They did. Soon two competing bills appeared in the Senate, both of them much friendlier to broadcasters, forcing Van Deerlin to rewrite his own bill.[90] The revised bill, H.R. 3333,[91] angered public-interest groups even more than the first had, and they successfully convinced some of the junior members of Van Deerlin's subcommittee—among them Democrats Tim Wirth, of Colorado; Al Gore, of Tennessee; and Edward Markey, of Massachusetts—to oppose it. On July 13, 1979, Van Deerlin gave up, and withdrew his second bill from consideration. A year later, he himself left the House, having lost his bid for reelection.

Van Deerlin accepted defeat of his bill, but he insisted that where he had failed others would follow. "As a long-time observer and participant," he said, "I can tell you this: things will never be the same again."[92] They weren't. For its part, the FCC, which Van Deerlin's bills had threatened with extinction, took the lead under Chairman Charles Ferris in deregulating the communications industries—including radio broadcasting—and in promoting competitive services. In 1981 a new administration came to Washington for which deregulation was not merely an interest but a passion. Under Chairman Mark Fowler, the FCC's new watchword for regulation—what there was of it—was "the market." Much as Van Deerlin had, Fowler characterized the old fiduciary model of the public interest as a collection of "legal fictions." His solution, however, was very different:

The perception of broadcasters as community trustees should be replaced by a view of broadcasters as marketplace participants.

Communications policy should be directed toward maximizing the services the public desires. Instead of defining public demand and specifying categories of programming to serve this demand, the Commission should rely on the broadcasters' ability to determine the wants of their audiences through the normal mechanisms of the marketplace. The public's interest, then, defines the public interest. And in light of the First Amendment's heavy presumption against content control, the Commission should refrain from insinuating itself into program decisions made by licensees.[93]

In essence, the FCC wanted to bring up to date the free-enterprise rationale that had once inspired Herbert Hoover—but without any of the presumptions about service or civic responsibility with which Hoover had invoked the public interest. Neither did the FCC wish to honor, as Van Deerlin had, the idea that the public owned the airwaves. Congress should have auctioned off airspace at the beginning, Fowler said, and since it would be too disruptive to do so in 1982, instead he urged that broadcasters be given property rights—he called them "squatter's rights"—in their frequency assignments. Moreover, broadcasters should be free to renew their licenses without fear of challenge and, as with any other private property, free to sell their licenses to whomever they wished, whenever they wished.[94]

The result of this vigorous new deregulation policy of the Reagan administration was to transform broadcasting virtually overnight from a public trust into one of the hottest businesses on Wall Street. In their celebration of the bottom line and their open contempt for traditional public-interest values, broadcasters began to restructure, dismantle, or simply abandon many of the features for which the public had admired them most—news divisions, children's programs, standards-and-practices departments. The number and volume of commercials increased, and broadcasters adopted an anything-goes programming policy.

To many of the people who had so vehemently opposed Congressman Van Deerlin only a few years before, the new FCC version of deregulation was far worse. In the new television marketplace, the currency of access was dollars, not spectrum scarcity. In such a system, interest groups were simply shut out, unable or unwilling to dent the ideological armor around the FCC. Children's programming, already far down on the list of priorities for Congress and the FCC, was cast to the winds. In December 1983, forced by a federal court to proceed with a rulemaking on children's television, Fowler's FCC issued a report on children's programming practices and said there was no need for action. Commissioner Henry M. Rivera, in a dissenting statement, was both incredulous and angry:

> I wish I had the eloquence of Mark Antony for this eulogy. Our federal children's television policy commitment deserves no less at this, its interment. Make no mistake—this is a funeral and my colleagues have here written the epitaph of the FCC's involvement in children's television . . . The majority has dishonored our most treasured national asset—children. It has set the notion of enforceable children's programming obligations on a flaming pyre, adrift from federal concern, in the hope that the concept will be consumed in its entirety and never return to the FCC's shores.[95]

3 : Children, Television, and the First Amendment

*You are all confused about what you have a right to do under the
Constitution and the right thing to do.* —*Justice Potter Stewart*

THE ISSUE OF CHILDREN'S TELEVISION RETURNED TO THE FCC IN
1990, as we have seen, in the form of the Children's Television Act.
No one should have been less surprised by this than the architects
of deregulation at the agency, for, despite their rejection of it for
a decade, they had anticipated that the marketplace would probably
not create very good children's programming, if any at all. In 1982,
Chairman Fowler and his colleague Daniel Brenner had predicted:

> An advertiser-supported system may be unable to meet the demand
> for children's programs because of the limited range of advertisers
> wishing to sponsor these programs. Although cable television pro-
> vides a way for parents to subscribe to programs for children, this
> service will not be offered in many communities. For some time
> to come, some child audiences will remain without access to spe-
> cialized cable services.[1]

Fowler and Brenner had recommended that children's programming become the responsibility of "non-commercial" broadcasting, and that children's programs be subsidized by a spectrum fee on commercial users. But that was a decision for Congress to make, they said, not the FCC. The commission's task was to make commercial broadcasting more economically rational, to promote competition, and to do away with what Fowler characterized as the "legal fictions" of the Communications Act's public-interest standard.

According to this new interpretation of the public-interest principle, the only acceptable basis for government regulation of television would be some sort of egregious market failure, such as occurred with children's programming; but even that could not be remedied without violating the First Amendment. As two FCC attorneys put it in 1988:

> While a rational basis is enough to justify economic regulation under the Constitution, the fact that a regulation seems to make sense—even if supported by a cost-benefit analysis—is not enough to satisfy the command of the First Amendment. For First Amendment rights to be restricted, let alone abrogated, the government has to establish first that the public has a compelling interest in the restriction of free speech.[2]

Though the argument in this case concerned the Fairness Doctrine, the FCC also applied it to children's programming, which meant that television's treatment of children, whether excessively violent or commercially exploitative, was not "compelling" in its view. Whatever the marketplace chose to offer children was by definition in the public interest, and the First Amendment foreclosed further discussion.

Despite the Children's Television Act, this rationale has only gained in currency in recent years. At a June 1994 FCC hearing on broadcaster compliance with the act, for example, Commissioner James Quello objected to suggestions that the commission clarify its policies with respect to the law's "educational and informational" component. "The more specific we get in clarifying the rules, the closer we are to violating First Amendment rights," he said.[3] A similar reluctance prevails when the issue is violence portrayed in television programs. In November 1993, for example, People for the American Way criticized several congressional bills on the issue, calling them a "clear violation of the First Amendment."[4] *Broadcasting and Cable* hyperbolically opined: "If this is a war on violence and we're going to suspend the Constitution while invoking a state of national emergency, then let's call it that and not pretend it's something else. And let's not stop there. Curfews, newspaper censorship, book burning . . . the whole nine yards."[5]

It would surely come as a surprise to those who wrote the First Amendment to see that Americans now cite it not to begin discussion of the public interest, but as a reason to *close* it. Yet this is the rationale by which we have abandoned our children in the furthest and most foul reaches of the television wasteland: we have accepted the proposition that the marketplace of ideas, however imperfect, cannot abide any form of government intervention, and that *any* intervention—even on behalf of children—is unconstitutional. This is the argument the FCC used in 1983 when it refused to reconsider its lack of a children's television policy; broadcasters, producers, and other television people continue to invoke it today. Bearing as it does on our most fundamental freedom, the argument merits serious attention, and its implications rightly give pause to many advocates of better children's television—whether congressmen or parents.

Should we accept the argument? Should we accept the idea that the First Amendment both prohibits us from protecting our children from the mass media *and* from nurturing them through the mass media? If we accept it, we have committed the perverse error of divorcing our commitment to free speech—the gift by which the Founding Fathers intended us to deliberate on the public interest—*from* our commitment to the public interest itself.

The First Amendment forbids the *government* from interfering with free speech; it does not prohibit citizens from voicing their displeasure at speech that, whether for good reason or bad, they do not like. The First Amendment protects the expression of ideas, but it does not make them all equal. We should not behave as if it does. On the one hand, we do not take the "marketplace of ideas" metaphor literally enough: we forget that markets are characterized by failures that they themselves cannot correct. On the other hand, we take the metaphor too literally: very often all that interests us about an idea is the dollar value that the market attaches to it. Thus it is, for example, that the chief executive of Time Warner, one of America's largest news and entertainment companies, characterized public disgust at a rap song about killing police officers as an attack on his and the singer's right of free speech. Thus it is that when officials at PBS canceled a documentary whose facts they believed had been doctored to suit its conclusion, the program's producer called the decision censorship. Thus it is that NBC *Nightly News* showed, without any attending report or explanation, the on-camera murder of a Miami woman by her estranged husband and responded to criticism of its decision with the true but irrelevant fact that the broadcast was protected by the First Amendment. Thus it is that when the Federal Communications Commission questioned where there was a public interest in allowing Infinity Communications to buy more radio stations after earning more than $1.2 million in indecency fines for the scatological humor of its top on-air personality, Infinity charged the FCC with censorship. Thus it is that when a dentist in Texas organized a letter-writing campaign to television stations across the country to ask whether strippers, transvestites, and serial killers were appropriate topics for children's after-school television, talk-show host Phil Donahue accused him of censorship. None of these events involved the government except the Infinity case. In none was there any serious threat to the speaker's right to speak. *All* simply raised the implicit or explicit question of how the speaker's communications served the public interest, and for that all were characterized as acts of "censorship."

Surely if ever a word were in need of rest, "censorship" is that word. So, too, its frequent advance man, "chilling," which serves as a verbal cue to would-be critics to back off and shut up. Both these words are used so often, and so casually, as to have lost much of their meaning. Every year, for example, a California university issues a list of the most underreported stories of the past year, which it calls "Project Censored." The list consists of events that have been ignored, underreported, inaccurately reported, unfairly reported, and even slanted—but by no means censored. To use the word so unthinkingly is not only wrong but dangerous, since it minimizes the many instances of *real* censorship that do occur, not only in the United States but throughout the world in nations where nothing close to First Amendment standards prevail.

Of course, broadcasters who depend on government-granted licenses to operate have a special reason to be concerned about censorship. The point is obvious enough to have inspired volumes of legal analysis, though the best documentation of the danger is Erik Barnouw's fine three-volume history of American broadcasting, which chronicles, among other things, the enormous and often insidious pressure the federal government brought to bear on radio and television during the "red scares" of the 1930s and 1950s and throughout the Cold War.[6] This is the history that broadcasters should cite when warning of "censorship," not the prospect of giving America's children decent programs to watch, or of protecting them from programs intended for adults. Both of these goals can be achieved without harming anyone's First Amendment rights.

The United States' policy with respect to children's television is mired in a rhetorical no-man's-land that, while nominally concerned with the First Amendment, often has no bearing on the First Amendment at all. In 1992, for example, a network representative complained that a nationally organized Turn Off the TV Day, during which parents were urged to turn off the set and engage their children in some family activity instead, violated the networks' free-speech rights. It's hard to imagine how—especially since broadcasters have for generations advised parents who object to what television offers their children simply to turn it off. A similar knee-jerk invocation of the First Amendment occurred in the summer of 1993, when Massachusetts congressman Edward Markey proposed that television sets be manufactured with a v-chip, a programmable computer chip that would allow parents to lock out programs they deemed unsuitable for their children. The technology represents an exponential expansion of the power of the remote-control device, and though it relies on some sort of rating system to work, there is no reason why the government has to be involved in the rating. Anyone could rate the programs, from the programmers themselves to local schools and community groups. So could companies that offer rating services for a profit, plans for which are under way. Broadcasters and Hollywood studios, however, characterized the technology—and Markey's proposal—as censorship. Typical was Fox Television chairwoman Lucie Salhany: "Quite frankly, the very idea of a v-chip scares me. I'm also very concerned about setting a precedent. Will we have an 's-chip' [for sex]?"[7]

Does it matter? If millions of parents want to block out *America's Most Wanted*, *Mighty Morphin Power Rangers*, or even the evening news, what concern is that of broadcasters, who for years have insisted that the public interest is whatever interests the public? More to the point, what threat is the v-chip to the First Amendment? It is a glorified on-off switch; if it is unconstitutional, so is the remote control and so, for that matter, are parents who care enough to monitor what their children watch.

The v-chip, in fact, has been for many years the fond wish of many First Amendment scholars, who worry that broadcast regulations designed to protect children infringe on the First Amendment rights of adults. While by no means a perfect solution, the chip overcomes that difficulty by making it possible to transfer what courts call the "plain-brown wrapper" principle from print to television. Books, magazines, and the like that are clearly not intended for children may be distributed to adults simply by concealing their contents, thereby limiting the exposure children are likely to have to them. The v-chip, along with a ratings system, would similarly extend the reach of free expression on television, allowing adults to watch whatever suited them while effectively eliminating children from the audience.

From a First Amendment standpoint it clearly makes a difference who does the rating, and it should not be the federal, state, or local government. But churches, PTAs, and other organizations could rate programs, giving parents a variety of private rating schemes to choose from.* Parents would still have to go to the trouble of locking out undesirable programs, and doubtless many would con-

---

* Congressman Markey's v-chip proposal required broadcasters themselves to transmit a rating signal, which would raise constitutional questions. We shall turn to this issue in further detail in the final chapter.

tinue to neglect their primary responsibility to monitor what their children watch. But the First Amendment would be satisfied: government would not be in the business of judging television content. The boundaries of expression on television would likely expand rather than contract, and parents would have a realistic opportunity to control what their children see.

What do broadcasters object to, then? The fact is, their interest in the First Amendment begins and ends with its effect on their bottom line: the v-chip could chip into advertising revenues. The cable industry, whose revenues depend less on advertising than on viewer subscriptions, has supported the v-chip proposal, and the National Cable Television Association promotes an exhaustive system of program descriptions designed to let viewers know what potentially offensive scenes will occur in films and in original programs. Individual cable companies may or may not use these descriptions, but many do. They do so because the cable industry sees its advisory system as a value-added feature for its subscribers. But broadcasters earn their revenues entirely from advertisers, and thus any sort of rating or advisory system—no matter who offers it— may well drain their revenues. It is those revenues, not ideas, that broadcasters defend when they speak in reverent tones about the marketplace of ideas. Unfortunately for them, manufacturers are already at work developing other technologies to screen programs. It happens that they are for finding programs in video-on-demand television systems, which one day will offer hundreds of channels and thousands of programs. A device that can lock a program service *in* can as easily lock it *out*; does that make it unconstitutional? Of course not, but to hear broadcasters tell it, Congressman Markey's proposal was the single greatest act of prior restraint since the Alien and Sedition Acts.

A second error in the broadcasters' argument against the v-chip is that it defies what we know about constitutional history and law. The First Amendment is considered a "preferred freedom"—one that, when balanced against other rights, gets the benefit of the doubt—but it is not an absolute freedom. It cannot be exercised at the expense of other constitutional rights or, in other narrowly defined categories, contrary to public safety or well-being. One area in which the First Amendment receives special scrutiny is where speech concerns children, whether as speakers or listeners. The assertion that a child's place in the "marketplace of ideas" is no different from an adult's, that a child's obvious need to be protected from harm and to be taught the lessons of civic society is not "compelling" enough to require broadcasters to honor it, is simply wrong. No matter what the medium, whether print or video, no matter how big the market or diverse its offerings, no matter whether there are five channels or five million, it is a well-settled principle of common law that children are a special case under the First Amendment.[8] That was true in 1983 when the FCC declined to rule on ACT's petition, and it will be true in 2033, when television as most of us know it will be a quaint artifact.

The truth is, if we really care about our children, invocations of the First Amendment should mark the beginning, not the end, of our discussion about children and television. The idea that the First Amendment forbids such debate—put forth by the FCC in 1982 and now almost universally embraced by broadcasters—is not only legally incorrect but historically ignorant.

As we know from the history of both the 1927 Radio Act and the 1934 Communications Act, few if any of the congressmen or industry figures who created the laws believed that their public-interest language violated the First Amendment. Indeed, as we have seen, the commercial broadcasters offered the most vigorous and eloquent defense of that language—particularly in 1934, in the debate over the Wagner-Hatfield amendment—and insisted that Congress had the right to require educational, cultural, and other types of public-interest programs. And the lawyers of the American Bar Association argued that such requirements were not censorship at all, but in "the best interests of the public." Virtually all the key players in the development of American broadcasting—Herbert Hoover, the networks and other for-profit broadcasters, the educational and other not-for-profit broadcasters—recognized that the public interest could not be served simply by turning the airwaves over to the market. That was why William Paley promised to set aside 70 percent of his network's airtime for sustaining programs, and why David Sarnoff used revenues from the Red network to support noncommercial programming on his Blue one. That is why Section 317 of the Communications Act requires commercials to be clearly labeled and distinct from programs, and why one of the first regulatory statements about the public interest in broadcasting (the 1929 Great Lakes Statement, issued by the Federal Radio Commission) concerned itself almost entirely with commercial abuse of the airwaves. In 1934, the juxtaposed requirements that private broadcasters provide for the public interest and that government refrain from censorship were not regarded as contradictory. Indeed, by the standards of the day, the Communications Act was a stroke of civic genius: it created a public good—broadcasting—by allowing private companies free use of public property, the airwaves.

Because the Supreme Court had only barely begun to explore the reach of the First Amendment and its protections, the Communications Act can be regarded as a statement of what Congress thought free speech *meant* in a world transformed by the new medium of radio. In 1934 the Court was only three years removed from its first major "free press" case, *Near v. Minnesota*, in which it held that prior restraints on the news media were generally impermissible. Only six years before that, in *Gitlow v. New York*, the Court had first extended the reach of the First Amendment to the states through the Fourteenth Amendment. Before *Gitlow*, and for virtually the entire nineteenth century, American thinking on the meaning of free speech had been shaped by state courts, some of which were considerably more libertarian in their interpretation than the Supreme Court was when it took up the matter around the time of World War I. Significantly, however, many states—both in their own constitutions and in their courts' rulings—regarded free speech as a right that, while sacred, was properly understood in terms of personal and social responsibility.[9] For that reason, the often-heard modern criticism that the Communications Act's public-interest requirement, and the Radio Act's before it, was a corrupt compromise, a willful intrusion of government into free speech that commercial broadcasters embraced for no other reason than to limit competition and promote their own interests, is considerably overstated—even if, under the burden of historical evidence, it appears to be true. In 1927, the politically and logistically difficult task of canceling spectrum assignments made the public-interest compromise not only necessary but, at the time, progressive. Indeed, as the legal scholar and former Yale president Benno Schmidt writes:

> It must be remembered that when broadcast regulation was cast, free speech principles had yet to win a victory in the Supreme Court. Up to that time, the courts had shown virtually complete deference to legislative prerogatives in regulating expression. Moreover, early radio made no pretense of being a news medium. It appeared to have more in common with motion pictures than with the print media, and the Supreme Court had held in 1915 that motion pictures, which were in its unanimous view more like "circuses" and "spectacles" than like the press, had nothing to do with the guarantee of free expression. The Radio Act, therefore, went well beyond what First Amendment notions of the day would have compelled when it barred censorship and included statutory protection for broadcasters' right of free speech.[10]

By 1934, the trusteeship system for broadcasting seemed essential if the new medium were to survive the Depression. If the public-interest clause in the Radio and Communications Acts has been vague to the point of constituting a "legal fiction," as critics of the law like to say, it was because the law too often went unenforced, not because broadcasters, the FCC, and Congress had no idea what it meant. From the industry's codes of good practice to FCC statements enumerating the elements of public service, clear (though unheeded) definitions of the public interest abounded. The history of the regulatory agencies indicates that marketplace success was one measure of the public interest, but by no means the *only* one. The drafters of the Communications Act believed that the public interest also depended on the deliberate judgments of responsible citizens, which would not necessarily submit to the mathematical calculations of the marketplace.

If we have forgotten all this it is because we have forgotten that the men and women who created American broadcasting did not believe, even in their most libertarian moments, that the public interest could be left to chance. When the Radio and Communications Acts were written, the meaning of the "public interest," writ large, was a subject of vigorous and visible debate in America. The country had emerged an international power from the industrial revolution and World War I, transformed technologically, economically, and culturally into a new nation. President Woodrow Wilson called it "the age of new relationships." New technologies in manufacturing, transportation, and communication made both the country and the world smaller, and spawned new political and economic ideas and institutions that would shape the twentieth century. These changes were so profound that many social commentators wondered whether democracy would survive them.

Americans approached this new age in two ways. On the one hand, under the guidance of men like Herbert Hoover, they worked to bring the social and material benefits of capitalism to many more people than had theretofore enjoyed them. On the other, they talked about the nature of a civic society, about the social and educational foundations of citizenship, and about the role of institutions, particularly the press, in making complex information meaningful.

Probably no two Americans personified this debate more than did the journalist Walter Lippmann and the educator John Dewey. To both men, the great question of the day was how to build and sustain an informed and principled public—and whether, indeed, it could be done at all. Their debate was not just an intellectual exercise confined to academic lecture halls or the pages of learned journals. Lippmann and Dewey were among the most widely read and admired authors of their day, and the debate was carried on in books, newspapers, and magazines. Moreover, despite their disagreements, both men recognized that, at bottom, the public interest was best defined in the lives and hopes of children. That is why Dewey is remembered today primarily as an educational reformer, the man who changed the way public schools approached children and their needs. As for Lippmann, this is how he summed up the meaning of "public interest" in 1955, toward the end of his career:

We cannot know what . . . infants in the cradle will be thinking when they go into the polling booth. Yet their interests, as we observe them today, are within the public interest. Living adults share, we must believe, the same public interest. For them, however, the public interest is mixed with, and is often at odds with, their private and special interests. Put this way, we can say, I suggest, that the public interest may be presumed to be what men would choose if they saw clearly, thought rationally, acted disinterestedly and benevolently.[11]

If Lippmann or anyone else offered this definition of the public interest today, his remarks might invite contemptuous snickers. Today the moral questions that Lippmann, Dewey, and their contemporaries believed defined the parameters of the public interest are rarely asked. In their place—in government and in industry, in think tanks and in universities, among conservatives and liberals alike—are economic theories of efficiency and equity, as if the public interest were merely a matter of distributive justice. This who-gets-what conceptualization of the public interest is antidemocratic at its core, since it assiduously avoids having to make the moral decisions that democracies, by definition, are supposed to make.[12] Children are the biggest losers of all in this calculus, because they lack economic and political power and are dependent on the moral discretion of adults for their safety and health, their civic and academic education—their future.

Small wonder that the well-being of our children counts among the greatest failures of American public and private life over the past thirty years. As a nation we are far less willing to make the investments in families that other advanced nations do. The United States ranks twenty-first in the world in infant mortality rates; almost 9 million American children have no health-care insurance. American children are the least likely in the developed world to be immunized. In addition, "risks of abuse or neglect by parents, including exposure in utero to alcohol or illegal drugs, reach record proportions. Children's own use of alcohol and illegal drugs produce immediate damage and correlate with violence. Large numbers of American children become parents as teens, drop out of school, commit crimes or commit suicide."[13] Among youths aged fifteen to nineteen, firearms cause more deaths than all natural causes combined. (Among African-Americans in that age group, firearms are the cause of 60 percent of all deaths.)

But the most telling indicator of our failure is that children—
14.3 million of them—are the largest single group of Americans
living in poverty. The United States reports the highest poverty rate
for children in any of the world's industrialized democracies: one
in five American children (22 percent) live below the poverty line;
of very young children, those under the age of six, one in four do.
Among African-American children, one in two live in poverty.
While in the United States' population as a whole poverty is no
more prevalent today than it was two decades ago, child poverty
has increased by about 20 percent.[14]

One reason for this horrifying state of affairs is that over the past
thirty years the percentage of children born outside of marriage has
quintupled, from 5 percent to 25 percent overall—18 percent for
whites and 63 percent for African-Americans;[15] over the same period divorce rates have tripled (one in every two marriages ends in
divorce);[16] and even parents who stay together spend, on average,
about 40 percent less time with their children than did their own
parents (the hours per week have gone from 30 to 17), in large part
because more than half of mothers with very young children have
jobs.

The causes of this dismal state of childhood and family life in
America are many, and conservatives and liberals often argue over
what they are. Frequently the argument turns on what the historian
James MacGregor Burns has called "second-level" moral issues—
the degree to which parents honor values like fidelity, honesty, and
responsibility, and whether, if they honored them more, America's
children would be better off. Doubtless they would be. But we
should also realize that many of our country's institutional struc-
tures are stacked against the parents who try. With regard to the
first-level moral question—the nation's commitment to its children—policy is piecemeal at best, negligent at worst.

One might well ask why, if the nation's failure of its children has
been so complete, anyone should care particularly about the role
of television. We have seen what the first and obvious answer to
this question is: millions of American children spend more time
watching television than they do with their parents; most children
between the ages of six and twelve watch 20 to 28 hours each week,

no matter what their social settings. The second answer is clear to anyone who stops to think about the central function that television fulfills in presenting the public questions that a free people are supposed to decide: until we can use the most powerful communications medium in the world to benefit all children, rather than to exploit them, all the other efforts we make in their behalf will be incomplete. In a nation where, increasingly, children spend more time with television than doing anything else, it is unacceptable that that time should be taken up principally by salesmen, animated assault artists, and leering talk-show hosts.

That our children have been abandoned to strangers for so long, that the abuse every year becomes more aggressive and avaricious, is a direct consequence of our myopic new belief that commercial competition is the only measure of free speech and civic health, that, as Bernard de Mandeville put it in 1706, "private vice is public virtue." Until very recently Mandeville's axiom had lain dormant as a principle of public life, having been put to rest in the late eighteenth century by a young philosopher named Adam Smith, who exposed the idea as dangerously simplistic. To refute it, Smith offered a powerful new explanation of free markets and his "invisible hand" theory of the public good, both of which he introduced in his famous treatise *Inquiry into the Nature and Causes of the Wealth of Nations*. Smith believed that of all forms of social organization, the market was probably the one with the greatest potential to make the largest number of people "decent, gentle, prudent and free." By free, he meant not free to indulge in private vices but, rather, free to control one's worst instincts and create a society that aspired to "imperfect but attainable virtues": self-control, the ability to place duty over desire, and the ability to recognize and act on the needs of others.[17] Smith had a great distrust of businessmen, and he certainly did not mean to equate profit-seeking with decency. He described those who lived by profit as "an order of men, whose interest is never exactly the same with that of the public, who have generally an interest to deceive and even to oppress the public and who accordingly have, upon many occasions, both deceived and oppressed it."[18]

The countless people who cite Smith to justify every injustice or barbarity created by the marketplace almost certainly have not read his work. Smith knew, as Walter Lippmann did, as the drafters of the Communications Act did, that the public interest is not merely the outcome of competition between partisan interests. James Madison, the author of the First Amendment, knew this, too. In *Federalist 10*, he argued that partisan interests are in fact *adverse* to the public interest. His hope was that they might, through conflict, mitigate their effects or even cancel one another out; he did not believe that their struggle in any way represented the public interest or that the "winners" in any way embodied it. The *public's* interest, Madison knew, could not be deduced through formulaic notions about competition, but required the moral judgments inherent to deliberation. If self-interest could not be controlled, he concluded in *Federalist 55*, "the inference would be that there is not sufficient virtue among men for self-government; and that nothing less than the chains of despotism can restrain them from destroying and devouring one another."

Properly understood, the marketplace metaphor with which we characterize the First Amendment speaks directly to Madison's concern. Justice Holmes, who introduced the metaphor to the Supreme Court's lexicon in 1919, did not believe in truth, but he did believe in the ability of free speech to expose falsehoods. For Holmes, as the legal scholar Rodney Smolla has written, "the benefit of the marketplace was not the end but the quest, not the market's capacity to arrive at a final and ultimate truth but rather the integrity of the process."[19] Holmes knew, as surely as Madison and the other Founders did, that upon that process depended the freedom of generations yet unborn.

The great constitutional scholar Alexander Bickel once observed that the "First Amendment is a series of compromises and accommodations, confronting us again and again with hard questions to which there is no certain answer."[20] That very lack of certainty defeats any claim that free speech is an absolute freedom. The First Amendment does not protect libel or slander, obscenity, or all forms of commercial speech. Its guarantee of freedom does not override the Sixth Amendment's guarantee that people charged with a crime shall have a fair trial, nor does it override legitimate concerns about public safety or national security. Wherever the exercise of First Amendment rights conflicts with some other compelling public interest, or with another of the Bill of Rights' protections, courts employ various tests to judge the merits of the speech at issue; whether the risks the expression poses are real; and whether, if they are, the expression should or can be restrained.

There are very few such "accommodations" that the Supreme Court has made in First Amendment jurisprudence; by and large it has been faithful to the Founders' liberal prescription that "Congress shall make no law" abridging free speech. It is significant, therefore, that one accommodation the Court has carved out of its constitutional interpretation concerns children.* The Court has made it clear that "safeguarding the physical and psychological well-being of a minor" is "compelling" enough to justify laws that serve that goal, especially when they do not unduly infringe on the rights of adults.[21] These exceptions occur when children are involved not only as listeners but as speakers, and they are particularly compelling where the government itself is, or is reasonably construed to be, the speaker (as it is in public schools); where parents (or others acting on parents' behalf, such as schools) wish their adult judgments to prevail over their children's; or where adult speech is directed toward children, not merely to a general audience.[22] There is a reason for this special treatment for children, explains the legal scholar and historian Thomas Emerson:

> The system of freedom of expression cannot and does not treat children on the same basis as adults. The world of children is not the same as the world of adults, so far as a guarantee of untrammeled freedom of the mind is concerned. The reason for this is

---

* The law also regards children as a special case in several areas unrelated to the First Amendment, of course. The law has established age-based distinctions that affect the regulation of sexual activity, marriage, employment, driving, curfews, alcohol and tobacco, access to bars and other adult spaces, medical consent, and abortion—to name a few. The justifications for all these restrictions are the same as in free-speech cases: protection of the parent-child relationship, protection of the child, and society's interest in protecting itself from the immature decisions of minors.

... that a child "is not possessed of that full capacity for individual choice which is the presupposition of the First Amendment guarantees" [*Ginsberg v. New York*]. He is not permitted that measure of independence, or able to exercise that maturity of judgment, which a system of free expression rests upon.[23]

Most of the Court's restrictions on what children may see or hear or say are based on what can only be described as a "maturity test," in essence an acknowledgment that there are a lot of things children may not do—like vote, marry, or drive cars—until they have first passed some threshold of emotional maturity and physical independence. Under that test, the Court has used two main justifications for creating what amounts to a "child's First Amendment," the first relating to education, the second to the need for protection.

The education of children is of course one of the primary responsibilities of a free people, and it falls variously on parents and schools, government and private institutions. Because our public schools are a crucible of our civic life, the First Amendment works in two almost contradictory ways in the public-school setting. The first is jealously to guard against improper intrusions by the state or by religious organizations into the schools' pedagogical decisions, so that children can enjoy a free and open learning environment. This is an issue the Supreme Court took up early in its modern development of First Amendment law, in *West Virginia Board of Education v. Barnette* (1943), which affirmed the right of children who were Jehovah's Witnesses not to salute the American flag or recite the Pledge of Allegiance, both of which the public school considered a necessary part of its pedagogical mission but which were inconsistent with the teachings of the children's religion.[24] The state's right to enforce its wishes over the deeply held convictions of students was also denied in a 1969 case, *Tinker v. Des Moines Independent Community School District*, in which the Court upheld the right of students to wear black armbands in protest of the Vietnam War, since the students did not "shed their constitutional rights to freedom of speech or expression at the schoolhouse gate."[25] In a more recent decision (and a much less clear one), the Court held that while school administrators do not have to supply controversial books to a school library, once the books are there they cannot remove them simply because someone thinks they are offensive.[26]

At the same time, however, the Court has recognized that some intrusions into elementary- and secondary-school activities—even into the pedagogical realm—are proper and necessary if public schools are to have any success in instilling the values these decisions are based on. For example, in 1988 the Supreme Court upheld the decision of a St. Louis high-school principal to stop publication of a school-financed student newspaper that contained an article on students who had had abortions and another on students with divorced parents. Indeed, said the Court:

> . . . a school may in its capacity as publisher of a school newspaper or producer of a school play "dissociate itself," not only from speech that would "substantially interfere with [its] work . . . or impinge upon the rights of other students," but also from speech that is, for example, ungrammatical, poorly written, inadequately researched, biased or prejudiced, vulgar, or profane, or unsuitable for immature audiences. A school must be able to set high standards for the student speech that is disseminated under its auspices—standards that may be higher than those demanded by some newspaper publishers or theatrical producers in the "real" world—and may refuse to disseminate student speech that does not meet those standards.[27]

Such a sweeping charge would be clearly unconstitutional in most other contexts, including one in which the students published their paper independently of the school. But the Court has upheld similar decisions by school administrators who have exercised their discretion about what students may say and even wear while in their charge.[28]

The other justification for reading the First Amendment in a special way for children has to do with protecting them from ideas that, because of children's immaturity, may do them psychological harm. For example, the Court ruled in a 1968 case, *Ginsberg v.*

New York, that the government has a legitimate interest in protecting children from exposure to magazines like *Playboy* and *Penthouse*. In *Ginsberg*, the Court recognized both the state's and the parents' interests in protecting the well-being of children and upheld a statute prohibiting the sale of "girlie" magazines to minors, even though the magazines were not obscene under adult standards.[29] In another case, *Young v. American Mini Theatres*, the Court upheld a Detroit "anti-skid row" ordinance requiring that adult theaters be located farther than 500 feet from residential areas and farther than 1,000 feet from certain other designated areas, deciding that the zoning ordinance was not an impermissible restraint on expression. The Court cited the ordinance's stated purpose—protecting children—and noted that even justices who "accord the greatest protection to [pornographic] materials have repeatedly indicated that the State could prohibit the distribution or exhibition of such materials to juveniles and unconsenting adults."[30]

The Supreme Court has taken a particularly dim view of obscene speech that, in its view, exploits children. In *New York v. Ferber*, for example, it held that a state could prohibit distribution of materials that depicted or promoted a child's sexual conduct.[31] The case involved a man who had been indicted for selling two films, both of which featured young boys masturbating, to an undercover police officer. In upholding the indictment, the Court found that child pornography bore "heavily and pervasively on the welfare of children engaged in its production," and determined that this evil far outweighed the importance of the expressive activity involved. More recently, the Court in 1990 upheld the constitutionality of an Ohio statute that makes the mere possession of child pornography a crime.[32]

These "child-protection" cases raise two issues relevant to children's television. The first, which divided the Court in its 1968 *Ginsberg* decision, is whether or not some forms of expression may harm children, and how, and whether, they can be restricted in any case. The second is whether expression can be restricted *at all* without infringing the First Amendment rights of adults.

The first issue is tricky, and the Court really has not answered it. In *Ginsberg*, for example, Justice William Brennan, writing for the five-justice majority, noted that obscenity was low on the list of protected speech, and so he asked merely "whether it was rational for [New York] to find that the minors' exposure to such material might be harmful." Two girlie magazines were in question, the buyer was a sixteen-year-old boy, and though the State of New York clearly thought the situation was a harmful one (since it had a statute prohibiting it), Brennan considered it "very doubtful that this [was] an accepted scientific fact." Nonetheless, he concluded, the state did not have to show "the circumstances which lie behind the phrase 'clear and present danger' "; it was enough that the Court "be able to say that it was not irrational for the legislature to find that exposure to material condemned by the statute is harmful to minors."[33] In short, the Court upheld the statute because it thought the statute expressed the community's judgment about what was appropriate for minors with regard to a form of expression that does not enjoy full First Amendment protection, and, that being so, because it was not "irrational."

The second question is not so difficult: the Court will not uphold what it considers overly broad restrictions. Even where it can be proved that the government has a compelling interest in protecting children, the means by which it does so "must be carefully tailored to achieve those ends."[34] The Court first made this point in a 1957 case, *Butler v. Michigan*, which concerned the misdemeanor conviction of a man who had sold a book with a "potentially deleterious influence upon youth" to a police officer (not a child). The Court threw out the conviction and invalidated the statute, saying it could not "reduce the adult population . . . to reading only what is fit for children." Whatever the state's good intentions, the Court said, its quarantine of the "general reading public" in order to "shield juvenile innocence" was "surely to burn the house to roast the pig."[35] Similarly, in a 1974 case the Court invalidated a Jacksonville, Florida, ordinance that made it illegal for a drive-in movie theater to show a film depicting nudity when the movie screen was visible from a public street or other place outside the theater. While noting that it "is well settled that a state or municipality can adopt more stringent controls on communicative materials available to youths than on those available to adults," the Court rejected the ordinance anyway, because it would "bar a film containing a picture of a baby's buttocks, the nude body of a war victim, or scenes from a culture in which nudity is indigenous."[36]

It is important to note that these last two Supreme Court decisions do not forbid restrictions on content that might be unsuitable for children though suitable for adults. Rather, they require that the government's aims be compelling and that its restrictions be reasonable, and by "reasonable" the Court means that statutes written to protect children may not unduly curtail the First Amendment rights of adults.

The requirement of reasonableness obviously works no hardship in some cases, as with adult movie theaters or bookstores: children aren't allowed in those places and adults can enter freely. With broadcasting, however, standards of reasonableness are notoriously difficult to apply, because programs intended for adults are equally available to children, given the easy accessibility of the broadcast signal—indeed its very ubiquity. Moreover, as we know, radio and television broadcasts reach where printed words cannot, into the hearts and minds of children too young to read or even to speak. That is why, long before the Supreme Court ever heard a case involving broadcasting, the first NAB codes of ethics and standards of practice identified children as an audience with special needs and deserving of special protections.

The reason for those codes, and for all the subsequent controversy, is that the pervasiveness of the broadcast signal, its flip-of-the-switch availability, makes the parents' task of shielding their children from offensive broadcast material (in the same way they keep them from, say, sexually explicit magazines) almost impossible. This was the problem the Supreme Court took up in 1978, after a father riding in the car with his son heard on the radio the comedian George Carlin's monologue "Seven Dirty Words" and complained to the FCC, which then fined the New York City station, WBAI, that had aired it. The station had warned listeners that the monologue might be offensive to some, and it aired the routine not as a lark but as part of a program on social attitudes toward language. Pacifica Foundation, which owned and operated the station, appealed the FCC's sanction, and the case made its way to the Supreme Court, where Justice John Paul Stevens upheld the commission's action.

The Court decided that, because of the pervasiveness of their signal, broadcasters had to take special care not to air material that might offend or shock children. "Of all the forms of communication," Justice Stevens wrote, "broadcasting has the most limited First Amendment protection," because it extends "into the privacy of the home" and "is uniquely accessible to children." As to the station's argument that people who were offended by the monologue could just turn off the radio, Justice Stevens said that was like "saying that the remedy for an assault is to run away after the first blow."[37] The Court ruled that indecent programming on the airwaves, while not prohibited, could lawfully be restricted to hours during which children were unlikely to hear it.

Many legal scholars found the Court's decision in the *Pacifica* case troubling, because it seemed to contradict the reasoning of *Butler, Erzoznik*, and other decisions in which the Court had thrown out ordinances intended to protect children but that had the effect of restricting what adults could see or hear. But the *Pacifica* decision did not ban adult programming; it simply made it less accessible to children. And whatever its faults, the decision spoke to the important truth that broadcasting relies for its success on public airwaves and that it reaches children in ways that almost no other medium can. Even Mark Fowler, who criticized the *Pacifica* ruling as an example of dangerous regulation, conceded that

> undoubtedly many children below the age of literacy watch television. This situation may justify regulation of indecent materials carried over the air. Indecent material can be withheld from distribution to children if it is in the form of print or film, and scheduling of adult programs for late-night viewing can and does give parents more control over what their children watch.[38]

If Fowler believed this, he did not act on it as FCC chairman until he was pressed to do so by Attorney General Edwin Meese. Broadcasters paid the warning no mind either, and focused instead on the FCC's view that even "narrow restrictions" meant to protect children were impermissible. Practically overnight parents had the sole responsibility for what their children saw on television or heard on the radio, and they were denied any help in controlling what programs entered their home and when.

Fowler's successors, first Dennis Patrick and then Alfred Sikes, both tried to reimpose restrictions on broadcast programs that viewers and listeners thought indecent, but they had little success. A decade after deregulation had come to the FCC, television broadcasters convinced themselves that the secret to "competition" lay not in distinguishing their programming from what was available on cable but in copying it. The competition, such as it was, was to reclaim the well-off younger viewers whom advertisers wanted to reach and who had migrated in significant numbers to cable. To lure them back, broadcasters began to experiment with programs on topics and issues once considered off-limits—much of the material, like cable programming, with strong sexual or violent content. Both the FCC and Congress voiced misgivings, but the entertainment industry characterized any effort to limit its experimentation as the "heavy hand of government slowly, steadily, remorselessly intruding into the outer perimeter of the First Amendment."[39]

To hear many broadcasters and Hollywood studios tell it, the Court's *Pacifica* decision is not only bad law but obsolete law. They note that federal courts have invalidated some *Pacifica*-like restrictions, and they argue that as broadcasting technology blurs with and gives way to digital technology—and people pay to receive television signals, whether through a wire or through the air—*Pacifica* will become irrelevant.

These arguments are, to use Mark Twain's term, "stretchers," based on an understanding of the world that is more technological than constitutional. It is true, for example, that the courts have invalidated some restrictions on indecent programming, but *Pacifica* is nonetheless good law. Programming restrictions have been invalidated when the courts found them too broad for their purpose; no court has ever questioned the *reason* for the restrictions—protecting children—and most have made it clear that carefully tailored restrictions would pass constitutional muster. The most recent case of this type, for example, came in November 1993, when a federal appeals court in Washington, D.C., threw out rules established by the FCC in 1991 that prohibited radio and television stations from broadcasting "indecent" material between 6 a.m. and midnight, a ban that was too broad to accomplish its purpose, the court said. The three-judge panel added that a more narrowly drawn statute —one that banned indecent material during specific times when large numbers of unsupervised children are known to be in the audience—might survive a court challenge.[40]

As for *Pacifica*'s obsolescence, that, too, is true only with respect to the law's *means*, not its *reasons*. Broadcasting remains a healthy and profitable business, and reports of its imminent death appear to be exaggerated, despite claims made in the last decade that the broadcast networks were "dinosaurs" destined for extinction in the digital age. The so-called Big Three—CBS, NBC, and ABC—are thriving enterprises, holding on to about $9 billion of the $25 billion spent on television advertising each year. Additionally, Fox has successfully created a fourth network, and at least two other networks—one by Paramount and another by Time Warner—began operation in early 1995. True, if at some future time "free" broadcast television were to disappear and be replaced entirely by pay-per-view television delivered over a wire or direct-broadcast satellite, *Pacifica*'s presumption about the broadcast signal's ubiquity would disappear and, with it, the technological basis for the Court's decision. (To some extent that has already happened: the reasoning of *Pacifica* cannot be applied, for example, to a premium cable service like HBO or the Playboy channel.) But even if such a dramatic technological switch were to occur, it is highly unlikely that fee-for-service, à la carte television would go ahead without regard for the substantial body of First Amendment law that recognizes children as a special class of citizens who require special protections.

One reason for this is self-evident to those who know communications history: each new technology, from the printing press to the computer, raises new problems in the application of common law and constitutional law, and these problems need solutions specific to the medium. The information superhighway, for example, combining as it does characteristics of both private and mass communications, of the technologies of print, television, telephone, and computers, will eventually challenge and in many cases change our understanding of the common law of libel, privacy, copyright, and so on. It will also challenge our understanding of the First Amendment's protections and limitations, not least because the superhighway's theoretical ability to make anyone a "publisher" will change our understanding of the "press."

The difficulty of applying today's free speech principles to tomorrow's technologies is aptly illustrated by the growing popularity, especially among children, of videos and video games. If the two taken together were a television network, says former NBC researcher Larry McGill, "it would be the number one network on television among kids 2 to 11."[41] Now imagine a video game that includes graphic violence and explicit sexual content: is it a publication, like a magazine whose sale to children a community can prohibit, or a form of television program it may not? In the very near future, the same question might be asked of programming available on television or on computers in the home. Reasonable people may disagree on the answer, but it cannot be answered by the facile application of what Justice John Paul Stevens calls "blackletter" rules about the First Amendment. Doing so creates the risks "that specific facts may be discounted and, as a result, that deserving speech may be left unprotected while unimportant speech is overprotected."[42]

Pacifica may indeed one day pass from usefulness. But does that mean that programmers, whoever and wherever they are, will be free to prey on children? This is the implication—if not the assertion—of the many fulsome appeals to the "marketplace of ideas" one hears not only in the communications industries but perhaps even more remarkably in many schools of journalism and mass communications. History and common sense suggest a different outcome: that the Court will adapt the child-protection principles in *Pacifica* to new circumstances, especially because the technologies of cyberspace will expose children to currently unknown forms of exploitation and abuse. Already, in fact, the Supreme Court has anticipated this; in a 1989 case, *Sable Com-*

munications v. FCC, it spoke about the issues posed by fee-for-service television. The *Sable* case involved an effort by Congress to ban so-called dial-a-porn telephone services, making it illegal even for adults to have them. The Supreme Court struck down the ban, and it distinguished the decision from *Pacifica* in two ways. First, the Court noted, the *Sable* case imposed an outright ban while *Pacifica* imposed only a time restriction. Second, telephone service is different in nature from broadcasting, which "can intrude on the privacy of the home without prior warning, . . . and is 'uniquely accessible to children, even those too young to read.'" But telephony raised no such "captive audience" problem:

> Placing a telephone call is not the same as turning on a radio and being taken by surprise by an indecent message. Unlike an unexpected outburst on a radio broadcast, the message received by one who places a call to a dial-a-porn service is not so invasive or surprising that it prevents an unwilling listener from avoiding exposure to it.[43]

In striking down the ban, the Court ruled only that it was too broad. Far from dismissing its intentions, the Court affirmed that the government's "compelling interest in protecting the physical and psychological well-being of minors extends to shielding minors from the influence of literature that is not obscene by adult standards." Then the Court went even further, offering suggestions as to how the government might achieve that goal. It recommended that dial-a-porn services have various obstacles to their access, such as credit-card numbers, access codes, or scrambling. These obstacles would be far from foolproof, the Court said, but might prevent all but "a few of the most enterprising and disobedient young people" from gaining access to dial-a-porn services.[44]

Congress wasted no time in acting on these suggestions, and in 1989 amended them to the Communications Act.[45] The FCC then drafted rules requiring that commercial dial-a-porn services relying on either telephone companies or common carriers for collection and billing must notify the carriers that their services are indecent; the carrier in turn must either block access to the service until subscribers submit written requests to unblock them, or scramble their messages and sell personal decoders. Dial-a-porn services that do their own billing and collection must require credit-card payment before transmitting their messages. Significantly, both the Second and Ninth Circuit courts have upheld these rules, saying that they comply with *Sable*, that they are neither too vague nor too broad, and that they do not constitute prior restraints.

If the dozens of Supreme Court cases that make up the "child's First Amendment" tell us anything, and whether they involve a school newspaper or access to dial-a-porn services, they tell us that where free speech is concerned, children are a special case under our Constitution and a reason for caution. Certainly not all the cases reviewed here concern issues that translate to television. The government's role in public schools, for example, is not the same as that of private broadcasters using the public airwaves. But the point is that in both of these settings and no matter what the medium—whether public-school library books, broadcast television, or telephone service—considerations arise where children are involved that do not arise with adults. Those considerations do not always carry the day, *but they are always present, always will be, and cannot be belittled or dismissed, no matter what the medium.*

It is simply not true, therefore, that any and all regulations to improve children's television are constitutionally suspect, that, as Media Institute staff attorney Andrew Auerbach put it, "It is the height of demagoguery to use the First Amendment to protect children."[46] If anything, the weight of historical and legal evidence suggests that the constitutional presumption should go the other way. And while the "reasonableness" standard often used in cases involving children is hardly what we would wish to use to decide most First Amendment questions, it nonetheless exists for a very good reason: children are special. Clearly there are legitimate and important First Amendment principles that militate against certain poorly drafted regulations, notably those that are too broad. But those issues cannot be used as a rationale for dismissing the welfare of our children, especially when we know that the First Amendment's regard for the status of children is itself a well-recognized and compelling reason for imposing restrictions on speech, especially adult speech directed to children, as is almost always the case with television.[47]

The "child's First Amendment" is especially important in broadcast television, which still uses the publicly owned spectrum, is still subject to the public-interest obligations of the Communications Act, and is still governed by the Supreme Court's ruling in *Pacifica*. Moreover even critics who believe that the FCC should be disbanded, that broadcasters should be given property rights in the spectrum and with them the same free-speech protections as print media, acknowledge that where children are concerned the government will still have legitimate First Amendment reasons to protect them.[48] These intersecting considerations should make clear to Congress, the FCC, and the public that regulations intended to improve children's television not only work very little hardship on the First Amendment but are supported by it. Writing in a recent issue of the *Yale Law Journal*, Justice Stevens noted that the *Pacifica* decision might have turned out differently

> if the broadcaster had simply contended that the particular order was erroneous because the evidence of actual or probable offense to the listening audience was so meager. Instead, however, the station took the position that the Commission was entirely without power to regulate indecent broadcasting, whatever the surrounding circumstances. Under that view, any program, no matter how inappropriate for children, could have been targeted at juvenile audiences so long as it was permissible fare for adults. Instead of attempting to sell the Court such a rigid and unattractive proposition of law, adopting a less ambitious strategy might have better served the interests of both the litigants and the law.[49]

Justice Stevens's observation that the confluence of the statutory law (on the question of the FCC's authority) and First Amendment principle (on the question of protecting children) creates a strong supposition in favor of children is important. First, television programmers who wave the free-speech flag are, on children's issues more than anywhere else, on doubtful legal ground. Second, the protection of children has real relevance with respect to the issue of televised violence. In the fall of 1993, Congress considered no fewer than eleven bills on this issue. Some of those bills, arguably, are unconstitutional on their face, though others may not be. In every case, their constitutionality almost certainly turns on the means they use to accomplish their objective, not on the objective itself—which is protecting children. In July 1992, for example, an appeals court for the Eighth Circuit threw out a Missouri statute that restricted the rental or sale to minors of videocassettes that depicted any type of violence. Why? Because the statute contained no "narrowly drawn, reasonable and definite" definition of a "violent act," and therefore could not "achieve its end without unnecessarily infringing on freedom of expression."[50] The court left open the possibility that a statute which carefully defined and proscribed a specific type of violence, such as "slasher films," might withstand constitutional scrutiny.

Interestingly, overcoming these definitional problems may be easier with violent material than with indecency, the area in which such restrictions have traditionally prevailed. True, "violence" does not share the common-law legacy of low repute that "obscenity" does, but obscenity is famously ill-defined, subject primarily to the "I'll know it when I see it" test, and restricted not because of any evidence that it causes psychological harm to minors—most social psychologists say it does not—but merely because of the presumption that it does. By contrast, the meaning of violence can be and has been adequately defined hundreds of times narrowly enough to exclude the many obvious instances (football games or the evening news) in which it is either unavoidable or serves a legitimate purpose.[51] Television people routinely claim that violence cannot be adequately defined, that seemingly innocuous definitions will quickly be the end not only of gratuitous blood and gore but also of NFL football games, PBS productions of *Hamlet*, National Geographic specials, Saturday-morning cartoons, and the like. This is a gross simplification intended to foreclose discussion. Moreover, it has been demonstrated that excessive violence on television causes real—not presumed—psychological harm to children. The philosopher Sissela Bok argues that the weight of evidence is so over-whelming that it presents "an interesting theoretical challenge to the familiar First Amendment doctrine of 'clear and present danger' "[52] (one of the traditional tests used by the Supreme Court, since 1919, to determine whether a particular expression can be restricted[53]). "If the American standard for judging speech is to be that you can't shout 'fire!' in a crowded theater," says Douglass Cater, "I think perhaps that standard should apply here. We live in an increasingly crowded society in which huge numbers of children die violent deaths, often at the hands of other children."[54] If Americans thought differently about the damage television violence does, such challenges would be unnecessary. All that would be required would be Justice William Brennan's reasoning in *Ginsberg v. New York*: one does not need to find a clear and present danger, Brennan wrote, only "that exposure to material condemned by the statute is harmful to minors."

Television programs and advertisements that are unsuitable for children abound on cable television, and broadcasters note correctly that many people—especially children—do not know broadcast channels from cable ones, or care. One thoughtful observer says that broadcasters are right to "complain that they are being held to a standard not always applied to the cable industry, motion picture companies and various video services."[55] Others argue that those standards are "premised on the asserted 'scarcity' of the electromagnetic spectrum," and that new technologies "have seriously eroded this scarcity rationale."[56] These technology-rooted arguments tend to view even legitimate efforts to protect children as a threat to free expression, especially because the technologies of print, broadcast, computer networks, and other distribution systems are increasingly the same.

These arguments have merits: they appeal both to intuition and to reason. They suffer, however, from two defects: they accept the exploitation of children as an unavoidable policy outcome, thereby capitulating to disaster; and their analysis ends at the very point where it should begin, since the disaster they accept is avoidable. *Especially* in the age of information superhighways, media directed at children will require special attention. New technologies will present us with new challenges and new difficulties in deciding how to protect and serve our children, but as *Sable* makes clear, they will not relieve us of the constitutional duty to do so—to say nothing of the moral one. The claim that "scarcity" no longer exists is irrelevant to this fundamental principle, and it also isn't true. There are today, as there have always been, many more people who want to broadcast than there are available frequencies. This scarcity—based not on the total number of broadcasters or a comparison with other kinds of media but on the number of would-be broadcasters compared to the number of available frequencies—is the "unique characteristic" that has always supported, and still supports, the Communication Act's public-interest standard.[57]

If anything, Americans should be thinking more seriously about how new technologies might be used to fortify that standard, particularly if they could relieve some of the tensions inherent in the broadcasting dilemmas posed by *Pacifica*. Here broadcasters' supposed constitutional objection to the v-chip, for example, falls on its sword. Clearly a technology that allows parents, rather than the government, to filter the information coming into American homes is not only constitutional but far preferable to regulation or judicial decree in the idea marketplace.[58] This is all the more true since the parental role is itself fully protected by the Constitution, which indeed takes full cognizance of parents' duty to raise children as they see fit.

Bringing the "child's First Amendment" into the volatile and extremely complex environment created by digital communications technologies will not be easy. Difficult questions abound, and answering them will require an earnest search. But the important thing, as Justice Holmes knew when he spoke of the marketplace of ideas, is the search. Where children are concerned, we have abandoned the search in favor of easy platitudes about the market that ignore what we know about the First Amendment. In so doing, we have also abandoned our children.

More than twenty years ago a young political scientist named Ithiel de Sola Pool was called before Congress to testify about the findings of the 1972 Surgeon General's report on the effects of television violence on children. Pool was a famous critic of broadcast regulation and the dangers it posed to free speech, and he had been one of the twelve social scientists to work on the report. Now, in the public confusion surrounding the report's conclusion, Rhode Island senator John Pastore wanted a definitive answer on the subject. On that day in 1973, when asked whether television violence adversely affected children, Pool told Pastore it did. Pastore pressed him further: what should be done about the problem? Pool thought for a moment, then responded:

> Too often scientists pontificate on public policy as if their science has given them answers when their answers come from their personal values. As to what needs to be done, I would rather say as a citizen than a scientist, because that is a civic question, not a scientific question.[59]

Pool was right. Our children are not economic abstractions, nor can their needs be neatly reduced to mathematical formulas. To serve them requires civic debate among free people. That is why the Founders gave us the First Amendment. It is past time we used it to serve and protect our children rather than as an excuse to exploit them.

4 : The Next Generation and the Age of SuperTube

We cannot always build the future for our youth, but we can build our youth for the future.   —*Franklin D. Roosevelt*

"CHANGE IS INEVITABLE," ADLAI E. STEVENSON ONCE SAID. "change for the better is a full-time job."[1] So it is with children's television: change is coming, as it is throughout television, but to be for the better it demands full-time attention—from all of us. Children's television cannot be left exclusively to the market, or to chance. Americans have missed many opportunities to make television better, and now, as television evolves into a medium that can be transmitted over a wire by cable and telephone, and through the air by microwave and direct-satellite broadcasts, we have another opportunity. Not only *can* Americans change television, we *must*. After decades of narrowing the definition of the "public interest" through technological change, industry practice, scholarly research, and constitutional challenge, we are at the one place where the meaning of public interest can narrow no further: children.

The larger question is, what kind of people do we want to be? Do we want to be the kind of nation, the kind of people, who abandon their children to a state of subhuman exploitation and regard them only as customers, recognizing them as citizens only when they arrive on the brink of constitutional protection?

Americans have never debated this question; rather, they have defaulted on it, and in so doing have in effect answered it in the affirmative. To be sure, the strangers who enter our homes through the gateway of the family television set do so because the United States has left its children's television policy, insofar as it has one, to the discretion of the television industry. But at the end of the day, the truth is that the strangers who dominate our children's lives can do so because we let them: parents, educators, foundations, and public officials—all of us—have abandoned the nation's children to their care. And we argue incessantly over the wrong question—over whose First Amendment rights are being gored—and ignore the question of what opportunities and gifts television might offer to make children's lives better. Our failure is a national disgrace, not merely an industry one: there is plenty of blame to go around. Better yet, there is plenty of responsibility to share.

It is self-evident that the primary responsibility for policing children's television viewing lies with parents. It is equally evident—to teachers, to law-enforcement authorities, to health-care professionals, and to many parents themselves—that too many parents neglect this responsibility. The people who ignore it fit no particular demographic profile; they come from all walks of life, rich and poor, educated and uneducated, white and black, yellow and brown. When Jack Valenti, president of the Motion Picture Association of America, is called on—before congressional committees, in interviews, and in editorials—to answer for the entertainment industry's exploitation of children, he asks, "Whose children are they, anyway?" He rarely gets an answer.

Parental neglect on such a broad scale has its roots in many places. One source can be found in schools, which for decades have scorned television as trash, regarding the medium as a pop-culture backwater undeserving of serious attention. The United States is the only major English-speaking country in the world that includes no formal media education in its primary and secondary schools. The critic Douglas Davis notes that when the Department of Education released its famous call-to-arms in the mid-1980s, *A Nation at Risk*, "its authors, the cream of the nation's educational establishment, did not once so much as mention the word *television*."[2] Robert Kubey, a longtime advocate of media education beginning in the earliest primary-school grades, writes:

> Over 2,300 years ago, Plato wrote that a "sound education consists in training people to find pleasure and pain in the right objects." But though most Americans now spend half their leisure time watching television and film, very few schools devote formal attention to helping students become more sophisticated media consumers. Schools do devote time to teaching students about poetry and short stories, but in reality, once they graduate, very few people will spend much time with these forms. This is not to say that we shouldn't continue to introduce students to poetry and short stories—we should—but that we do not spend time helping students similarly appreciate, interpret and analyze the mass media that surround them is nothing short of educational neglect . . . If most children are going to continue to spend 1,000 hours of television every year of their young lives, and 1,000 hours every year for the rest of their adult lives, isn't it a mistake for them not to receive formal media education?[3]

Good teachers not only teach their students about television but make imaginative use of television as a pedagogic tool. John Merrow, once the *MacNeil-Lehrer NewsHour* education reporter and a former vice president of the Learning Channel, argues that "television itself belongs in schools, not as an end in itself, but as a means to mastery of essential skills."[4] A former high-school English teacher himself, Merrow advocates the use of educational videotapes or, even better, what he calls "assigned viewing":

> Every history teacher worth his or her salt certainly assigned *The Civil War*, Ken Burns' PBS series. Savvy teachers regularly check the TV listings for opportunities to supplement their courses. In addition, networks like A&E, Discovery and the Learning Channel have well-organized efforts to inform teachers of programs that might help their teaching.

Another form of assigned teaching is what one sixth-grade teacher I know calls "going with the flow." He knew his students watched *The Simpsons* and *ALF*, so he made them an assignment. One week his students had to write several paragraphs describing what one character did, and why. Another week students had to listen for, and keep a list of, adverbs. Another assignment had students keeping track of commercials and writing paragraphs explaining which they felt were best, and why.[5]

One reason for the neglect of television in our schools is that our teachers colleges also ignore it. Indeed, higher education in general pays little attention to television, until fairly recently studying almost exclusively its effect on pop culture, and either minimizing or ignoring its dominance in American life. Even now, many standard college-level texts on American history or political science make only cursory mention of broadcasting's development in the twentieth century or say nothing at all. The subject matter is left to the curricula of schools of journalism and communications, even the best of which are often treated as second-class citizens, mere "trade" schools in their home universities. Too often the characterization rings true: at a time when Congress is considering the most substantial, far-reaching changes to the Communications Act since it was written in 1934, our communications and journalism schools are as silent as stones on the issue of what constitutes the public interest. To be sure, a great deal of study and discussion goes on within these schools, but little of real consequence to policy or public debate comes out of them. The situation is reminiscent of what the political scientist Theodore Lowi found a quarter century ago, when he wrote his classic examination of what had happened to the concept of the public interest in modern America, and despaired for his fellow political scientists. Modern political science, he wrote, had elevated "rigor over relevance" and in doing so had become "a defender of the status quo"; too often, "those who are trying to describe reality tend to reaffirm it." In looking at the demise of Madisonian public-interest principles, he warned that if someday the public interest were to lose all meaning, "it will be the critics, not the politicians, who are to blame."[6]

Of course, politicians do bear their share of the blame. When

Congress effectively banished educators from helping to make any meaningful decisions in broadcasting between 1927 and 1934, it took the first important step toward creating the deplorable environment of children's television today. While Congress was careful to craft a special provision for itself—the Equal Time rule contained in Section 315 of the Communications Act[7]—and has for sixty years sporadically supervised the administration of the airwaves through its oversight of the FCC, it gave no focused attention to children and their needs until 1990. Its regular visitations on the subject of television violence—every few years for the last forty years—and its equally predictable inaction suggest to parents and broadcasters alike that it is trotting out the problem merely to score publicity points.

This pattern of neglect is a self-fulfilling prophecy. But it does not have to be like this. Long before television found its way into American homes, some commentators saw in the new medium a harbinger of social disaster, others the promise of social progress; only a very few argued that what television was, or might become, was a matter not of fate but of *choice* and therefore deserving of public debate. In 1938, the writer E. B. White hoped that television would be a "saving radiance in the sky," but at the same time he worried that it would make Americans turn inward, away from each other and from the questions and challenges of public life. But Congress never seriously discussed what Americans might want from television, or might need. For decades, the word *television* was not even added to the Communications Act. What little debate went on in Washington about television's future revolved, as we have seen, around industry battles for competitive advantage. In 1959, only a few years after television sets had penetrated into more than half of America's homes, Congress spent more time investigating rigged quiz shows than it ever spent on examining how television might be used for public benefit, whether for children or for adults. These events, combined with evidence of corruption at the Federal Communications Commission during the middle and late 1950s, led many to conclude that whatever promises television once had, the greatest of them had already been lost. But a few, echoing E. B. White, saw the matter differently. The sociologist Leo

Bogart was unambiguous: "Television is a wholly neutral instrument in human hands. It is and does what people want."[8]

No one paid attention. In 1975, Douglass Cater made an observation similar to Bogart's, but tinged with incredulity: "One might think we would by now have devoted serious attention to the effects of this medium on our culture, our society, our lives . . . Yet, as the prescient Mr. Marconi predicted a long time ago, telecommunications has become part of the 'almost unnoticed working equipment of civilization.' " Looking ahead to today's television environment—and tomorrow's—Cater described what he called "multiple output telecommunications home end resources," or MOTHER:

> . . . she will offer infinitely more channels—via microwave, satellite, cable, laser beam—than the present broadcast system provides. There will also be greater capacity crammed within each channel—more information "bits" per gigahertz—so that one can simultaneously watch a program and receive a newspaper printout on the same channel . . . MOTHER will be "interactive," permitting us to talk back to our television set by means of a digital device on the console. Recording and replay equipment will liberate us from the tyranny of the broadcast schedule, and computer hookup and stop-frame control will bring the Library of Congress and other Gutenberg treasures into our living room.[9]

Much of what Cater foresaw in television's future—the recording of television programs, for example—had already started in 1975, and few doubted that new technologies would soon throw the traditional communications industries into turmoil and, with them, the Communications Act itself. That is why California congressman Lionel Van Deerlin tried to rewrite the Communications Act in the late 1970s, and the technology transformation served as justification for the FCC's deregulatory efforts in the 1980s. But if there was a single turning point when Cater's prediction moved from possibility to probability, it was 1984. That was the year in which it all began.

"It" is "The Giant Tug of Wire," "The Light Fantastic," or "The End of TV as We Know It," as various news and business magazines have characterized it. "It" is the result of two formerly separate but now converging events: the breakup of the American Telephone and Telegraph Company, which opened telephone services to new forms of competition, resulting in the creation of seven regional telephone companies, or "Baby Bells"; and the passage of the 1984 Cable Act, which freed the cable industry from the domination of broadcasters and turned it loose to wire America, at the same time prohibiting the new telephone companies from owning cable franchises or offering their own information services.* In the decade since, telephone and cable companies have been on a crash course, fighting both between and among themselves, as well as with newspaper companies and broadcasters, to claim a position of dominance in an electronic communications market that is expected to be worth more than $3 trillion—about half the current GNP of the United States—by the early twenty-first century. "It" is SuperTube.

The age of SuperTube arrived in Cerritos, California, in 1989, when the GTE Corporation, a phone company, came to town with a permit from federal and state regulators to test an experimental, interactive, video information service called Main Street. GTE signed up 500 Cerritos residents, who used the service to browse electronic encyclopedias, play games, shop, buy and sell stocks, get news, sports, and weather twenty-four hours a day—to use any of sixty-five services—all for $9.95 a month, a price roughly equal to what home-computer owners now pay for similar fare on Prodigy or America OnLine.[10] But there was a big difference: Main Street was delivered through television sets in cooperation with the local cable company. In testing the market for Main Street's services, GTE relied on simple arithmetic: 99 percent of American homes have at least one television set, while then only about 15 percent had home computers (today closer to 30 percent have them).[11]

The age of SuperTube arrived in England in 1991, also through

* The seven regional Bell companies are NYNEX, BellSouth, Pacific Telesis, Bell Atlantic, USWest, Southwestern Bell, and Ameritech. The Baby Bells were created by the 1984 consent decree that dissolved the phone service monopoly held by AT&T. By its terms, the Baby Bells were to provide local telephone service in their respective regions; they were not to offer long-distance service (which remained the domain of AT&T, MCI, Sprint, and other long-distance companies) or manufacture telephone equipment. Today the consent decree's terms are being reexamined, both by the courts and by Congress.

joint ventures of telephone and cable companies, and with the blessing of the British government. Three of our seven regional phone
companies—NYNEX, USWest, and Southwestern Bell—operate
cable television systems in England; USWest in partnership with
Telecommunications Inc. (TCI), and Southwestern Bell with Cox
Cable. All three offer telephone service over the same fiber-optic
lines that carry cable television, and for about 15 percent less than
British Telecom, the nation's dominant telephone company. While
so far the American companies have offered no-frills service to only
about 150,000 customers, they expect to wire nearly all of the 6
million homes in their English franchise areas by the end of the
decade. The reason for such rapid growth, says Eugene Connel,
chief executive of NYNEX Cablecomms (the NYNEX venture in
England), is that "it's not going to be just basic voice and cable
and more of the same. You will see an explosion of diversity in
programming and an opportunity for accessing data bases, you
name it."[12]

No mere pipe dreams, these. The so-called boob tube of past
generations is already well on its way to becoming a smart set. In
Montreal, Expos fans can pay $8 a month for the privilege of
controlling a button that allows them to call up instant replays,
choose camera angles from which to watch a game, review a pitch-
er's speed and the location of his pitches, check the batter's statistics
against his opponent—and the salaries of both. In Toronto, businesses use cable television to conduct video conferences and share
spreadsheets. Television viewers in Littleton, Colorado; Orlando,
Florida; and New York City are all experimenting with video-on-
demand services, joint ventures of cable and telephone companies
that allow them to watch movies of their choice at their convenience.
Your Choice TV, a test project of the cable-programming service
Discovery and its founder, John Hendricks, allows 2,500 viewers
in West Palm Beach, Florida, to order and watch, for a dollar, any
episode, anytime, of any one of the major broadcast networks' top
twenty weekly shows. In Sterling Heights, Michigan, 115 fourth
graders use an electronic network installed by Ameritech, another
regional Bell company, to complete and submit homework, and to
receive nature and geography videos, encyclopedias, and games, on
their home television sets. Blockbuster, king of home-video rentals,

announced in May 1993 that it was teaming up with computer giant IBM to create an electronic megastore, a digital file of movies and music that can be summoned at the click of a button from almost anywhere, copied to a compact disc, and sold.

These experiments in limited interactivity constitute what Robert Pepper, chief of plans and policy at the FCC, calls television's third stage, beyond terrestrial broadcasting and cable. A fourth stage, of full interactivity, is emerging, but is still far off. Even farther off—sometime in the next century—is a fifth stage, when technologies such as video holography and virtual reality will make television not just interactive but *active*, allowing people to experience media beyond the sensations of sight and sound. So revolutionary is this technological transformation that it hardly seems correct to call the result "television."

Neither is it quite correct to call its products "programs." Of all SuperTube's visionaries, perhaps the first to realize this was Barry Diller. The former chief executive of both a major movie studio (Paramount) and a broadcast network (Fox), Diller surprised everyone in February 1992 with the sudden announcement that he was leaving Fox, which he had helped to make not just an upstart in the network television business but a major competitor. Ten months later, Diller announced that he had become a partner, with the cable companies TCI and Comcast, in a twenty-four-hour shopping network called the Quality Value Convenience Network, QVC. He had done so, according to the journalist Ken Auletta, because

> as [he] thought about the competing interests of the cable companies, Hollywood studios, TV networks, computer hardware and software companies, publishers, telephone companies and assorted consumer-electronics powerhouses, . . . he realized that each one hoped someday to control either the wire highway to each home or the switching mechanism that would someday direct video traffic or the computer databases that would serve as a library or the technology that converted pictures and programming to digital signals and back again.[13]

Barry Diller's purchase of QVC pointed up the now familiar shortcoming in this technological revolution: content. While cable and telephone companies may be bursting with the delivery potential of thousands of channels, they have very little to deliver on them. *Forbes* magazine has estimated that if five hundred channels were programmed with reruns of every prime-time network show ever made and with every American movie ever made, the programming inventory would be exhausted in about nine weeks.[14] In buying QVC, Diller clearly had a different kind of television in mind and, with it, a different kind of content: not just programming, but services, all of it delivered from vast video databases.

The basis for such a system is precisely what Douglass Cater predicted: interactivity, the revolutionary technological transformation of the family television set into the family telecomputer. Diller, inspired by his own use of an Apple Powerbook computer, imagined the world of television turned inside out, where individual viewers, not cable companies or broadcasters, decide what's on and when. In Diller's world, viewers will scroll through a menu of programs and services, click on their choices, and devise a viewing schedule of their very own. Instead of passively watching TV, we will use it or play it, just as we might a cash machine or a video game. The future, Diller said, isn't about "500 channels or 800 or whatever. It's really one channel. It's your channel."[15] It's SuperTube.

Diller's experience with his Apple Powerbook underscores the most critical difference between broadcast television and Super-Tube: broadcasting is a mass medium, built around spectrum usage; SuperTube is a personal one, built around computers. Microsoft president and chairman Bill Gates has said that "interactive TV" is actually a misnomer,

a really bad name for the in-home device connected to the information highway. The bottom line is that two-way communication is a very different beast than one-way communication . . . A phone that has an unbelievable directory and lets you talk or send messages to lots of people, and works with text and pictures is a better analogy than TV . . . Because TV had very few channels, the value of TV time was very high so only things of a very broad interest could be aired on those few channels. The information highway will be the opposite of this—more like the Library of Congress, but with an easy way to find things.[16]

The centrality of computers to the information highway is key for two reasons. The first is that computers drop in cost and increase in effectiveness in exponential proportions every year; every eighteen months the number of transistors on a single chip nearly doubles.* When combined with digitization—the ability to break information of any kind into the 1's and 0's of binary code, the native eloquence of computers—computers allow unimaginably huge amounts of information to be stored, compressed, and transmitted along copper telephone lines, coaxial cable, and the radio spectrum. The second reason is related: there is as yet no computer powerful enough to do the job on the scale of an "information highway." The biggest mainframe computer can handle only about one hundred customers in the kind of true video-on-demand system envisioned by Barry Diller. A computer that could handle 10,000 or more requests simultaneously is an engineering feat that has yet to be met. In Littleton, Colorado, for example, where the cable giant TCI is trying to gauge subscriber interest in using an on-demand video library, the system's interactivity is decidedly low-tech. Viewers can make their choices by clicking away at their television screens, but the requests aren't handled by a computer. Instead they cause a bell to go off in a TCI building miles away, letting an attendant know that he has five minutes to find a video-tape and load it into a VCR.

At present, when most people talk about the information super-highway, what they really mean is a nation wired together with fiber-optic cable, the third technological component—along with digitization and computers—of the information highway. A single fiber-optic cable, a strand of glass only slightly thicker than a human hair, can simultaneously carry the phone conversations of a hundred people, along with enough video programming to supply them all with a hundred channels of cable television. Unlike computers, however, the problem with fiber-optic cable is cost-effectiveness. The estimated cost of wiring the entire United States is very large,

---

* The process by which chips double in computing power every eighteen months, known as Moore's Law, also applies to television sets as we move into the next century. The family television will very soon also be an advanced digital terminal, its power and versatility far greater than anything imaginable today.

in the hundreds of billions of dollars.* That cost, as much as anything else, is at the core of the debate about who will build the information highway and whom it will serve.

Some answers to the question are already clear. Like the railroads of the nineteenth century, the information highway of the twenty-first century will be built with private resources using public rights-of-way. And the companies building the information highway, like those that built the railroads, will actively seek government regulation to protect their markets from competition and give them the greatest return on their investment.

The question of whom the information highway will serve, and with what services, is more difficult, but promises abound. In the months after Barry Diller's ascendancy to the top of SuperTube's visionary heap, virtually every major American newspaper, news-weekly, and business magazine featured a cover story on the information highway's potential to enrich our lives.[17] Typical of the fantastic scenarios each offered was this one from *Newsweek*:

> You come home from work and grab the remote. As you putter around, removing tie or pantyhose, and occasionally checking the picture, your personal video navigator brings you up to date. You find out what TV shows the kids watched after school, and hear a reminder from the florist: it's time to send out Aunt Agnes's birthday bouquet; how about this arrangement? You look at a copy of Tommy's report card, issued that day, and a list of movies you could watch that night, based on how much you loved *The Age of Innocence*. You click on the beef bourguignon how-to that you selected this morning; you've got all the ingredients because the program automatically faxed a list to Safeway, which delivered.[18]

Brandon Tartikoff has described television's future with similar enthusiasm, but, notably, without using the term *television*:

---

* Published estimates of the cost of wiring the nation with fiber-optic cable run from $200 billion to $1 trillion, but no one knows for sure. AT&T, which manufactures fiber-optic cable, says that about 4 percent of traditional copper access lines wear out every year, and that for each $1,000 of copper replacement cost fiber-optic cable can be used instead for only $750 plus $50 for video capability, with far less maintenance costs than copper. The cable industry disputes these figures, but it is nonetheless true that opto-electronics is, like computers and television, becoming more cost-effective. Even so, the cost of wiring the nation is still formidably high.

Someday, maybe even before the year 2000, you'll come home from a hard day at the office, flip on your computer and fire up a video menu. Let's say you're in the mood to watch *Northern Exposure*. Working with your remote-control device, you'll be able to preview scenes from the series, or call up brief plot descriptions, from five available episodes. Later that night, you can watch the news—not just the news that some local station wants to feed you, but a selection of reports listed on the video menu and pretailored, based on past viewing habits, to your interests. After that, you can round out the night with a movie—one of several thousand available titles.[19]

Among SuperTube's most glowing predictions is that it will be a particular benefit to children. TCI executive J. C. Sparkman said:

The things this is going to do for our children, for our children's children . . . are going to be phenomenal. Think of what it will do for education. Think of how any person in any town, in any community, the smallest or the largest in this nation, can dial up and get any course on any subject they would like to hear about or like to learn about on a moment's notice.[20]

Yes, indeed, think about it. It is hard to read these descriptions without recalling the similar hopes that people like David Sarnoff, Paul Porter, Pat Weaver, and CBS president Frank Stanton once held for television. It is telling, at least, and probably a lot closer to the truth, that virtually all the projections of SuperTube's blessings are predicated on the success of entertainment programming and home-shopping channels. Children's programming is at best an afterthought, a vague promise pinned onto the much more lucrative services that excite Wall Street. Television shopping, for example, was a $2.5 billion business in 1993 and is expected to reach $30 billion within the decade (taking a huge bite out of the $60 billion mail-order catalog and $250 billion retail businesses).[21] Sensing the change already upon them, giants like Spiegel and R. H. Macy have announced plans to begin home-shopping programs. *Technology Review* notes that so far the information highway "has less the character of a highway than a strip mall, focusing on services with proven consumer demand that can rapidly pay for themselves."[22] Movies are perhaps the least of those services. More likely targets are the $4 billion Americans spend each year for video games, the $100 billion they spend on basic telephone service, and, biggest by far, the more than $500 billion they spend each year on gambling. Bell Atlantic chairman Raymond Smith and TCI chief executive John Malone have both said they want SuperTube to bring off-track betting and lotteries to every American home.[23]

To the extent that any of these services will cater to children, they will regard them merely as marketing opportunities, not as students or citizens, nor even as young and impressionable human beings; some services clearly are not suitable for children at all. It is as if SuperTube were merely a better way to sell things, as if the public interest had nothing to do with children but was measured in sales receipts. In 1993, USWest chairman Richard McCormick told a congressional committee as much: "The market," he said, "*is* the public interest."[24] Barry Diller's epiphany had come when he went with his friend the clothes designer Diane Von Furstenberg to visit QVC and watched while it sold more than $1 million worth of her designs to more than 19,000 people in less than two hours. He announced his intention to buy a controlling share of the network a month later. Diller told reporters, "I have seen the future, and it is retail."[25]

If Barry Diller, Richard McCormick, Raymond Smith, and John Malone are right, the future of television, far from being an electronic cornucopia, will be much worse than its past. The strangers who enter our home by the hundreds will enter by the thousands; parents who find it difficult to monitor the access those strangers have to their children today will find it impossible tomorrow. Quality children's programming, expensive to produce and nowhere near so profitable as product-based programming, will be available only to those who can afford to pay for it. Elsewhere—if it exists at all—it will have to depend on the trickle-down from commercial programming profits.

But of course the market alone is not the public interest. If there is any lesson Americans can take from the age of broadcasting, and from the Radio Act of 1927 and the Communications Act of 1934, it is that the market is but one factor in determining the public interest, not the thing itself. And expanding the market to include more players hawking more goods and services does not alone constitute or enlarge the public interest.

Yet anyone who has followed the debate about SuperTube in Washington knows that our politicians have defined the public interest primarily in terms of "competition" among the various industries—broadcast, cable, telephone, newspapers, and others— that have financial stakes in the policy outcome. Each industry offers a different version of the "public interest," carefully wrapped in pieties about free speech and free enterprise, with itself as the regulation-protected standard-bearer of the new order and the political power to veto any regulatory scheme it does not like. In September 1994, that is exactly what happened: one part of the communications industry (news reports pinned responsibility on the Baby Bells) blocked passage of a sweeping effort to bring the Communications Act into the information age, arguing that the bill was too generous to rival industries.

The most remarkable thing about this debate—and the most disturbing—is how similar it is, in its assumptions and even in its cast of characters, to the debates that preceded the Radio and Communications Acts more than a half century ago. Americans are fulfilling George Santayana's prediction about those who are ignorant of history: we are repeating it. At best, ours is an enormously shortsighted approach to public policy. SuperTube, after all, is not merely a better form of television. It is an altogether different medium, the core of a communications revolution that is as significant an advance over broadcasting as radio was over print, as print was over writing, as writing was over speech. Some scientists have compared the changes portended by SuperTube to the changes in the history of life billions of years ago when primitive organisms evolved into multicellular animals. Like the atom at mid-century, communication is about to fission and change the world.

When the atom was split, and within a year of the atomic bombings of Hiroshima and Nagasaki, Albert Einstein warned that the powerful technology of nuclear fission was so unlike anything that had ever come before that it exceeded mankind's capacity for moral calculation. Everything has changed, he wrote in 1946, except the way we think. What we need to do now is change the way we think about television, and its place in our children's lives.

5 : Changing the Way We Think

Train up a child in the way he should go; and when he is old, he will not depart from it.   —*Proverbs, 22:6*

THE PROSPECTS FOR CHANGE IN A WORLD OF WIRED "INFORMATION highways" are full of promise. As traditional communications regulations are made obsolete by the development of new technologies, a sound and effective children's telecommunications policy can and should be strengthened by First Amendment principles. The single most important thing Americans should do is think less about the technology that makes the next communications revolution possible and more about what direction we want the revolution to take. This means acknowledging that we can shape the future that is at hand. How should we do so? In this book, we have argued that the guiding principle should be the public interest—and that we all know what the public interest is: it is the best interests of our children. In its Madisonian sense, to care about the public interest means to address issues of civic responsibility. And nothing is more central to that responsibility than protecting and educating children.

Thus the foremost principle for realizing the public interest is to put children first. They are our future; before long, they will be our governors. At the minimum, therefore, public policy should focus on three goals:

- It should meet the child's need to be prepared for life as a productive citizen. Television, the nation's most powerful teacher, should be a conduit for the generational transmission of democratic values and the values of simple decency.
- It should meet the child's need to be protected from harm that comes from continuous exposure to violence whose primary purpose is to serve as a conveyance for commercial matter.
- It must give every advantage to parents, helping them not only to control the passage of strangers in and out of their home but also to be better parents; it should place a premium on parent education and support, including parent-to-parent support.

Though in this book we have focused primarily on broadcast television, these principles are equally applicable to SuperTube. For the present, and for the foreseeable future, broadcasting channels command far larger audiences of children than cable channels do, but the habits of mind and practice that dominated children's broadcast television for so long will almost certainly find their way into television's next generation if they are left unchallenged and unchanged today. It will not do to put off for the future what must be done now, before another generation of children is abandoned for sale in the marketplace. The evidence for such urgency is in the words and deeds of the men and women now running the television and interactive communications industries, and in the many years we have listened to them insist that any children's television—even bad children's programming—isn't worth the trouble unless the children who are watching can be delivered to advertisers as marketable products. The principles above, therefore, and the recommendations that follow from them concern the present, what Robert Pepper calls television's second and third stages. Our recommendations focus on broadcasting, but have implications for cable and for the world of SuperTube. Our principles, on the other hand, have *nothing* to do with television per se, and *everything* to do with the well-being of American children. As a nation we cannot ignore what Sissela Bok describes as the "call for all concerned—parents, educators, industry officials and . . . government, to come to grips" with the television environment which our children grow up in, where they learn so much, so young, about the values of the adult world.[1] If we cannot honor these simple principles—worse, if we cannot agree on their importance—then we are not worthy of calling the United States the world's standard-bearer for democracy.

There is a little-noted episode in American broadcast history that suggests how deeply all of us already know this, and can act on what we know. Of the preeminent children's television systems in the world, one is Japan's, another Germany's. Both countries make extraordinary use of television in their national educational systems. Both put a premium on parent involvement and on education. But Japan's system was not created by the Japanese, nor Germany's by the Germans. The foundation for each was laid after World War II by others who knew all too well the dangers of leaving the public interest exclusively to the whims of private power in the marketplace—by the occupying Americans. Now it is time for Americans to rebuild our own television system. Translating the public interest into a commitment to our children will take time and public debate. We challenge the American people to demand that debate and participate in it, for in the long run it will take a combination of broad education, wise parenting, corporate responsibility, and smart and forceful lawmaking to improve children's telecommunications.

We propose these recommendations:

1. **Congress should fulfill the promise of the 1990 Children's Television Act.** It should explicitly define the Communications Act's "public interest" standard in terms of broadcasters' service to children, then give broadcasters two alternatives: either make an enforceable commitment to meet a specified standard of programming service for children on each of however many channels they operate, or forgo public service to children and pay for their use of the spectrum.

With the first alternative, Congress needs to make the "educational and informational" requirements of the Children's Television Act explicit and require broadcasters to make public the record of their compliance. Without clear requirements in the law, the alternative will be a failure—for the simple reason that the FCC has never successfully enforced any public-interest requirements over a long period of time, instead changing its interpretation of the law with each new presidential administration and congressional hearing. Explicit requirements for service to children need to be clear, so as to be enforceable; farsighted, recognizing that broadcasters will soon be using additional channels in the spectrum for purposes other than traditional programming; broad, to permit experimentation; and narrow, to prevent their being ignored or circumvented, regardless of who is in the White House or controls Congress.

Since 1993, the FCC under Chairman Reed Hundt has somewhat clarified the meaning of the Children's Television Act's "educational and informational" requirement. In June 1994, the commission took testimony from children's advocates, industry representatives, parents, and other concerned citizens. In April 1995, it issued several proposals for public comment, including one that would allow broadcasters within each market to pay other broadcasters to meet their children's programming obligations for them. At a minimum, said children's advocates, that obligation should be one hour a day of quality programming during times when children might actually be watching.

The proposal is a good start. But if history is any guide, even this mild recommendation will pass with the political winds. It will work only if two conditions are met. The first is that Congress grant broadcasters an antitrust exemption so that they may cooperate in the production and scheduling of quality children's programming. Requiring broadcasters to meet such a minimal public service is reasonable, but asking them to take financial lumps in the name of public service is counterproductive—and, more important, competition in this area will *not* benefit children. Far better that a network such as Fox, which has already had success with its preschool series *Cubhouse*, continue to program for younger viewers, while CBS serves six- to ten-year-olds and NBC, perhaps, young teens. Broadcasters might also differentiate their programs by subject matter. CBS, for example, airs the wonderfully wacky science show *Beakman's World* for older children and young teens; ABC might offer a science show for younger viewers, or perhaps a reading or news program. If broadcasters could discuss scheduling and avoid concurrent airtimes, children would also be able to watch all the quality programs made just for them, providing children themselves a brighter palette of weekly programming (and avoiding the kind of ghettoization that occurs when children's programs are all bunched into the same time period) and giving broadcasters a realistic opportunity to build a loyal viewership for their programs. Finally, says David Kleeman, director of the American Center for Children's Television,

> If kids knew that every day, at a consistent time, there would be a full hour of television just for them, broadcasters wouldn't need to be tied to the convention of half-hour and hour programs. The sixty minutes could include any number of shorter pieces, each a length that suited its content. A ten-minute drama, a five-minute documentary, a 12-minute game show—these just fit the attention span of young viewers, and writers, excited by the prospect of designing programming that broke all the rules, would love the challenge of creating shorter, tighter stories . . . The children's hours could become the most innovative on television.[2]

The need for an antitrust exemption in this area is obvious: a diverse and quality children's programming service cannot be summoned out of thin air; broadcasters should be allowed to cooperate if an hour-a-day requirement is to benefit children.

No such initiative will work without a critical second step: that the hour of required programming be clearly labeled as the broadcaster's compliance with the law. The label should work just as the signs do that millions of Americans post prominently in the windows of their homes and businesses, letting children know that these places are safe refuges. The programming label indicates that the program's primary purpose is to educate, not to sell toys or junk food, and that it is safe, that there is a friend in the house instead of a stranger. In October 1994, ABC began experimenting with something very much like what we propose when it announced that it would use a special on-air logo to designate programs that are "particularly enjoyable for family viewing," according to ABC entertainment president Ted Harbert. The new "Family Viewing Logo" is to appear in the lower-right hand corner of the screen at the beginning of family programs and for several seconds after each commercial break. The label is a marketing device, not an advisory, says ABC's Chris Hikawa. But a similar label on educational programs would help parents or children who are searching for something to watch to find it easily. A label of this kind is friendly to viewers, to broadcasters, *and* to the First Amendment: it notifies parents that a program has special value, thus drawing attention to it and increasing its chances for success; it gives the public clear notice not only that the law's requirements are being met but how they are being met; and it protects broadcasters from constant government inquiries into programming practices and policies that do offend the First Amendment.

If broadcasters choose the second alternative, they will effectively be relieved of their public-interest obligations to children under the 1934 Communications Act; but, in return, they will have to pay a percentage of their annual revenues—between 1 and 3 percent—for spectrum leases. The money from those leases should, in turn, be required by statute to go to the production of children's programming on public broadcasting.

This second alternative has not been seriously considered since Congressman Van Deerlin's attempt to rewrite the Communications Act in the late 1970s. Its most ardent advocate today is Henry Geller, former FCC general counsel and head of the National Telecommunications and Information Administration—and also principal proponent of the 1990 Children's Television Act. Geller argues that sixty years of the Communications Act's public-interest standard have been a failure, and a particularly dismal failure where children are concerned. No amount of coaxing, cajoling, or threatening has produced an adequate or sustainable amount or quality of children's programming, nor is it ever likely to, he believes. Minimal requirements, such as an hour a day, are still woefully insufficient, Geller argues, and broadcasters will heed them with as little imagination, effort, and cost as possible. Far better, he says, to charge broadcasters a fee for the publicly owned spectrum they now use for free, and put that money toward funding noncommercial, not-for-profit children's programming.

In July 1994, Congress and the administration discovered just how valuable the spectrum could be when, for the first time ever, the FCC auctioned off a "narrowband" portion of the radio spectrum, soliciting bids for ten nationwide licenses for use with electronic pagers. The auction was expected to earn the government approximately $20 million; instead, after days of furious bidding, it earned nearly *thirty times that much*, almost $600 million. "My little socks are knocked off," said FCC commissioner Rachelle Chong. In the fall of 1994, a second narrowband auction earned more than $489 million. Finally, the FCC began an auction of "broadband" spectrum for wireless telephone service in December 1994, which, when it finally ends sometime in 1995, is expected to earn about $10 billion; in its first week it earned more than $800 million. Such a windfall, says Geller, should wake Americans up to "what six megahertz of valuable spectrum is worth." Six megahertz is the valuable chunk of spectrum used by each commercial broadcaster, and Geller believes that Congress and the administration will inevitably ask broadcasters to pay for its use.

The important question is: where does the money go once the federal government gets it? Currently it disappears into the $1.5 trillion federal budget. The enormous lost opportunity that money represents is illustrated by the case of Austrian immigrant Stanley S. Newberg, who came to the United States in 1906, succeeded in manufacturing and real estate, and, when he died in 1986, bequeathed his fortune of $5.6 million to the United States government "in deep gratitude for the privilege of residing and living in this kind of government—notwithstanding many of its inequities." After Newberg's will was finally settled in 1994, the money went directly to the U.S. Bureau of Public Debt, where it lasted about ninety seconds.[3] And then it was gone, spent in the service of who knows what.

Coming as they do from publicly owned telecommunications resources, the revenues from the auctions ought to be invested in improving telecommunications for children. The idea of taking the money earned from the administration of a valuable public resource and investing it in another is not unprecedented. In 1965, Congress created the Land and Water Conservation Fund to provide federal financing for the acquisition of parks and other public lands by using money from offshore oil and gas leases. Later, in 1978, the Urban Parks and Recreation Recovery Program included similar financing provisions. The principle in both cases is the same: use the revenues from one irreplaceable resource to protect another.

Why should the revenues raised from spectrum auctions be used any differently, without some sort of real payback to the public? The money generated by a spectrum fee on broadcasters, for example, could go a long way. Edward Palmer, a noted observer of children's television practices throughout the world, has calculated that the cost of creating four years' worth of first-rate children's programs—an hour of original programming each weekday for each of three different age groups (two to five, six to nine, and ten to thirteen)—is about $63 million a year (or $1.50 per child per year).[4] Markle Foundation president Lloyd Morrisett, who has chronicled the meanderings of telecommunications policy for a quarter century, estimates that the cost is higher, between $200 million and $300 million. Either way the point is the same: even the most modest spectrum fee could easily turn children's television from a wasteland into a garden of delights. Today, annual gross television broadcasting revenues in the United States are conservatively estimated at about $25 billion, radio at $9 billion; *by itself, a bare minimum of 1 percent of broadcast television revenues would pay annually for $250 million of children's programming; 3 percent* would provide $750 million, a sum with which Americans could transform not only children's television, but childhood itself, and bring to fruition some of the extraordinary advances in education, health care, and family support that futurists predict for SuperTube. Currently, the Children's Television Endowment, created by the Children's Television Act in 1990 to support high-quality, educational programming, is pitifully underfunded. In 1994 it asked for $24 million to do its job, but Congress appropriated $1 million; for 1995, it appropriated $2.5 million. A similarly underfinanced effort to improve the lot of America's children is the Ready-to-Learn programming and satellite service, a virtual blueprint for dedicated, educational children's television. Congress created the service in 1993 but appropriated less than $7 million—after authorizing $30 million—with which to start it.*

Why not take some of the money from the administration or auction of telecommunications resources and put it toward children's services? Is there a better investment in our children's future? We should learn from past mistakes, such as the misuse of cable franchise fees, which cable companies must pay to make use of public streets, telephone poles, and other rights-of-way. Those fees yield about $800 million annually, but there is no stipulation that the money be used to support public-service programming, as was originally intended. Cities can spend the money any way they choose. Based on 5 percent of revenues, cable fees provide a city like Chicago more than $7.6 million a year. In most places this money simply disappears, as Geller says, into "pensions and potholes."

In every instance where the auction or administration of telecommunications resources yields revenues—whether from broadcast, cable, or even SuperTube—Congress should require by statute that at least a portion of the money be earmarked for children. The larger the tax base, the lower the percentage rate needed in any one medium; and the rate required to serve our children well is very small to begin with. Of the $10 billion minimum the federal gov-

---

* In 1995 Congress was considering rescinding the Ready-to-Learn budget even further.

ernment expects to earn from its spectrum auctions, for example, 2 to 3 percent would meet the annual programming costs that Morissett has calculated. A larger portion of the windfall could be given to connecting America's primary and secondary schools to the information highway, to testing new electronic educational services and to training teachers to use them.

If instead the federal government does with that $10 billion what it did with Stanley Newberg's bequest—spend it—the money will last about forty-four hours. And then it, too, will be gone. By even the most conservative cost-benefit analysis, a much superior alternative would be to make that money last a lifetime—many millions of them. Invest public telecommunications revenues in our children.

2. Parents should monitor their children's television viewing and, whenever possible, watch television with them. This recommendation seems obvious, but remarkably few parents actually *do* it. Political and philosophical opposites—such as Charles Murray and Roger Wilkins—agree that if there is one thing that might make a genuine difference in the lives of America's children, it is parents who are effective and nurturing. "No job is more important to our nation's future than that of a parent," the Carnegie Corporation has recently reported, "and no job is more challenging."[5] Certainly one place to begin is in front of the family television set.

Experts on children's television agree that the importance of the role of parents in making television better for children cannot be overestimated, and they begin and end their advice with one imperative: Sit down and watch with them.[6] Peggy Charren, former president of Action for Children's Television, has argued for years that if parents actually knew and cared about what their children watched, her job would be a lot easier. Research supports her view. The psychologist Patricia Marks Greenfield writes that an adult presence encourages a child to be an active, critical viewer:

A pervasive finding in television research is that the effects of television programs on knowledge are stronger if an adult interacts with the child during the viewing process. The adult can encourage the children to pay attention, can make interpretations, and can explain things the child finds incomprehensible. Watching with the child is not enough; it is crucial to talk about the show being watched.[7]

What do you talk about? Experts recommend many different questions, comments, and activities, depending on the age of the children. Some can focus on teaching children to differentiate between TV and reality ("How come Theo on *The Cosby Show* seldom studies? Do you think he has as much homework as you?"). Some can get kids interested in the basics of television production ("Does the music make the story more exciting?" or "Have you noticed that the music always seems less happy whenever the bad guy comes on?"). Some can spur creative thinking ("How would you have preferred to see the story end?"), while others may point out racial or sexual stereotyping or educate children about TV commercials ("They're trying to make you think that all that sand and ocean and sun come with Barbie. Did you fall for it?"). Many activities suggested by experts to complement TV viewing are didactic. For example, one resource suggests, "Teach your youngster the habit of writing down words he or she doesn't understand while watching television. Help your child to look those words up in the dictionary."[8] Of course, every time a child watches television the experience does not need to become a lesson in critical viewing. Like adults, children often want only to be entertained. One parent found that "it works well to intersperse several comments in one show, then leave the subject alone for several shows or days afterwards."[9]

Perhaps the most important reason parents should watch television with their children is that people like Dick Wolf, the producer of such programs as *Miami Vice* and *Law & Order*, dismiss the idea that the industry has any responsibility whatsoever toward parents or children. His own children, Wolf said, have "never seen any of the shows I've ever produced. They shouldn't be watching them."[10] Wolf may well be a fine parent, but the problem remains that millions of children *do* watch his programs. If their parents watched with them, they would have a chance to offset the messages they disagree with (such as gender or racial stereotyping) or find confusing or frightening (such as portrayals of sex and/or violence).

To mitigate the effects of televised violence, the American Psychological Association suggests that parents discuss why the violence happened and how painful it is; ask the child how the conflict might have been solved without violence; and explain how violence in entertainment is "faked" and not real. Parents should encourage children to watch programs with characters that cooperate with, help, and care for one another, and they should watch at least one episode of a program their children watch regularly to judge for themselves the program's suitability for their children.[11]

Parents who watch television with their children know that programs aren't the only thing to worry about. On commercial channels, children are bombarded with advertisements, many of them intended for adults. In a country where 85 percent of households own a VCR, one way to solve this problem is to establish a family video library, since parent-approved "family library" tapes need no future screening for replays. The television critic David Bianculli writes that he vigilantly screens what his children watch. "When they were younger," he says, "the only 'live' TV shows my children watched were *Mister Rogers' Neighborhood*, *Sesame Street*, and old *Looney Tunes* cartoon showcases. Otherwise, their TV came pretaped and prescreened."[12]

Parents who don't have the time to screen individual shows and episodes often wish they had the power to screen out entire channels. What they often do not know is that by law cable companies must offer parents some type of device that allows them to block out channels. Some technologically advanced cable companies offer sophisticated electronic equipment that allows one to program channels one would like to receive (CNN and C-SPAN are perennial parent favorites) and block out those not wanted (usually MTV or movie channels). In Evanston, Illinois, for example, such a device is available for an extra $2.95 per month.

Of course, many parents are dismayed less by what their children watch than by how much time they spend watching it. Their concern is not unfounded. Research shows that children who watch excessive amounts of television are less likely to do well in school, and that they are more likely to develop the kinds of health problems associated with a sedentary lifestyle and a diet high in junk food.[13] Parents who simply want to reduce their children's viewing time might consider purchasing a "mechanical disciplinarian" such as TV Allowance. In order to turn on a set equipped with TV Allowance, a child punches in his or her individual code; the machine then deducts each minute the television is on from a total number of minutes allotted by a parent. According to Randal Levenson, its creator, TV Allowance "allows children to budget their time, to learn to make choices, and to control their viewing."[14] Some strong advocates of TV rationing, such as the pediatrician and writer T. Berry Brazelton, recommend that children watch no more than an hour of television on school days and two hours a day on weekends. Brazelton, however, admits to a certain ambivalence about devices like TV Allowance. "Parents," he says, "ought to have the guts to do it themselves and not do it by a machine."[15]

In either case, the larger point is the same: parents must, in some way, take primary responsibility for what their children see on television. Very often the source of the problem is parents themselves, who on average watch between five and ten *more* hours of television a week than their children do.[16] Parents cannot control their children's viewing unless they also control their own, and when they do that they discover something else—the power of a good example.

3. Help parents protect their children from television violence and other programming they find objectionable. As Congress thinks about television's adaptation to the world of information highways, it should keep in mind that on real highways the law requires infant seats and seat belts to ensure children's safety. Children should travel the information highway with at least as much protection. Therefore Congress should, as Massachusetts congressman Edward Markey has proposed, empower parents to the fullest extent possible with the technological means of blocking unwanted strangers from their home, including those whom they consider violent, crude, and harmful. One such technological means is the v-chip, and it should be a required component of all television sets. The Electronics Industries Association has already endorsed the chip as a component of new television sets, and at least one company, Spruce

Run Technologies, already manufactures a program-screening chip—which the company calls a c-chip (*c* standing for choice). Other manufacturers and programmers offer channel-lockout capability. A set-top box called TeleCommander, manufactured by Protelcon, generates an on-screen menu with which parents can select programs and times they want blocked out; the United States Satellite Broadcasting Company (USSB), a digital satellite broadcaster, offers a feature called Locks and Limits that allows parents to set rating limits for their television, screening out, for example, any films with a Motion Picture Association of America rating other than G or PG. Choice technology, under whatever name it goes, is here to stay.

Parents need to be aware of its availability, however; more important, there should be multiple sources of judgment about which programs are violent or otherwise unsuitable for children, since parents will differ in their views on this. While Congress should call on broadcast networks, independent television stations, and cable and satellite programmers to place parental advisories on material they may consider unsuitable for children, the government should not itself get into the business of rating programs. The best source of parental information must be parents themselves, using their own personal taste and discretion. Community groups—schools, PTAs, churches—can also rate programs, and other organizations may find a way to make such rating schemes profitable. The most ambitious and inventive such effort to date is OKTV Inc., which uses an independent advisory board of experts in children's issues to rate programs as either "OK" or "NOT OK" for each of two age groups (one to six, and seven to twelve), matches those ratings to local television viewing schedules, and then uses chip technology in TV set-top units to display either general programming (whatever happens to be on television) or children's programs that have been judged "OK." Significantly, OKTV works with cable and broadcast-only television service, and it does more than merely block out programs unsuitable for children—it can also lock in those that are good for them. Says OKTV creator Richard Leghorn:

> With OKTV service parents retain complete control of the system and can conveniently override it for whatever reason whenever

they like. They can override OKTV ratings based on their own assessment of what is suitable or not suitable for their children based on press critiques, word-of-mouth opinion, or ratings and monitoring reports of others such as the motion picture classifications of MPAA or the violence warning labels planned by the cable and broadcast industries. But OKTV service, which will be biased in favor of protection rather than permissiveness, will always be there to handle most, and for many parents all, of the tremendous burden parents now have in trying to protect their children from harmful programs and guide their viewing toward beneficial programs.[17]

Undoubtedly many parents will not take advantage of choice technology, and others will not consult either a ratings scheme or their own judgment. But so long as Congress sees to it that they have every opportunity to block programs they do not want their children to see, and does not itself engage in making content decisions, the First Amendment will be satisfied. Parents will have a realistic way of keeping unwelcome strangers out of their homes, and the range of programming available to adults on television will expand.

4. End Television's Commercial Exploitation of Children. Of all the research findings about children and television, the one on which there is virtually no disagreement is that small children do not understand the difference between programs and commercials. The FCC and the FTC have implicitly recognized in the past that commercials aimed at the very young are inherently deceptive. Congress should reconsider the commercial time constraints in the Children's Television Act, and forbid commercials in programming directed primarily at preschool children, those younger than six.

Objections to this recommendation will be of two kinds. The first, from broadcasters, will be that a commercial ban is economically irrational, that in the absence of commercials to support good programming for the very young, such programs will not exist. This is another way of saying that although they have received a valuable economic privilege for free in return for serving the public interest, broadcasters must now violate that interest in order to maximize profit levels. Is the idea of "sustaining time" first proposed by David Sarnoff and William Paley now a crime against nature? Were Adam Smith available for consultation on the matter, he would say that the burden of irrationality in this matter lies with broadcasters.

A second objection will be that a prohibition like this is unworkable. Those who believe so need only look to Canada for proof that it can work. The Canadian Association of Broadcasters, in cooperation with the Canadian Advertising Foundation (a private industry organization), voluntarily created a broadcast code for advertising to children twelve and under. Written in 1971 and revised in 1993, the code was created to

> serve as a guide to advertisers and agencies in preparing commercial messages which adequately recognize the special characteristics of the children's audience. Children, especially the very young, live in a world that is part imaginary, part real and sometimes do not distinguish clearly between the two. Children's advertising should respect and not abuse the power of the child's imagination.

The code, neither vague nor toothless, is an eleven-page document with specific restrictions regarding the "factual presentation" of products; the use of "undue pressure"; the scheduling of ads; the discussion of price and purchase terms; endorsements by program characters and celebrities; the promotion of "values inconsistent with the moral, ethical or legal standards of contemporary Canadian society"; the portrayal of unsafe toys or toy use; and comparison claims with other products. The Canadian Advertising Foundation can require an advertiser to substantiate any claim it makes for a children's product, and has the authority to administer the code anywhere in Canada—except Quebec, which bans broadcast advertising to children altogether. Broadcasters who air commercials for children that do not meet the CAF's standards can have their licenses revoked.

Do American children deserve any less protection than Canadian children do? It should no longer be acceptable for the programmers to claim, as the Fox Children's Network does in its trade advertisements, "We deliver more young viewers than anyone." Children are human beings, not commercial opportunities.

5. Congress should exempt broadcasters and other programmers from the antitrust laws for the purpose of developing a code of professional standards. The earlier code of the National Association of Broadcasters was abandoned in 1982 after an overeager, short-sighted, and ideologically driven Justice Department succeeded in destroying it. The Justice Department's action made effective self-regulation virtually impossible in the industry, and left the government in the position of being the only judge of programming practices, a situation clearly unfavorable to the First Amendment.

Congress should not only permit the creation of a code of practice but require membership of all licensed broadcasters. A code of professional standards for broadcasters would be analogous to similar codes in other industries, from real estate to manufacturing, that prohibit deceptive, discriminatory, or abusive practices. The code of the National Association of Securities Dealers, for example, specifies what brokers may not say or do in their dealings with the public and with each other. Other professionals—such as lawyers and doctors, engineers and teachers—have to meet minimum standards of professional practice. Journalists, of course, are not professionals in this sense of the term, but most broadcasters are not journalists; instead, they are licensed operators of a publicly owned spectrum. Are their character and performance any less important than that of other professionals? Broadcasters and cable operators should be held to a standard of practice that meets their own best professional judgments.

Business groups, particularly, have an important role to play here, since their advertising influences so much television programming. Sanford McDonnell, chairman emeritus of McDonnell Douglas, is a proponent of what he calls "character education" in schools, but worries that "television is creating a very strong headwind into which we character education proponents must fly." For that reason McDonnell has wisely urged his colleagues in the influential Business Roundtable to use their influence "to leverage the cable and television industries into establishing a self-policing mechanism," but so far has had no success.[18] If the members of the roundtable sat with their children and grandchildren and watched and discussed the programs sponsored by their companies—if all advertisers did—they would change their policies. Producers and advertising executives should similarly spend time with their children and grandchildren, watching the programs they have produced and funded. Are they proud of what they're doing?

Recently a number of business associations announced their commitments to "children's best interest," as one group, the New American Revolution, put it in a full-page *New York Times* advertisement in September 1994. The New American Revolution includes among its members top executives from several communications companies, including Time Warner CEO Gerald Levin and USA Network president Kay Koplovitz, both of whom, in different circumstances, have publicly denied their own companies' responsibility to children and parents. Inconsistencies like these raise questions about whether the revolution was launched in the boardroom or the marketing department. Now the real question is whether these executives and the companies they represent will make good on their promises.

6. **The nonprofit community, especially foundations and universities, should become more active in the debate over children's television and its place in the new world of SuperTube.** About seventy-five not-for-profit groups have been active in the Telecommunications Policy Roundtable, a consortium that lobbies to guarantee equal and affordable access to the information superhighway. Others have sponsored projects related either to SuperTube or to children's television. Laudable as these efforts are, they need to be brought together lest their debate—and their message—go unheard. In the years between 1927 and 1934, divisiveness among educators, labor unions, churches, and foundations was perhaps the single most important reason why the Wagner-Hatfield amendment was defeated and the success of commercial broadcasters assured in controlling virtually the entire radio spectrum. Today we are in danger of repeating the mistake. If Americans compound the error they made in 1934, it will be because the institutions that fought so resolutely in the 1930s are now sitting silently on the sidelines.

Our foundations and think tanks have offered few imaginative ideas about SuperTube except the standard homilies about competition and free speech. They have said virtually nothing about the place of children in television's next generation. Some members of the American Academy of Arts and Sciences, the organization that supported the writing of this book, expressed doubts about the importance of television serving the public interest, and even asked whether the public interest can be defined except in economic terms. Would George Washington, Thomas Jefferson, and John Adams, three of the academy's founders, have spoken in the same way?

Perhaps the most remarkable absentees in the debate over SuperTube—and least forgivable—are the nation's educators. The two failed information highway bills in the 103rd Congress, H.R. 3636 and S. 1822, both barely mentioned children except to consider linking schools to the National Information Infrastructure as cheaply as possible, an undertaking that few people familiar with the costs of such linkage think feasible.[19] Just how these linkages should be financed is a critical public-policy question, one that the nation's educational establishment has scarcely acknowledged.* Until it does, the billions of dollars that will come from spectrum auctions will simply disappear into federal spending, with no benefit whatsoever to children.

Finally, the nation's colleges and universities, which should be leading the fight on this issue, have been content to follow instead. "The universities are letting the business community set the agenda," says Jeffrey Chester of the Center for Media Education. "They have abdicated their responsibility. Where are the intellectuals, the innovative models, where are the studies—other than those that are funded by big business?"[20] An urgent question, and as yet unanswered.

---

* Among the educational organizations that have proposed funding mechanisms for wiring the nation's schools are the National Association of School Principals, the National School Boards Association, the American Library Association, the National Education Association, and the Council of Chief State School Officers. In 1994, these groups proposed that the FCC use the "consumer productivity dividend" derived from the access charges local phone companies collect from long-distance companies to wire the schools. The groups estimated the annual revenue from such charges to be about $300 million.

7. **The news media should distinguish legitimate concerns about free speech from equally legitimate concerns about the health and well-being of children.** No one makes this point better than Sissela Bok, who writes that, in the debate over television violence particularly, journalists too easily accept a number of poorly thought-through rationalizations about the problem as reasons for doing nothing about it.[21] In doing so, Bok says, they fail to advance public understanding or debate, indeed become obstacles to debate.

It is true, for example, that America has a history of violence; that other factors besides television contribute to violence; that the link between televised violence and real violence, as with smoking and cancer, is not infallibly conclusive; that television violence is in some measure a reflection of violence in society; that "violence" is hard to define; that SuperTube may eventually create many hundreds more outlets for video violence; that parents have primary responsibility for what their children watch; and that public policy should not tread lightly on free expression. Yet none of these truths, Bok correctly argues, justifies ignoring the legitimate concern that television violence is inappropriate for, and possibly damaging to, children. It was rationalizations such as these, Bok notes, that once sustained such abhorrent practices as slavery and child labor. Similar rationalizations would not permit toy manufacturers to make dangerous toys, pharmaceutical companies to neglect childproof packaging, contractors to build homes with asbestos ceilings and lead-based paint, or stores to sell weapons or explosives to minors. When journalists allow the First Amendment to foreclose debate on the issue of children's television, Bok says, the free speech argument

> produces a chilling effect all its own. It will matter, therefore, for the press to scrutinize its own role in covering the debate over television, . . . to be on the lookout for rationales and rationalizations, . . . and to explore the obstacles that stand in the way of providing better coverage. On such a basis, it ought to be possible, when reporting on contributions to this debate by public interest groups, industry officials, office-holders and others, not only to convey more thoroughly what is being said and done (something which would already represent a significant improvement) but to

provide the type of analysis routinely offered with respect to other societal problems.[22]

8. A program for media education should be developed and supported in the nation's primary and secondary schools. In the end, the best people to judge the way television treats children are parents. Schools, universities, and foundations, therefore, must give much more attention and support to media education for parents as well as for children. Elizabeth Thoman, a former English teacher and the director of the Los Angeles-based Center for Media Literacy, says, "Today, you have to teach the underlying messages around the visuals . . . Media literacy as an organizing discipline incorporates sociology, political science, literary criticism, economics and political analysis. It's an organizing umbrella for seeing problems in a different light and for seeing solutions, all of which are interrelated."[23]

Thoman is by no means alone. The state of New Mexico, at the urging of Governor Bruce King and state educational leaders, formally introduced media literacy programs to its K-through-12 curriculum in 1994. Harvard University has for several summers operated a Media Education Institute, a program for elementary- and secondary-school teachers that introduces them to the principles and methods of media education, and Yale began research on the uses of media for children in 1976.[24] In 1990, the American Academy of Pediatrics formally recommended that parents, teachers, and pediatricians place greater emphasis on "critical television-viewing skills," and the Harvard psychologist Ronald Slaby has for years urged Congress and parents to call upon a variety of institutions, from the television industry to the nation's schools, to help children develop those skills that can reduce the damaging effects of television violence.

At times, the television industry has responded thoughtfully to such encouragement. In 1993, for example, the television journalist Linda Ellerbee did a special program for Nickelodeon in which she interviewed children about their perceptions of televised violence. HBO, in cooperation with *Consumer Reports*, produced its award-winning *Buy Me That*, a film for children about the half-truths and deceptions hidden in advertising.

To be effective over the long term, media literacy programs need to become a basic part of the school curriculum, just as schools now include courses on the potential uses and abuses of the Internet. At a minimum, media education should introduce pupils to the classic techniques of persuasion and propaganda, and to the art classics of film and television. Wherever possible, media education should also familiarize children with the techniques of telling stories using the grammar and syntax of the moving image. Says Kubey,

> With the growing availability of video cameras and the extremely low cost of videotape, this can be done more readily than ever before. Even if cameras aren't available, students can also learn by "storyboarding" scenes and writing scripts . . . One of the ways to increase students' interest in literature is to help them recognize that many of the same storytelling techniques used in the classics are also used in the popular programs and films with which they are already familiar.[25]

Many of the people who advocate media literacy programs have little or no connection to the people who write school curricula; and the media literacy movement as a whole has little understanding of the research on how children of different ages watch television and process its messages.[26] To solve these problems, the nation that creates more media product than any other cannot continue to neglect media education.

9. Congress should commit to a deadline for updating and amending the Children's Television Act, to serve the needs of children both now and in the age of SuperTube. Inevitably, congressional efforts to rewrite the 1934 Communications Act will focus largely on competition between the cable industry, the Baby Bells, long-distance companies like AT&T, broadcasters, and others. In this morass of private interest and technical details, the needs of children will be minimized (as they were in 1994) or forgotten altogether. Congress should therefore refine and expand its finding in the Children's Television Act that the public interest requires special attention to young viewers. The new world of telecommunications is amenable to human choice in direction; the right direction to go is the one consistent with the public interest; and the public interest is the protection and development of children. Congress should therefore establish a deadline by which time it will report to the American people how it is meeting the national commitment to children in the new communications revolution.

Specifically, Congress should begin public discussion and debate on these topics: protecting children from the harm of violence; promoting parenting skills through television; promoting media education for parents and children; determining the obligations and professional standards of broadcasters, narrowcasters, producers of video games, and other purveyors of new communications technologies; ending television's commercial exploitation of children; and engaging universities, foundations, and other nonprofit institutions in the active debate over the future. A new Children's Telecommunications Act, an overhaul of the 1990 act, should be passed into law within two years.

As we approach the age of SuperTube and its glowing promises, we would do well to remember the reservation expressed by the great journalist and broadcaster Edward R. Murrow as he looked at television's future in 1958. "This instrument can teach," he said, "it can illuminate; yes, it can even inspire. But it can do so only to the extent that humans are determined to use it to those ends. Otherwise it is merely lights and wires in a box."[27] The technology that delivers pictures and other information to our home has changed since Murrow's day to include coaxial cable, fiber-optic cable, cellular and other wireless systems, and direct broadcast satellites. But the box is still a box. What we use it for is still up to us. The telecommunications revolution already under way in America and around the world demands sustained attention, lest its promise go unfulfilled. If it does, the cost of our failure will be borne by our children.

When Douglass Cater looked ahead to the age of SuperTube, he called the new technology MOTHER out of his concern that it would become an instrument of control—by the government, perhaps, but more likely by private commercial interests—rather than an instrument of freedom and creativity. But it doesn't have to be that way. If we act wisely, SuperTube can bring the First Amendment fully into the digital age, empower real mothers and real fathers to decide what is best for their children, and establish children themselves—as the Communications Act did not—as the principal beneficiaries of our nation's communications policy. Though SuperTube may eventually dispense with many of the public-interest obligations that marked the age of broadcasting, our responsibility to protect and educate our children will never be among them. Even skeptics who believe the public interest is beyond definition know that it lies in the hearts and minds of children. If as a nation we cannot figure out what the public interest means with respect to those who are too young to vote, who are barely literate, who are financially and emotionally and even physically dependent on adults, then we will never figure out what it means anywhere else. Our children *are* the public interest, living and breathing, flesh and blood.

Or will we, once again, abandon our children to the wasteland?

Appendix 1 : A Bill for Children's Telecommunications

The 1990 Children's Television Act is incorporated into the 1934 Communications Act as Section 303(b). We propose the following additions to that section in accordance with the principles and recommendations laid out in Chapter 5.*

A Bill

To amend the Communications Act of 1934 to increase the availability of educational and informational television programs for children and to afford greater control to parents to deal with violence in television programs.

Be it enacted by the Senate and House of Representatives of the United States of America in Congress assembled,

* The authors thank Henry A. Geller for his help in preparing this draft legislation.

TITLE I—REGULATION OF CHILDREN'S TELEVISION

Section 1. Short Title.

This Act may be cited as the "Children's Television Protection and Education Act of 1995."

Section 2. Findings.

The Congress finds that

(1) By the time the average student graduates from high school, that child has spent more time watching television than in the classroom.

(2) It has been clearly demonstrated that television can assist children in learning important information, skills, values, and behavior, while entertaining them and exciting their curiosity to learn about the world around them.

(3) Commercial television is the most effective and pervasive mass medium.

(4) The potential of commercial television programming for making a positive impact in improving the education of children has been inadequately realized.

(5) As public trustees, commercial television licensees have a legal obligation to provide public service to children.

(6) Commercial television has inadequately met its obligation to provide educational and informational programming to children as a crucial part of its obligation to serve the public interest, and this has occurred despite the enactment of the Children's Television Act of 1990.

(7) The Federal Communications Commission, in implementing that Act, has not taken effective steps to increase educational and informational programming designed for children on commercial television and has instead left the broadcaster's obligations to serve children vague.

(8) Preschool children cannot distinguish between advertising and programming material, and therefore advertising in programming specifically designed for the preschool child audience is inherently deceptive.

Section 3. Consideration of Children's Television Service in Broadcast License Renewal.

There is added to Section 303 the following subsections:

"(c) In fulfilling the above obligation in subsection (b), each television broadcasting station shall broadcast a substantial amount of programming:

(1) which serves the educational and informational needs of children who are 12 years of age or younger through programming that is specifically designed to meet such needs,

(2) which is reasonably scheduled throughout the week, and

(3) which is directed to specific age groups of children.

(d) (1) The Commission shall establish a presumptive quantitative guideline for serving the child audience, which broadcasters must meet to obtain renewal of license or establish good cause for not doing so. That guideline is the broadcast of a minimum of one hour each day [or seven hours a week, five hours of which shall occur Monday through Friday,] of programming that is described in subsections (c)(1), (2), and (3).

(2) Alternatively, the commercial television licensees shall make a contribution to the public interest through efforts described in subsection (b)(2) that are directed to the noncommercial television sector, specifically by contributing 1.5 percent of their gross advertising revenues to the Corporation for Public Broadcasting, which shall use the sums so received exclusively for the production and distribution of programming specifically designed to educate and inform the child audience.

(e) The Commission shall prescribe such regulations as are necessary to carry out the purposes of this section. Such regulations shall be initially prescribed not later than 180 days after the date of enactment of the Children's Television Act of 1995.

(f) In the annual report required by Section 4(k), the Commission shall list those television broadcast station licensees whose licenses were renewed, notwithstanding a failure to meet the level of programming set forth in section (d)(1) or the alternative contribution described in section (d)(2), and set out in detail the reasons for the renewal."

Section 4. Regulation of Commercials in Children's Programming.

(a) After January 1, 1998, no commercial television broadcast licensees shall include commercial matter in conjunction with programming that is specifically designed for, or directed to, the preschool child audience.

(b) As used in this section, the term "commercial television broadcast licensee" includes a cable operator, as defined in Section 602 of the Communications Act of 1934 (47 U.S.C. 522).

(c) The Commission shall prescribe such regulations as are necessary to carry out the purposes of this section.

Title II—Ready-to-Learn Cable Television Education Channel

Section 1. Short Title.

This title may be cited as the "Ready-to-Learn Cable Television Education Channel Act of 1995."

Section 2. Findings.

The Congress finds that

(1) Cable television is rapidly emerging as a most important source of video programming, passing 93 percent of U.S. television households and subscribed to by over 60 percent of such households.

(2) Because of its multichannel capacity, which is increasing rapidly through such developments as use of fiber-optic cable and compression techniques, cable television is in a unique position to make available educational and informational programming for children.

(3) While several cable programmers significantly and commendably do contribute in this respect, there is generally no one channel devoted entirely to the education of young children, particularly preschool children.

(4) Franchising authorities have the authority to require a channel devoted to educational purposes, but the number of such channels is estimated to be very low (i.e., less than 15 percent of cable systems have such channels).

(5) In view of the problems now confronting the educational system in many areas, it is a compelling national interest to foster the development of a "ready-to-learn" channel for preschool children, where parents, preschool teachers, and day-care directors could turn with confidence throughout the day.

(6) A reasonable portion of the franchise fee now imposed on cable systems, and passed on to cable subscribers, should be devoted to support this channel, so vitally needed in the community in which the cable system operates.

(7) Public television stations have a special opportunity and indeed duty to work with cable systems and local educational groups to aid in bringing this concept to successful fruition; if at all feasible, such stations could also use portions of the programming for wider dissemination to a child audience not linked to the cable television service.

Section 3. Establishment of a Ready-to-Learn Education Channel.

There is added to Section 621 the following subsections:

"(g) Within one year after the date of enactment of the 'Ready-to-Learn Cable Television Education Channel Act of 1995,' each franchising authority shall establish an education channel devoted to preschool children. In later evening hours, such channel may be used for informational material for parents to assist them in the education of their children.

(h) To provide funds for the channel, the franchising authority shall allocate 1.5 percent of the franchise fee imposed on the cable system. Half of the sum so obtained shall be used for local assistance, and the other half shall be transmitted to the Corporation for Public Broadcasting, to be used exclusively for the production and distribution to cable systems of programming specifically designed for this channel. To the extent feasible, portions of the programming so produced shall also be available for broadcast over public television stations or for distribution in other ways, so as to ensure that a significant amount is available to the child audience not linked to cable systems.

(i) The Commission shall adopt such regulations as may be necessary to ensure the timely implementation of this section, but shall in no way address the content or manner of distribution of such programming."

TITLE III—TELEVISION VIOLENCE AND CHILDREN

Section 1. Short Title.

This Act may be cited as the "Television Violence Reduction Through Parental Empowerment Act of 1995."

Section 2. Findings.

The Congress finds the following:

(1) To the fullest extent possible, parents should be empowered with the technology to choose to block the display on their televisions of programs they consider too violent for their children.

(2) Violence now touches the lives of American children more than adults. From 1982 through 1984, teenagers were the victims of 1,800,000 violent crimes, twice the annual rate of the adult population over age twenty. According to the American Academy of Pediatrics, one of every eight deaths among children ten to fourteen years old in 1990 was caused by a shooting. Among teenagers and young adults, that figure rose to one of every four deaths.

(3) Children watch an extensive amount of television. It is estimated

that a child watches approximately 15,000 hours of television before finishing high school, about 4,000 more hours than he or she has spent in the classroom.

(4) The amount of violence on television has reached epidemic levels. The American Psychological Association estimates that the average child witnesses 8,000 murders and 100,000 acts of violence before finishing elementary school.

(5) Three Surgeons General, the National Institute of Mental Health, the Centers for Disease Control, the American Medical Association, the American Academy of Pediatrics, and the American Psychological Association have concurred for nearly twenty years as to the deleterious effects of television violence on children.

(6) Despite periodic television industry efforts to reduce the amount of television violence, reductions in the level of televised violence have never been long-lasting.

(7) Parents who are working are unable to constantly monitor the television viewing habits of their children. Advanced television technologies such as channel compression and digitization will allow the expansion of channel capacity to levels even more unmanageable for parents who want to protect their children from televised violence.

(8) The major broadcast networks and a large number of cable channels have agreed to place parental advisories on programs they consider to be too violent for children.

(9) Congress calls upon the broadcast networks, independent television stations, cable programmers, and satellite programmers to promote the parental right to guide the television viewing habits of children by placing parental advisories on programs they consider to be too violent for children.

(10) Other sources have issued and can be expected in the future to issue advisories on such programs.

(11) These parental advisories are of limited use to parents if they are not watching television with their children. The technology now exists to equip television sets at a nominal cost to permit parents to block the display of television programs they consider too violent for children. However, this technology will only be effective if (A) the equipment is very user-friendly and (B) parents are informed as to its use, including the need therefor and the various sources of information concerning programs considered too violent for children, through such organizations as Parent-Teacher Associations.

Section 3. Equip Televisions to Block Programs

Section 303 of the Communications Act of 1934 (47 U.S.C. 303) is amended by adding to the end thereof the following:

"(v) Require that apparatus designed to receive television signals be equipped with circuitry designed, in the most user-friendly way possible, to enable viewers to block the display of channels, programs, and time slots. The requirements of this subsection shall apply when such apparatus is manufactured in the United States or imported for use in the United States, and its television picture screen is 13 inches or greater in size, measured diagonally."

Section 4. Shipping or Importing

(a) Regulations.—Section 330 of the Communications Act of 1934 (47 U.S.C. 330) is amended—

(1) by redesignating subsection (c) as subsection (d); and

(2) by adding after subsection (b) the following new section:

"(c) No person shall ship in interstate commerce, manufacture, assemble, or import from any foreign country into the United States any apparatus described in Section 303(v) of this Act except in accordance with rules prescribed by the Commission pursuant to the authority granted by that section. Such rules shall provide performance standards for such blocking technology. As new video technology is developed, the Commission shall take such action as the Commission determines appropriate to ensure that blocking service continues to be available to consumers. This subsection shall not apply to carriers transporting such apparatus without trading it."

(b) Conforming Amendment.—Section 330(d) of such Act, as redesignated by this Act, is amended by striking "Section 303(s) and section 303(u)" and inserting in lieu thereof "and sections 303(s), 303(u) and 303(v)."

Section 5. Effective Date.

The amendments made by Sections 3 and 4 of this Act shall take effect one year after enactment of this Act.

Section 6. Rules.

The Federal Communications Commission shall promulgate rules to implement the amendments made by this Act within 180 days after the date of its enactment.

Appendix 2 : The Wasteland Speeches, by Newton N. Minow

Address to the National Association of Broadcasters, May 9, 1961

Thank you for this opportunity to meet with you today. This is my first public address since I took over my new job. When the New Frontiersmen rode into town, I locked myself in my office to do my homework and get my feet wet. But apparently I haven't managed to stay out of hot water. I seem to have detected a certain nervous apprehension about what I might say or do when I emerged from that locked office for this, my maiden station break.

First, let me begin by dispelling a rumor. I was not picked for this job because I regard myself as the fastest draw on the New Frontier.

Second, let me start a rumor. Like you, I have carefully read President Kennedy's messages about the regulatory agencies, conflict of interest, and the dangers of *ex parte* contracts. And, of course, we at the Federal Communications Commission will do our part. Indeed, I may even suggest that we change the name of the FCC to the Seven Untouchables!

It may also come as a surprise to some of you, but I want you to know that you have my admiration and respect. Yours is a most honorable profession. Anyone who is in the broadcasting business has a tough row to hoe. You earn your bread by using public property. When you work in broadcasting, you volunteer for public service, public pressure, and public regulation. You must compete with other attractions and other investments, and the only way you can do it is to prove to us every three years that you should have been in business in the first place.

I can think of easier ways to make a living.

But I cannot think of more satisfying ways.

I admire your courage—but that doesn't mean I would make life any easier for you. Your license lets you use the public's airwaves as trustees for 180 million Americans. The public is your beneficiary. If you want to stay on as trustees, you must deliver a decent return to the public—not only to your stockholders. So, as a representative of the public, your health and your product are among my chief concerns.

As to your health: let's talk only of television today. In 1960 gross broadcast revenues of the television industry were over $1,268,000,000; profit before taxes was $243,900,000—an average return on revenue of 19.2 percent. Compare this with 1959, when gross broadcast revenues were $1,163,900,000 and profit before taxes was $222,300,000, an average return on revenue of 19.1 percent. So, the percentage increase of total revenues from 1959 to 1960 was 9 percent, and the percentage increase of profit was 9.7 percent. This, despite a recession. For your investors, the price has indeed been right.

I have confidence in your health.

But not in your product.

It is with this and much more in mind that I come before you today.

One editorialist in the trade press wrote that "the FCC of the New Frontier is going to be one of the toughest FCCs in the history of broadcast regulation." If he meant that we intend to enforce the law in the public interest, let me make it perfectly clear that he is right—we do.

If he meant that we intend to muzzle or censor broadcasting, he is dead wrong.

It would not surprise me if some of you had expected me to come here today and say in effect, "Clean up your own house or the government will do it for you."

Well, in a limited sense, you would be right—I've just said it.

But I want to say to you earnestly that it is not in that spirit that I come before you today, nor is it in that spirit that I intend to serve the FCC.

I am in Washington to help broadcasting, not to harm it; to strengthen it, not to weaken it; to reward it, not punish it; to encourage it, not threaten it; to stimulate it, not censor it.

Above all, I am here to uphold and protect the public interest.

What do we mean by "the public interest"? Some say the public interest is merely what interests the public.

I disagree.

So does your distinguished president, Governor Collins. In a recent speech he said, "Broadcasting, to serve the public interest, must have a soul and a conscience, a burning desire to excel, as well as to sell; the urge to build the character, citizenship, and intellectual stature of people, as well as to expand the gross national product . . . By no means do I imply that broadcasters disregard the public interest . . . But a much better job can be done, and should be done."

I could not agree more.

And I would add that in today's world, with chaos in Laos and the Congo aflame, with Communist tyranny on our Caribbean doorstep and relentless pressure on our Atlantic alliance, with social and economic problems at home of the gravest nature, yes, and with technological knowledge that makes it possible, as our president has said, not only to destroy our world but to destroy poverty around the world— in a time of peril and opportunity, the old complacent, unbalanced fare of action-adventure and situation comedies is simply not good enough.

Your industry possesses the most powerful voice in America. It has an inescapable duty to make that voice ring with intelligence and with leadership. In a few years this exciting industry has grown from a novelty to an instrument of overwhelming impact on the American people. It should be making ready for the kind of leadership that newspapers and magazines assumed years ago, to make our people aware of their world.

Ours has been called the jet age, the atomic age, the space age. It is also, I submit, the television age. And just as history will decide whether the leaders of today's world employed the atom to destroy the world or rebuild it for mankind's benefit, so will history decide whether today's broadcasters employed their powerful voice to enrich the people or debase them.

If I seem today to address myself chiefly to the problems of television, I don't want any of you radio broadcasters to think we've gone to sleep at your switch—we haven't. We still listen. But in recent years most of the controversies and crosscurrents in broadcast programming have swirled around television. And so my subject today is the television industry and the public interest.

Like everybody, I wear more than one hat. I am the chairman of the FCC. I am also a television viewer and the husband and father of other television viewers. I have seen a great many television programs that seemed to me eminently worthwhile, and I am not talking about the much-bemoaned good old days of *Playhouse 90* and *Studio One*.

I am talking about this past season. Some were wonderfully entertaining, such as *The Fabulous Fifties*, the *Fred Astaire Show*, and the *Bing Crosby Special*; some were dramatic and moving, such as Conrad's *Victory* and *Twilight Zone*; some were marvelously informative, such as *The Nation's Future*, *CBS Reports*, and *The Valiant Years*. I could list many more—programs that I am sure everyone here felt enriched his own life and that of his family. When television is good, nothing —not the theater, not the magazines or newspapers—nothing is better.

But when television is bad, nothing is worse. I invite you to sit down in front of your television set when your station goes on the air and stay there without a book, magazine, newspaper, profit-and-loss sheet or rating book to distract you—and keep your eyes glued to that set until the station signs off. I can assure you that you will observe a vast wasteland.

You will see a procession of game shows, violence, audience participation shows, formula comedies about totally unbelievable families, blood and thunder, mayhem, violence, sadism, murder, western badmen, western good men, private eyes, gangsters, more violence and cartoons. And, endlessly, commercials—many screaming, cajoling, and offending. And most of all, boredom. True, you will see a few things you will enjoy. But they will be very, very few. And if you think I exaggerate, try it.

Is there one person in this room who claims that broadcasting can't do better?

Well, a glance at next season's proposed programming can give us little heart. Of seventy-three and a half hours of prime evening time, the networks have tentatively scheduled fifty-nine hours to categories of "action-adventure," situation comedy, variety, quiz, and movies.

Is there one network president in this room who claims he can't do better?

Well, is there at least one network president who believes that the other networks can't do better?

Gentlemen, your trust accounting with your beneficiaries is overdue. Never have so few owed so much to so many.

Why is so much of television so bad? I have heard many answers: demands of your advertisers; competition for ever higher ratings; the need always to attract a mass audience; the high cost of television programs; the insatiable appetite for programming material—these are some of them. Unquestionably these are tough problems not susceptible to easy answers.

But I am not convinced that you have tried hard enough to solve them.

I do not accept the idea that the present overall programming is aimed accurately at the public taste. The ratings tell us only that some people have their television sets turned on, and of that number, so many are tuned to one channel and so many to another. They don't tell us what the public might watch if they were offered half a dozen additional choices. A rating, at best, is an indication of how many people saw what you gave them. Unfortunately, it does not reveal the depth of the penetration, or the intensity of reaction, and it never reveals what the acceptance would have been if what you gave them had been better—if all the forces of art and creativity and daring and imagination had been unleashed. I believe in the people's good sense and good taste, and I am not convinced that the people's taste is as low as some of you assume.

My concern with the rating services is not with their accuracy. Perhaps they are accurate. I really don't know. What, then, is wrong with the ratings? It's not been their accuracy—it's been their use.

Certainly I hope you will agree that ratings should have little influence where children are concerned. The best estimates indicate that during the hours of 5 p.m. to 6 p.m., 60 percent of your audience is composed of children under twelve. And most young children today, believe it or not, spend as much time watching television as they do in the schoolroom. I repeat—let that sink in—most young children today spend as much time watching television as they do in the schoolroom. It used to be said that there were three great influences on a child: home, school, and church. Today there is a fourth great influence, and you ladies and gentlemen control it.

If parents, teachers, and ministers conducted their responsibilities by following the ratings, children would have a steady diet of ice cream, school holidays, and no Sunday school. What about your responsibilities? Is there no room on television to teach, to inform, to uplift, to stretch, to enlarge the capacities of our children? Is there no room for programs deepening their understanding of children in other lands? Is there no room for a children's news show explaining something about the world to them at their level of understanding? Is there no room for reading the great literature of the past, teaching them the great traditions of freedom? There are some fine children's shows, but they are drowned out in the massive doses of cartoons, violence, and more violence. Must these be your trademarks? Search your consciences and see if you cannot offer more to your young beneficiaries, whose future you guide so many hours each and every day.

What about adult programming and ratings? You know, newspaper publishers take popularity ratings, too. The answers are pretty clear; it is almost always the comics, followed by the advice-to-the-lovelorn columns. But, ladies and gentlemen, the news is still on the front page of all newspapers, the editorials are not replaced by more comics, the newspapers have not become one long collection of advice to the lovelorn. Yet newspapers do not need a license from the government to be in business—they do not use public property. But in television—where your responsibilities as public trustees are so plain—the moment that the ratings indicate that westerns are popular, there are new imitations of westerns on the air faster than the old coaxial cable could take us from Hollywood to New York. Broadcasting cannot continue to live by the numbers. Ratings ought to be the slave of the broadcaster, not his master. And you and I both know that the rating services themselves would agree.

Let me make clear that what I am talking about is balance. I believe that the public interest is made up of many interests. There are many people in this great country, and you must serve all of us. You will get no argument from me if you say that, given a choice between a western and a symphony, more people will watch the western. I like westerns and private eyes too—but a steady diet for the whole country is obviously not in the public interest. We all know that people would more often prefer to be entertained than stimulated or informed. But your obligations are not satisfied if you look only to popularity as a test of what to broadcast. You are not only in show business; you are free to communicate ideas as well as relaxation. You must provide a wider range of choices, more diversity, more alternatives. It is not enough to cater to the nation's whims—you must also serve the nation's needs.

And I would add this—that if some of you persist in a relentless search for the highest rating and the lowest common denominator, you may very well lose your audience. Because, to paraphrase a great American who was recently my law partner, the people are wise, wiser than some of the broadcasters—and politicians—think.

As you may have gathered, I would like to see television improved. But how is this to be brought about? By voluntary action by the broadcasters themselves? By direct government intervention? Or how?

Let me address myself now to my role, not as a viewer, but as chairman of the FCC. I could not if I would chart for you this afternoon in detail all of the actions I contemplate. Instead, I want to make clear some of the fundamental principles which guide me.

First: the people own the air. They own it as much in prime evening time as they do at 6 o'clock Sunday morning. For every hour that the people give you, you owe them something. I intend to see that your debt is paid with service.

Second: I think it would be foolish and wasteful for us to continue any worn-out wrangle over the problems of payola, rigged quiz shows, and other mistakes of the past. There are laws on the books which we will enforce. But there is no chip on my shoulder. We live together in perilous, uncertain times; we face together staggering problems; and we must not waste much time now by rehashing the clichés of past controversy. To quarrel over the past is to lose the future.

Third: I believe in the free enterprise system. I want to see broadcasting improved and I want you to do the job. I am proud to champion your cause. It is not rare for American businessmen to serve a public trust. Yours is a special trust because it is imposed by law.

Fourth: I will do all I can to help educational television. There are still not enough educational stations, and major centers of the country still lack usable educational channels. If there were a limited number of printing presses in this country, you may be sure that a fair proportion of them would be put to educational use. Educational television has an enormous contribution to make to the future, and I intend to give it a hand along the way. If there is not a nationwide educational television system in this country, it will not be the fault of the FCC.

Fifth: I am unalterably opposed to governmental censorship. There will no suppression of programming which does not meet with bureaucratic tastes. Censorship strikes at the taproot of our free society.

Sixth: I did not come to Washington to idly observe the squandering of the public's airwaves. The squandering of our airwaves is no less important than the lavish waste of any precious natural resource. I intend to take the job of chairman of the FCC very seriously. I believe in the gravity of my own particular sector of the New Frontier. There will be times perhaps when you will consider that I take myself or my job *too* seriously. Frankly, I don't care if you do. For I am convinced that either one takes this job seriously—or one can be seriously taken.

Now, how will these principles be applied? Clearly, at the heart of the FCC's authority lies its power to license, to renew or fail to renew, or to revoke a license. As you know, when your license comes up for renewal, your performance is compared with your promises. I understand that many people feel that in the past licenses were often renewed *pro forma*. I say to you now: Renewal will not be *pro forma* in the future. There is nothing permanent or sacred about a broadcast license.

But simply matching promises and performance is not enough. I intend to do more. I intend to find out whether the people care. I intend to find out whether the community which each broadcaster serves believes he has been serving the public interest. When a renewal is set down for hearing, I intend—wherever possible—to hold a well-advertised public hearing, right in the community you have promised to serve. I want the people who own the air and the homes that television enters to tell you and the FCC what's been going on. I want the people—if they are truly interested in the service you give them—to make notes, document cases, tell us the facts. For those few of you who really believe that the public interest is merely what interests the public—I hope that these hearings will arouse no little interest.

The FCC has a fine reserve of monitors—almost 180 million Americans gathered around 56 million sets. If you want those monitors to be your friends at court—it's up to you.

Some of you may say, "Yes, but I still do not know where the line is between a grant of a renewal and the hearing you just spoke of." My answer is: Why should you want to know how close you can come to the edge of the cliff? What the commission asks of you is to make a conscientious good-faith effort to serve the public interest. Every one of you serves a community in which the people would benefit by educational, religious, instructive, or other public-service programming. Every one of you serves an area which has local needs—as to local elections, controversial issues, local news, local talent. Make a serious, genuine effort to put on that programming. When you do, you will not be playing brinkmanship with the public interest.

What I've been saying applies to broadcast stations. Now a station break for the networks:

You know your importance in this great industry. Today, more than one-half of all hours of television-station programming comes from the networks; in prime time, this rises to more than three-fourths of the available hours.

You know that the FCC has been studying network operations for some time. I intend to press this to a speedy conclusion with useful results. I can tell you right now, however, that I am deeply concerned with concentration of power in the hands of the networks. As a result, too many local stations have forgone any efforts at local programming, with little use of live talent and local service. Too many local stations operate with one hand on the network switch and the other on a projector loaded with old movies. We want the individual stations to be free to meet their legal responsibilities to serve their communities.

I join Governor Collins in his views so well expressed to the advertisers who use the public air. I urge the networks to join him and undertake a very special mission on behalf of this industry: You can tell your advertisers, "This is the high quality we are going to serve—take it or other people will. If you think you can find a better place to move automobiles, cigarettes, and soap—go ahead and try."

Tell your sponsors to be less concerned with costs per thousand and more concerned with understanding per millions. And remind your stockholders that an investment in broadcasting is buying a share in public responsibility.

The networks can start this industry on the road to freedom from the dictatorship of numbers.

But there is more to the problem than network influences on stations or advertiser influences on networks. I know the problems networks face in trying to clear some of their best programs—the informational programs that exemplify public service. They are your finest hours, whether sustaining or commercial, whether regularly scheduled or special; these are the signs that broadcasting knows the way to leadership. They make the public's trust in you a wise choice.

They should be seen. As you know, we are readying for use new forms by which broadcast stations will report their programming to the commission. You probably also know that special attention will be paid in these reports to public-service programming. I believe that stations taking network service should also be required to report the extent of the local clearance of network public-service programming, and when they fail to clear them, they should explain why. If it is to put on some outstanding local program, this is one reason. But if it is simply to carry some old movie, that is an entirely different matter. The commission should consider such clearance reports carefully when making up its mind about the licensee's overall programming.

We intend to move—and as you know, indeed the FCC was rapidly moving in other new areas before the new administration arrived in Washington. And I want to pay my public respects to my very able predecessor, Fred Ford, and my colleagues on the commission who have welcomed me to the FCC with warmth and cooperation.

We have approved an experiment with pay TV, and in New York we are testing the potential of UHF broadcasting. Either or both of these may revolutionize television. Only a foolish prophet would venture to guess the direction they will take, and their effect. But we intend that they shall be explored fully—for they are part of broadcasting's new frontier.

The questions surrounding pay TV are largely economic. The questions surrounding UHF are largely technological. We are going to give the infant pay TV a chance to prove whether it can offer a useful service; we are going to protect it from those who would strangle it in its crib.

As for UHF, I'm sure you know about our test in the canyons of New York City. We will take every possible positive step to break through the allocations barrier into UHF. We will put this sleeping giant to use, and in the years ahead we may have twice as many channels operating in cities where now there are only two or three. We may have a half dozen networks instead of three.

I have told you that I believe in the free enterprise system. I believe that most of television's problems stem from lack of competition. This is the importance of UHF to me: with more channels on the air, we will be able to provide every community with enough stations to offer service to all parts of the public. Programs with a mass-market appeal required by mass-product advertisers certainly will still be available. But other stations will recognize the need to appeal to more limited markets and to special tastes. In this way we can all have a much wider range of programs.

Television should thrive on this competition—and the country should benefit from alternative sources of service to the public. And, Governor Collins, I hope the NAB will benefit from many new members.

Another, and perhaps the most important, frontier: Television will rapidly join the parade into space. International television will be with us soon. No one knows how long it will be until a broadcast from a studio in New York will be viewed in India as well as in Indiana, will be seen in the Congo as it is seen in Chicago. But as surely as we are meeting here today, that day will come—and once again our world will shrink.

What will the people of other countries think of us when they see our western badmen and good men punching each other in the jaw in between the shooting? What will the Latin-American or African child learn of America from our great communications industry? We cannot permit television in its present form to be our voice overseas.

There is your challenge to leadership. You must reexamine some fundamentals of your industry. You must open your minds and open your hearts to the limitless horizons of tomorrow.

I can suggest some words that should serve to guide you:

> Television and all who participate in it are jointly accountable to the American public for respect for the special needs of children, for community responsibility, for the advancement of education and culture, for the acceptability of the program materials chosen, for decency and decorum in production, and for propriety in advertising. This responsibility cannot be discharged by any given group of programs, but can be discharged only through the highest standards of respect for the American home, applied to every moment of every program presented by television.
>
> Program materials should enlarge the horizons of the viewer, provide him with wholesome entertainment, afford helpful stimulation, and remind him of the responsibilities which the citizen has toward his society.

These words are not mine. They are yours. They are taken literally from your own Television Code. They reflect the leadership and aspirations of your own great industry. I urge you to respect them as I do. And I urge you to respect the intelligent and farsighted leadership of Governor LeRoy Collins and to make this meeting a creative act. I urge you at this meeting and, after you leave, back home, at your stations and your networks, to strive ceaselessly to improve your product and to better serve your viewers, the American people.

I hope that we at the FCC will not allow ourselves to become so bogged down in the mountain of papers, hearings, memoranda, orders, and the daily routine that we close our eyes to the wider view of the public interest. And I hope that you broadcasters will not permit yourselves to become so absorbed in the chase for ratings, sales, and profits that you lose this wider view. Now more than ever before in broadcasting's history the times demand the best of all of us.

We need imagination in programming, not sterility; creativity, not imitation; experimentation, not conformity; excellence, not mediocrity. Television is filled with creative, imaginative people. You must strive to set them free.

Television in its young life has had many hours of greatness—its *Victory at Sea*, its Army-McCarthy hearings, its *Peter Pan*, its *Kraft Television Theatre*, its *See It Now*, its *Project 20*, the World Series, its political conventions and campaigns, the Great Debates—and it has had its endless hours of mediocrity and its moments of public disgrace. There are estimates that today the average viewer spends about 200 minutes daily with television, while the average reader spends thirty-eight minutes with magazines and forty minutes with newspapers. Television has grown faster than a teenager, and now it is time to grow up.

What you gentlemen broadcast through the people's air affects the people's taste, their knowledge, their opinions, their understanding of themselves and of their world. And their future.

The power of instantaneous sight and sound is without precedent in mankind's history. This is an awesome power. It has limitless capabilities for good—and for evil. And it carries with it awesome responsibilities—responsibilities which you and I cannot escape.

In his stirring inaugural address, our president said, "And so, my fellow Americans: ask not what your country can do for you—ask what you can do for your country."

Ladies and Gentlemen, ask not what broadcasting can do for you —ask what you can do for broadcasting.

I urge you to put the people's airwaves to the service of the people and the cause of freedom. You must help prepare a generation for great decisions. You must help a great nation fulfill its future.

Do this, and I pledge you our help.

HOW VAST THE WASTELAND NOW?

Address at the Freedom Forum Media Studies Center, Columbia University, May 9, 1991

After finishing that speech to the National Association of Broadcasters (NAB) thirty years ago today, I remained near the podium talking with LeRoy Collins, a former governor of Florida who was serving as NAB president.* A man from the audience approached us and said to me, "I didn't particularly like your speech." A few moments later the same man returned with, "The more I thought about it, your speech was really awful." A few minutes later he was back a third time to say, "Mr. Minow, that was the worst speech I ever heard in my whole life!"

Governor Collins gently put his arm around me and said, "Don't let him upset you, Newt. That man has no mind of his own. He just repeats everything he hears."

Thirty years later I still hear about that speech. My daughters threaten to engrave on my tombstone "On to a Vaster Wasteland."

My old law partner, Adlai E. Stevenson, loved to tell a favorite story about the relationship between a fan and a fan dancer: There is really no intent to cover the subject—only to call attention to it. Like a fan dancer, it is not my intent today to cover every part of that speech, but rather to use its anniversary to examine, with thirty years' perspective, what television has been doing to our society and what television can do for our society.

Thirty years cannot be covered fully in thirty minutes, but let us begin by reminding ourselves of the times, circumstances, and optimistic spirit of the Kennedy administration in the early 1960s. What was broadcasting like at that stage of development?

President Kennedy started off with a dream of a New Frontier, but made a major blunder on April 17, 1961, at the Bay of Pigs. A few weeks later, on May 5, there was a great triumph: the successful launch of the first American to fly in space, Commander Alan Shepard. Commander Shepard returned from his flight to meet President Kennedy and Congress on May 8. On the same day, President Kennedy was to speak to the National Association of Broadcasters and invited me to

* Governor Collins died in 1991—after an exceptionally distinguished career of public service of the highest quality.

accompany him when he gave his speech. I was to meet him outside the Oval Office in the morning and to ride with him to the Sheraton Park Hotel.

As I waited there, President Kennedy emerged and said, "Newt, how about taking the Shepards with us to the broadcasters?" Of course, I said, and the president went back into his office to make the arrangements. He returned to say, "It's all set. Now come with me, I want to change my shirt. And what do you think I should say to the broadcasters?"

Although I had known Jack Kennedy before he was president, it was the first time that I was in the bedroom of the president of the United States watching him change shirts and being asked to advise him on what to say. Nervously, I mumbled something about the difference between the way we handled our space launches compared to the Soviets: that we invited radio and television to cover the events live, not knowing whether success or failure would follow. On the other hand, the Soviets operated behind locked doors. President Kennedy nodded, took no notes, and led me back to his office, where Commander and Mrs. Shepard and Vice President Lyndon Johnson were waiting. We went out to the cars. The vice president and I ended up on the two jump seats in the presidential limousine, with the president and the Shepards in the back seat in an ebullient mood as we rode through Rock Creek Park. After we arrived, President Kennedy gave a graceful, witty, thoughtful talk about the value of an open, free society, exemplified by the live radio and television coverage of Commander Shepard's flight. The broadcasters responded with a standing ovation.

The next day I returned to that same platform for my first speech as chairman of the Federal Communications Commission. Many people think I should have asked President Kennedy to watch me change my shirt and give me advice on my speech because, as you know, the audience did not like what I had to say.

That night, at home, there were two phone calls. The first was from President Kennedy's father, Joseph Kennedy. When I heard who was calling I anticipated sharp criticism; instead Ambassador Kennedy said, "Newt, I just finished talking to Jack and I told him your speech was the best one since his inaugural address on January 20. Keep it up; if anyone gives you any trouble, call me!" The second call was from Edward R. Murrow, then director of the U.S. Information Agency. He said, "You gave the same speech I gave two years ago. Good for you —you'll get a lot of heat and criticism, but don't lose your courage!"

Those two calls gave me the backbone I needed.

What was the situation at the time? In the late 1950s, scandals damaged both the FCC and the television industry. President Eisenhower had to replace an FCC chairman who had accepted lavish entertainment by industry licensees. Broadcasters had to explain quiz-show and payola scandals in congressional hearings. Television was still new—in its first generation of programming. The word "television" did not yet appear in the Federal Communications Act.

While at the FCC, we followed two fundamental policies: (1) to require that broadcasters serve the public interest as well as their private interest; and (2) to increase choice for the American home viewer. In the long run, we believed that competition was preferable to governmental regulation, especially where a medium of expression was involved. So we worked to open markets to new technologies, to help build a noncommercial television alternative, and to provide educational opportunities through television. Satellites, UHF, cable—we encouraged them all.

Today that 1961 speech is remembered for two words—but not the two I intended to be remembered. The words we tried to advance were *public interest*. To me, the public interest meant, and still means, that we should constantly ask: What can television do for our country?—for the common good?—for the American people?

Alexis de Tocqueville observed in 1835: "No sooner do you set foot on American soil than you find yourself in a sort of tumult . . . All around you everything is on the move." What would Tocqueville have said about the explosive expansion of telecommunications—particularly the electronic media—during the thirty years between 1961 and 1991?

In 1961 there were 47.2 million television sets in American homes; by 1990 that number had more than tripled, to 172 million. Fewer than 5 percent of the television sets in 1961 were color; in 1990, 98 percent of American homes receive television in color. Cable television, which started by bringing television to people who could not receive signals over the air, now brings even more television to people who already receive it. In 1961, cable television served just over a million homes; now it reaches more than 55 million. Between 1961 and 1991, the number of commercial television stations in America doubled, from 543 to 1,102. Noncommercial—now called public—television stations quintupled, from 62 to 350.

Americans spend more time than ever watching television. Since 1961 the U.S. population has risen from 150 million to 245 million, and the amount of time Americans spend watching television has skyrocketed from 2.175 hours a day to a staggering 7.3 hours per day. In 1961, television viewers spent more than 90 percent of their viewing time watching the three commercial networks; today that figure is around 62 percent.

While the U.S. government slipped from a $3 billion surplus in 1960 to a deficit of more than $161 billion today, total advertising revenues for the television industry rose twentyfold in the same period, from $1.2 billion to $24 billion. In 1961 cable advertising revenues were zero; in 1988 cable advertising revenues were $1.16 billion. And cable subscribers, who paid an average of $4 per month in 1961, today pay around $25 for cable service. Cable subscriptions accounted for revenues of $51 million in 1961; now they amount to almost $20 billion.

Video revenue in the movie industry, which was zero thirty years ago, is now $2.9 billion—more than $700 million larger than current movie theater receipts. VCRs—unavailable commercially in 1961—are now in more than 58 million American homes.

Children today grow up with a remote-control clicker, cable, and a VCR. Former NBC president Bob Mulholland says that these children don't remember the days when television signals came to the home through the air to an antenna on the roof as God and General Sarnoff intended. My own children used to say, "Is it time for *The Mickey Mouse Club* yet?" My grandchildren say, "Can I watch the tape of *Peter Pan* again?"

Today, new program services like CNN, C-SPAN, HBO, Showtime, Disney, Nickelodeon, Discovery, Lifetime, Arts and Entertainment, ESPN, USA, TNT, Black Entertainment TV, Bravo, Cinemax, TBS, Home Shopping, Weather Channel, Univision, CNBC, Galavision, Nashville, MTV, FNN, American Movie Channel—and even more—enter the home by wire for those who can pay the monthly cable bill. Choice has skyrocketed. The VCR means you can watch a program when you want to see it, not just when the broadcaster puts it on the schedule. If you are a sports fan, a news junkie, a stock-market follower, a rock-music devotee, a person who speaks Spanish, a nostalgic old-movie buff, a congressional-hearing observer, a weather watcher—you now have your own choice. The FCC objective in the early 1960s to expand choice has been fulfilled—beyond all expectations.

Yet, to many of us, this enlarged choice is not enough to satisfy the public interest. There are several reasons. Although some viewers have gone from a vast emptiness to a vast fullness, others have been excluded. Choice through cable comes at a price not all can afford, and cable is still not available to the entire nation. (Where I live in Chicago, we did not receive cable service until last year, and of course many parts of New York City and Washington, D.C., do not have cable either.) And as CBS president Howard Stringer said last year, "We see a vast media-jaded audience that wanders restlessly from one channel to another in search of that endangered species—originality . . . more choices may not necessarily mean better choices."

One evening as I watched, with my remote control in hand, I flipped through the channels and saw a man loading his gun on one channel, a different man aiming a gun on a second, and another man shooting a gun on a third. And if you don't believe me, try it yourself. Remember Groucho Marx's advice: "Do you believe me or your own eyes?" I think the most troubling change over the past thirty years is the rise in the quantity and quality of violence on television. In 1961 I worried that my children would not benefit much from television, but in 1991 I worry that my grandchildren will actually be harmed by it. One recent study shows that by the time a child is eighteen he has seen 25,000 murders on television. In 1961 they didn't make PG-13 movies, much less NC-17. Now a six-year-old can watch them on cable.

Can this be changed where television is concerned? My own answer is yes. If we want to, we can provide the American people with a full choice, even if the marketplace does not meet the demands of the public interest. I reject the view of an FCC chairman in the early 1980s who said that "a television set is merely a toaster with pictures." I reject this ideological view that the marketplace will regulate itself and that the television marketplace will give us perfection. The absolute free-market approach to public good has been gospel in our country in the case of the savings-and-loan industry, the airline industry, the junk-bond financing industry, and in many other spheres of commerce and common interest. If television is to change, the men and women in television will have to make it a leading institution in American life rather than merely a reactive mirror of the lowest common denominator in the marketplace. Based on the last thirty years, the record gives the television marketplace an A+ for technology, but only a C for using that technology to serve human and humane goals.

Bill Baker, president of Thirteen/WNET here in New York (and like me a veteran of both commercial and public television), said it all in two short sentences: "To aim only at the bottom line is to aim too low. Our country deserves better." Felix Rohatyn, a star of the marketplace, was on target when he said, "Though I believe the marketplace knows best most of the time, I am skeptical that it should always be the ultimate arbiter of economic action, and I am more than willing to interfere with it when it becomes a distorting rather than a benign influence."

In the last thirty years, the television marketplace has become a severely distorting influence in at least four important public areas. We have failed (1) to use television for education; (2) to use television for children; (3) to finance public television properly; and (4) to use television properly in political campaigns.

First, education. Suppose you were asked this multiple-choice question: Which of the following is the most important educational institution in America? (a) Harvard, (b) Yale, (c) Columbia, (d) the University of California, (e) none of the above. The correct answer is e. The most important educational institution in America is television. More people learn more each day, each year, each lifetime from television than from any other source. All of television is education; the question is, what are we teaching and what are we learning? Sometimes, as in the case of the splendid Annenberg/CPB-sponsored educational course on the Constitution (created here at Columbia by Professor Fred Friendly), we see what television can do to stretch the mind and the spirit. In Ken Burns's brilliant programs about the Civil War, millions of Americans learned more about that terrible period in American history than they ever learned in school. We are slowly doing better each year in using television for education, but too much of the time we waste television's potential to teach—and viewers' to learn.

Second, television for children. Bob Keeshan, our Captain Kangaroo for life, has seen how television for children all over the world is designed to be part of the nurturing and educational system. But "in America," he says, "television is not a tool for nurturing. It is a tool for selling." True, there are glorious exceptions like Joan Cooney's work, starting with *Sesame Street*. But far too often television fails our children. And it fails them for more hours each day than they spend with a teacher in a classroom.

Competition, it is said, brings out the best in products and the worst in people. In children's television, competition seems to bring out the worst in programs and the worst in children. Children lack purchasing power and voting power, and the television marketplace and the political process have failed them. Cooperation instead of competition—

among broadcasters and cable operators—could do wonders for children. Congress last year and the FCC this year have finally started to address these issues, and the attention is long overdue. If they would give the same time and attention to policies for children's television as they give to industry fights about the financial interest and syndication rules, our children would begin to receive the priority concern they deserve.

Third, public television should become just as much a public commitment as our public libraries, hospitals, parks, schools, and universities. Yet it is a stepchild, struggling to provide outstanding public service while remaining in the role of a perpetual beggar in the richest country in the world. We have failed to fund a strong independent alternative to commercial television and thus failed, in Larry Grossman's words, to "travel the high road of education, information, culture and the arts."

There are many ways to establish a sound economic base for public broadcasting. For example, Congress could create a spectrum-use or franchise fee for all commercial broadcast and cable operators to fund public broadcasting on a permanent basis. If this were set in the range of a 2 percent annual fee on broadcasting and cable's $50 billion total annual revenues, it would produce about $1 billion a year. Even at that figure, we'd still be behind Japan. If we added $5 as a tax on the sale of new television sets and VCRs and earmarked the funds to match private contributions to public broadcasting, we could catch up to Japan—which now spends twenty times as much per person for public broadcasting as we do!

Finally, the use of television in political campaigns. Studies of the 1988 campaign show that the average block of uninterrupted speech by a presidential candidate on network newscasts was 9.8 seconds; in 1968 it was 42.3 seconds. As Walter Cronkite observed, this means that "issues can be avoided rather than confronted." And David Halberstam adds, "Once the politicians begin to talk in such brief bites . . . they begin to think in them."

A United States senator must now raise $12,000 to $16,000 every week to pay for a political campaign, mostly to buy time for television commercials. A recent United Nations study revealed that only two countries, Norway and Sri Lanka (in addition to the United States), do not provide free airtime to their political parties. If we are to preserve the democratic process without corrupting, unhealthy influences, we must find a bipartisan way to provide free time for our candidates and stop them from getting deeply in hock to special interests in order to pay for television commercials.

More than twenty years ago, I served on a bipartisan commission for the Twentieth Century Fund which recommended the concept of "voters' time" for presidential candidates. Voters' time would be television time purchased with public funds at half the commercial-time rates and given to candidates. In exchange, we would prohibit by law the purchase of time by the candidates. And while we're at it, we should institutionalize the presidential debates—make them real debates by eliminating the panels of journalists. And we should clean up our political campaigns—once and for all.

In these four areas, the television marketplace has not fulfilled our needs and will not do so in the next thirty years. These four needs can be met only if we—as a nation—make the decision that to aim only at the bottom line is to aim too low. If we still believe in the concept of the public interest, we can use television to educate, we can stop shortchanging our children, we can fund public broadcasting properly, and we can provide free television time for our political candidates. My generation began these tasks, and the time has now come to pass the responsibility on to the next generation—the first generation to grow up with television.

What will happen in television in the next thirty years—from now until 2021? As Woody Allen says, "More than any other time in history, mankind faces a crossroads. One path leads to despair and hopelessness. The other to total extinction. Let us pray we have the wisdom to choose correctly."

In the next thirty years, four main forces—globalization, optical fiber, computers, and satellite technology—will illuminate the crossroads.

Today's able FCC chairman, Al Sikes, is wisely trying to keep public policy in pace with rapidly changing technologies. As Al observes, "Today we can see the new world ... In it, tomorrow's communications networks will be dramatically improved. Copper and coaxial cables are giving way to glass fibers, and wavelengths are being replaced by digits ..."

Well before 2021, I believe, there will be convergence of the technologies now used in telephones, computers, publishing, satellites, cable, movie studios, and television networks. Already we see tests of optical fiber demonstrating the future. In Montreal tonight, a home viewer watching the hockey game on television can use his remote control to order his own instant replay, order different camera angles—and become his own studio director. In Cerritos, California, a viewer today can participate in an experiment to summon any recorded show at any time, day or night; and he can stop it, rewind it, or fast-forward it.

Here in New York City, Time Warner is building a two-way, interactive cable system with 150 channels. People will be able to order any movie or record album ever produced and see and hear it when they themselves want to see and hear it. We see 400- and 500-channel systems on the horizon, fragmenting viewership into smaller and smaller niches, and we need to remember that for all their presumed benefits these developments undermine the simultaneous, shared national experiences that comprise the nation's social glue.

At the Annenberg Washington Program of Northwestern University, we are developing a blueprint for the future of optical fiber. As this new technological world unfolds, the risk remains that we will create information overload without information substance or analysis, of more media with fewer messages, of tiny sound bites without large thoughts, of concentrating on pictures of dead bodies instead of thinking human beings. Henry Thoreau warned us more than 125 years ago: "We are in great haste to construct a magnetic telegraph from Maine to Texas; but Maine and Texas, it may be, have nothing important to communicate."

When we launched the first communications satellite in 1962, we knew it was important—but we had little understanding of its future use. I did tell President Kennedy that the communications satellite was more important than launching a man into space, because the satellite launched an idea, and ideas last longer than human beings. The last thirty years have taught us that satellites have no respect for political boundaries. Satellites cannot be stopped by Berlin Walls, by tanks in Tiananmen Square, or by dictators in Baghdad. In Manila, Warsaw, and Bucharest, we saw the television station become today's electronic Bastille.

Thirty years is but a nanosecond in history. If President Kennedy were alive today, he would celebrate his seventy-fourth birthday later this month. He would be seven years older than President Bush. He would be astonished by the technological changes of the past thirty years, but he would be confident that the next thirty years will be even more advanced.

Before he was elected president, Kennedy once compared broadcasters and politicians in these words, "Will Gresham's law operate in the broadcasting and political worlds, wherein the bad inevitably drives out the good? Will the politician's desire for reelection—and the broadcaster's desire for ratings—cause both to flatter every public whim and prejudice, to seek the lowest common denominator of appeal, to put public opinion at all times ahead of the public interest? For myself, I reject that view of politics, and I urge you to reject that view of broadcasting."

I went to the FCC because I agreed then and agree now with President Kennedy's philosophy of broadcasting. As I think back about him, and also think of our future, I propose today to the television and cable industries: Join together to produce a unique program to be on all channels that will have enduring importance to history. Seldom in history have we had five living American presidents at the same time: Right now, Presidents Reagan, Carter, Ford, and Nixon are with us, in addition to President Bush. You can bring all of them to the Oval Office in the White House to discuss their dreams of America in the twenty-first century, and you can give every American the opportunity to see and hear this program and to share a vision of our future.

The 1960s started with high hopes, confronted tragedy, and ended in disillusion. Tragically, our leaders—President John F. Kennedy, Reverend Martin Luther King, Jr., and Pope John XXIII—left too soon. We cannot go back in history, but the new generation can draw upon the great creative energy of that era, on its sense of national kinship and purpose, and on its passion and compassion. These qualities have not left us—we have left them, and it is time to return.

As we return, I commend some extraordinary words to the new generation. E. B. White sat in a darkened room in 1938 to see the beginning of television—an experimental electronic box that projected images into the room. Once he saw it, Mr. White wrote: "We shall stand or fall by television—of that I am sure . . . I believe television is going to be the test of the modern world, and that in this new opportunity to see beyond the range of our vision, we shall discover either a new and unbearable disturbance to the general peace, or a saving radiance in the sky."

That radiance falls unevenly today. It is still a dim light in education. It has not fulfilled its potential for children. It has neglected the needs of public television. And in the electoral process it has cast a dark shadow.

This year, television enabled us to see Patriot missiles destroy Scud missiles above the Persian Gulf. Will television in the next thirty years be a Scud or a Patriot? A new generation now has the chance to put the vision back into television, to travel from the wasteland to the promised land, and to make television a saving radiance in the sky.

Notes

CHAPTER I
1. Dr. Jerome Singer, quoted in *On Television: Teach the Children*, produced by Mary Megee, On Television Ltd., New York.
2. "Television Usage in Child-Care Centers," Statistical Research Inc., May 1994.
3. From the Fox Children's Network's advertisements celebrating its fifth season on the air. The ads ran in *Broadcasting and Cable* in October and November, 1994.
4. See Henry Hansmann, "The Role of Nonprofit Enterprise," *Yale Law Journal*, Vol. 89, 1980, pp. 835–901.
5. "On Television: Teach the Children," PTV Publications, Kent, Ohio, 1992.
6. In the Matter of Policies and Rules Concerning Children's Television Programming, Federal Communications Commission, MM Docket No. 93-48. Released March 2, 1993. No stations were penalized for their deception on the question of the law's "educational and informational" requirement, though the FCC eventually fined more than a dozen stations around the country a total of $345,000 for violations of the commercial time limits of the Children's Television Act.
7. "Congress Pushes for Kids Rules," *Electronic Media*, June 13, 1994.
8. Howard Stringer, address before the International Radio and Television Society Newsmaker Luncheon, September 23, 1993.
9. Editorials hostile to Attorney General Reno ran in the same week in the

Los Angeles Times, The New York Times, the Chicago Tribune, The Washington Post, and The Wall Street Journal. See, for example, "A Dangerous Cure for TV Violence," Chicago Tribune, October 23, 1993; and Michael Gartner, "Warning to the Attorney General," USA Today, October 26, 1993.

10. Ken Tucker, "Reno and Butt-Head: Do Movies and Television Have an Image Problem?" Entertainment Weekly, November 5, 1993.

11. CBS News, 48 Hours, June 2, 1993.

12. "Lawmaker Campaigns Against TV Violence," The Boston Globe, August 3, 1993.

13. "Hitting TV Violence with the 'Off' Switch," Los Angeles Times, November 12, 1992.

14. Quoted in "Program 'v-blocks' No Answer, Nets Tell Congress," The Hollywood Reporter, July 2, 1993.

15. Neil Hickey, "How Much Violence Is There?" TV Guide, June 1992.

16. Child viewing data from Nielsen Total Viewing Sources Report, February 1993.

17. See "Reading, Writing and Murder," People, June 14, 1993.

18. See David A. Hamburg, Today's Children: Creating a Future for a Generation in Crisis (New York: Random House, 1992), and William Dietz and Victor Strasburger, "Children, Adolescents and Television," Current Problems in Pediatrics, Vol. 21, No. 1, 1991, pp. 8–14.

19. Surgeon General's Scientific Advisory Committee on Television and Social Behavior, Television and Growing Up: The Impact of Televised Violence (Washington, D.C.: U.S. Government Printing Office, 1972).

20. "TV Violence Held Unharmful to Youth," The New York Times, January 11, 1972.

21. Quoted in Douglass Cater and Stephen Strickland, TV Violence and the Child: The Evolution and Fate of the Surgeon General's Report (New York: Russell Sage Foundation, 1975), p. 80.

22. "Violence on Air and in Life: No Clear Link," Broadcasting, January 17, 1972.

23. Quoted in Cater and Strickland, op. cit., p. 88.

24. Ibid., p. 3.

25. "TV Violence Labels Not Expected to Affect Kids," The Hollywood Reporter, July 1, 1993.

26. Violence on Television: A Symposium and Study Sponsored by the Editors of TV Guide, June 1992, pp. 9–10.

27. Quoted in Peter Biskind, "Drawing the Line," Premiere, November 1992.

28. Quoted in Ken Auletta, "What Won't They Do?" The New Yorker, May 17, 1993.

29. These figures are from Nielsen Data Research for the period from September 14, 1992, to September 13, 1993. See Larry McGill, "By the Numbers—What Kids Watch," Media Studies Journal, Fall 1994, pp. 95–96. Some researchers believe that smaller children, aged two to eleven, watch as much as twenty-eight hours of television each week. See Aletha

Huston et al., *Big World, Small Screen: The Role of Television in American Society* (Lincoln: University of Nebraska Press, 1992).

30. See J. P. Tangney and S. Feshbach, "Children's Television-Viewing Frequency: Individual Differences and Demographic Correlates," *Personality and Social Psychology Bulletin*, Vol. 14, 1988, pp. 145–58; and Ronald Kuby and Mikael Csikszentmihalyi, *Television and the Quality of Life: How Viewing Shapes Everyday Experience* (Hillsdale, N.J.: Earlbaum, 1990).

31. Huston et al., op. cit., p. 53. These per-hour figures are also cited by Edward Donnerstein, Ron Slaby, and Leonard Eron in *Violence and Youth: Psychology's Response* (Washington, D.C.: American Psychological Association, 1994).

32. National Institute for Mental Health, *Journal*, Vol. 1, 1982.

33. See "Number of Violent Scenes on TV Drops by Half," *Los Angeles Times*, July 29, 1993. The definition is the one used by George Gerbner and his colleagues; other researchers use similar definitions. The 1992 study done for *TV Guide* by the Center for Media and Public Affairs defined an act of violence as "any deliberate act involving physical force or the use of a weapon in an attempt to achieve a goal, further a cause, stop the action of another, act out an angry impulse, defend oneself from attack, secure a material reward, or intimidate others."

34. Brandon Centerwall, "Television and Violent Crime," *The Public Interest*, Spring 1993, pp. 56–58.

35. Ibid., pp. 65–66.

36. The idea that there was no such thing as childhood in the Middle Ages was first put forward by the French scholar Philippe Ariès in his 1962 book *Centuries of Childhood: A Social History of Family Life*. The implications of Ariès's argument have since been examined by scholars in many fields. See, for example, Martha Minow, "Rights for the Next Generation: A Feminist Approach to Children's Rights," *Harvard Women's Law Journal*, Vol. 9, 1986; and Cedric Cullingford, "Children's Social and Moral Claims," *Society*, November-December 1993.

37. This is another way of saying that communications technologies are not neutral with respect to the messages they convey. This point has been made by many communications scholars, most notably James Carey of the University of Illinois, who argues that the way we think is constantly reshaped to parallel the structure of the way we communicate. For a general discussion of television's impact on childhood, see Neil Postman's *The Disappearance of Childhood* (New York: Delacorte Press, 1982).

38. *Nielsen Total Viewing Sources Report*, February 1993. Children's television viewing peaks between 7:30 p.m. and 8 p.m., when a *third* of all children aged two to eleven are watching. See McGill, op. cit., p. 99.

39. "TV Talk Shows: A Four-Day Summary of Content," *Hotline*, American Political Network, May 28, 1993.

40. "TV Violence: More Objectionable in Entertainment Than in Newscasts," *Times Mirror Media Monitor*, March 24, 1993.

41. Bob Greene, "The Death of the Backyard Fence," *Chicago Tribune*, June 22, 1993.

42. The two cable channels that are perhaps consistently the best where children are concerned are Nickelodeon and Disney, the former a basic service, the latter often a premium one offered at a price above and beyond basic cable subscription rates.

43. "TV's Top 10s," *TV Guide*, February 27, 1993.

44. An April 1992 content analysis by the Center for Media and Public Affairs found, for example, that 144 music videos shown on MTV during a single eighteen-hour time block contained as much violence as the programs of the Big Three commercial networks combined.

45. Quoted in Lynn Spigel, "Seducing the Innocent: Childhood and Television in Postwar America," in *Ruthless Criticism: New Perspectives in U.S. Communication History*, ed. William Solomon and Robert McChesney (Minneapolis: University of Minnesota Press, 1993), p. 267.

46. Lynn Spigel, *Make Room for TV: Television and the Family Ideal in Postwar America* (Chicago: University of Chicago Press, 1992), pp. 38–59.

47. Mary Ann Watson, *The Expanding Vista: American Television in the Kennedy Years* (New York: Oxford University Press, 1990), p. 154.

48. Stephen Kline, *Out of the Garden: Toys and Children's Culture in the Age of TV Marketing* (New York: Verso Press, 1994), p. 119.

49. See Spigel, "Seducing the Innocent," op. cit., pp. 266–67.

50. Gerald Lesser, "The Positive Potential of Children's Television: The Scientific Evidence," report to the trustees of the Carnegie Corporation of New York, September 21, 1984.

51. See Lloyd N. Morrisett, "Television: America's Neglected Teacher," Markle Foundation Annual Report, 1983.

52. Joan Ganz Cooney, "*Sesame Street*: International Applications and Findings," report to the trustees of the Carnegie Corporation of New York, October 13, 1994.

53. "Kids' Brainpower: Use It or Lose It," *Technology Review*, November-December, 1993.

54. Lesser, "The Positive Potential of Children's Television," op. cit.

55. David Britt, report to the trustees of the Carnegie Corporation of New York, October 13, 1994.

56. "Curtis Conference on Advertising for Children Brings Heated Exchanges," *Advertising Age*, July 19, 1965.

57. Eugene Mahaney, "Partners for Profit: Children, Toys and TV," *Broadcasting*, June 30, 1969.

58. In 1969, Mattel was one of the three largest sponsors of children's television. Together with Kellogg and General Mills, it accounted for 25 percent of the annual broadcast revenues from children's programs, then about $70 million.

59. Quoted in Barry Cole and Mal Oettinger, *Reluctant Regulators: The FCC and the Broadcast Audience* (Reading, Mass.: Addison-Wesley Co., 1978), p. 249.

60. Ibid., p. 248.
61. Ibid., p. 254.
62. Ibid., p. 258.
63. *Broadcasting*, October 28, 1974.
64. Kline, op. cit., pp. 222–23.
65. See John B. Summers, "The Judicial Death of the NAB Codes," *Gannett Center Journal*, Winter 1988, p. 100.
66. Ibid., p. 106.
67. "Rules Mulled for Kiddie TV: Critics Blast Captain Power," *Advertising Age*, September 21, 1987.
68. "Telcomsubcom Holds Hearings on Children's TV," *Broadcasting*, September 21, 1987.
69. "With Power Rangers Scarce, Parents Are in Buying Frenzy," *The New York Times*, December 5, 1994.
70. This system of payment was reported by the Center for Media Education in testimony before a House subcommittee in June 1994. See Patricia Aufderheide and Kathryn Montgomery, "The Impact of the Children's Television Act on the Broadcast Market," Center for Media Education, June 1994; see also "The Children's Half-Hour: Hostage to Toy Makers?" *The Washington Post*, June 10, 1994.
71. Total television advertising, broadcast and cable, targeted to children is estimated at $550 million. See "We'll Be Right Back . . . ," *Total TV*, August 27–September 9, 1994.
72. "No TV Till You Do Your Responding," *Los Angeles Times*, May 4, 1993.
73. Quoted in "On Kid TV, Ploys R Us," *Newsweek*, November 30, 1992.
74. Quoted in "Broadcasters Say Ad Limits Limit Kids Programming," *Broadcasting and Cable*, March 15, 1993.
75. "The Government Can't Do Quality . . . at All," *Broadcasting and Cable*, August 15, 1994.

CHAPTER 2
1. These figures are based on Nickelodeon's full range of programming, which draws a significant *adult* audience with its nightly Nick at Nite block of old situation comedies.
2. "A Cable Challenger for PBS as King of the Preschool Hill," *The New York Times*, March 21, 1994.
3. Ibid.
4. "Fox Kids Net Flush with Ad $," *Variety*, April 6, 1994.
5. "And the Children Shall Lead Them," *Total TV*, May 6, 1994.
6. Quoted in "World Summit on Television and Children," a pamphlet distributed by Australian Children's Television Foundation, 1994.
7. "A Cable Challenger for PBS."
8. Lewis J. Perelman, "Toward Turbocharged Learning," *Signals*, Ameritech Corporation, Winter 1992. Perelman is also the author of *School's Out* (New York: William Morrow, 1993).

9. *Linking for Learning: A New Course for Education*, Office of Technology Assessment, United States Congress, 1989.
10. "Classrooms Without Walls," *The Wall Street Journal*, May 18, 1992.
11. "Classrooms on the Information Highway," *The New York Times*, July 20, 1994.
12. "Superhighway Planners Bet on Gambling," *Broadcasting and Cable*, December 13, 1993.
13. Quoted in John Rodden, "Ma Bell, Big Brother and the Information Services Family Feud," *Media Studies Journal*, Spring 1992, p. 16.
14. Robert E. Cushman, *The Independent Regulatory Commissions* (New York: Octagon Books, 1972), p. 20.
15. See *Charles River Bridge v. Warren Bridge*, 11 Peters 341 (1837), and *Munn v. Illinois*, 94 U.S. 113 (1877).
16. Willard D. Rowland, Jr., "The Meaning of 'The Public Interest' in Communications Policy, Part I," paper presented at the International Communication Association, May 28, 1989.
17. Cited by Bernard Schwartz, *Economic Regulation of Business and Industry*, Vol. 3 (New York: Chelsea House, 1973), p. 1731.
18. See William Leach, *Land of Desire* (New York: Pantheon Books), pp. 370–72.
19. Erik Barnouw, *Tube of Plenty* (New York: Oxford University Press, 1990), p. 23.
20. Ibid., pp. 43–47.
21. *United States v. Zenith Radio Corporation*, 12 F.2d 614 (N.D. Illinois), April 16, 1926.
22. Robert W. McChesney, "Conflict, Not Consensus: The Debate over Broadcast Communication Policy, 1930–1935," in *Ruthless Criticism*, ed. William Solomon and Robert McChesney (Minneapolis: University of Minnesota Press, 1993), p. 224.
23. *Proceedings of the Fourth National Radio Conference and Recommendations for Regulation of Radio*, Department of Commerce, Washington, D.C., November 9–11, 1925, p. 60.
24. Ibid., p. 56.
25. Willard Rowland, Jr., "The Meaning of the Public Interest in Communications Policy, Part II," paper presented at the International Communication Association, May 28, 1993, p. 12.
26. *Proceedings*, p. 84.
27. Rowland, op. cit., p. 7.
28. See Robert McChesney, "Free Speech and Democracy! Louis G. Caldwell, the American Bar Association and the Debate over the Free Speech Implications of Broadcast Regulation, 1928–1938," *The American Journal of Legal History*, October 1991.
29. *In the Matter of the Application of Great Lakes Broadcasting Co.*, FRC Docket No. 4900, 3FRC Ann. Rep. 32 (1929).
30. See McChesney, "Conflict, Not Consensus," p. 227.
31. Ibid., p. 225.

32. Barnouw, op. cit., pp. 55–56.
33. Erik Barnouw, *The Golden Web: 1933–1953*, Vol. 2 of *A History of Broadcasting in the United States* (New York: Oxford University Press, 1968), p. 26.
34. The story of the broadcast reform movement in the late 1920s and early 1930s is superbly told in Robert McChesney, *Telecommunications, Mass Media and Democracy* (New York: Oxford University Press, 1993).
35. See Margaret Blanchard, "Filling in the Void: Speech and Press in State Courts Prior to *Gitlow*," in *The First Amendment Reconsidered: New Perspectives on the Meaning of Freedom of Speech and Press*, ed. Bill F. Chamberlin and Charlene J. Brown (New York: Longman, 1982), pp. 14–59.
36. William S. Paley, "Radio and the Humanities," *Annals of the American Academy of Political and Social Science*, January 1935, pp. 23–24.
37. Quoted in McChesney, "Conflict, Not Consensus," p. 238.
38. Quoted in Barnouw, *The Golden Web*, p. 25.
39. National Advisory Council on Radio in Education and the American Political Science Association, *Four Years of Network Broadcasting* (Chicago: University of Chicago Press, 1937), pp. 49, 73.
40. William S. Paley, "The Viewpoint of the Radio Industry," in *Educational Broadcasting 1937*, ed. C. S. March (Chicago: University of Chicago Press, 1937), p. 6.
41. Paul Lazarsfeld, *The People Look at Radio* (Chapel Hill: University of North Carolina Press, 1946), p. 89.
42. Quoted in *The Literary Digest*, November 6, 1926.
43. Barnouw, *Tube of Plenty*, pp. 17–49.
44. Quoted in ibid., pp. 64–66.
45. The *New York Times* commentator was Orrin E. Dunlap, Jr., who wrote a regular Sunday column for the paper in the 1930s and 1940s and who chronicled many of the early technological advances in television, including RCA's television pavilion at the 1939 World's Fair; he consistently found the new medium wanting. See "Batter Up! Baseball Telecast Seen in a Dark Room on a Sunny Afternoon in May," *The New York Times*, May 21, 1939.
46. E. B. White, "Removal," in *One Man's Meat* (New York: Harper Bros., 1944), an essay originally published in *Harper's* magazine in 1938.
47. David Sarnoff, "The Future of Television," *Popular Mechanics*, 1939.
48. Eugene Lyons, *David Sarnoff: A Biography* (New York: Harper & Row, 1966), p. 279.
49. Quoted in *Televiser*, Summer 1945.
50. Quoted in *Television*, June 1949.
51. "Television's Impact," *Radio & Television News*, July 1949.
52. Quoted in *Variety*, July 16, 1952. Weaver had come to the NBC presidency by way of the advertising agency Young & Rubicam, where for several years he had produced television programs for distribution to the networks, as was commonly done in those days. It was largely through Weaver's

efforts at NBC that responsibility for programming moved from ad agencies to the networks themselves.

53. See "Mid-Century America and the Growth of Television," Chapter 1 of Leo Bogart, *The Age of Television* (New York: Frederick Ungar, 1956).

54. Quoted in Newton Minow, *Equal Time: The Private Broadcaster and the Public Interest* (New York: Atheneum, 1964), p. 14.

55. "Revelation of Former Network Presidents," *TV Guide*, April 19, 1972.

56. Senator Benton knew whereof he spoke. In 1929 he had been a founder of the great advertising agency Benton and Bowles, which for many years produced programs for radio. Benton left the agency in 1935 and went to the University of Chicago, where he served as vice president under Robert Hutchins. It was through Benton's efforts that the university created the popular and critically distinguished radio series "University of Chicago Roundtable."

57. Quoted in Henry Morgenthau, "Doña Quixote: The Adventures of Frieda Hennock," *Television Quarterly*, Summer 1992.

58. The nation's first noncommercial educational station went on the air on May 12, 1953. A decade later there were sixty-three such stations, accounting for one out of every ten stations in the country.

59. *National Broadcasting Co., Inc., et al. v. United States*, 319 U.S. 190 (1943).

60. Ibid., at 226.

61. Much is made of Justice Frankfurter's remark that the Communications Act "does not restrict the Commission merely to the supervision of [broadcasting] traffic," but that "it puts on the Commission the burden of determining the composition of that traffic." Chairman Porter, among many others, interpreted this to refer to content, when most scholars now agree that by "traffic" Frankfurter was referring to licensees.

62. Commission on Freedom of the Press, *A Free and Responsible Press, A General Report on Mass Communication: Newspapers, Radio, Motion Pictures, Magazines and Books*, ed. Robert D. Leigh (Chicago: University of Chicago Press, 1947).

   The commission's members were: Robert Hutchins, chancellor, University of Chicago; Zechariah Chafee, Jr., professor of law, Harvard University; John Clark, professor of economics, Columbia University; John Dickinson, professor of law, University of Pennsylvania; William Hocking, professor of philosophy, Harvard; Harold Lasswell, professor of law, Yale University; Archibald MacLeish, former assistant secretary of state; Charles Merriam, professor of political science, University of Chicago; Reinhold Niebuhr, professor of ethics and philosophy of religion, Union Theological Seminary; Robert Redfield, professor of anthropology, University of Chicago; Beardsley Ruml, chairman, Federal Reserve Bank of New York; Arthur Schlesinger, Sr., professor of history, Harvard University; and George N. Schuster, president, Hunter College.

63. Ibid., pp. 31, 35.

64. Ibid., pp. 63–73.

65. *The Public Service Responsibility of Broadcast Licensees*, Federal Communications Commission, March 7, 1946. Reprinted in *Documents of American Broadcasting*, ed. Frank J. Kahn (Englewood Cliffs, N.J.: Prentice-Hall, 1984), pp. 148–64.

66. Ibid., p. 154.

67. Erik Barnouw, *The Image Empire: From 1953*, Vol. 3 of *A History of Broadcasting in the United States* (New York: Oxford University Press, 1970), p. 109.

68. See James L. Baughman, *Television's Guardians: The Federal Communications Commission and the Politics of Programming, 1958–1967* (Knoxville: University of Tennessee Press, 1985).

69. Edward R. Murrow, address to the Radio and Television News Directors' Association Convention, October 15, 1958, reprinted in Harry J. Skornia, *Television and Society* (New York: McGraw-Hill, 1965).

70. *Variety*, June 21, 1961.

71. "Creeping Mediocrity Brings Boredom to TV," *Advertising Age*, November 4, 1957.

72. *The New York Times Magazine*, August 4, 1957.

73. Quoted in Gary Steiner, *The People Look at Television: A Study of Audience Attitudes* (New York: Alfred A. Knopf, 1963), p. 235.

74. Educational television in the United States got a $32 million boost when Congress passed the ETV Facilities Act in 1962 (Public Law 87-477, May 1, 1962); and UHF prospects improved considerably with passage of the All-Channel Receiver Law (Public Law 87-529, July 10, 1962) and Sections 303(s) and 330 of the Communications Act.

75. *Office of Communication of the United Church of Christ v. Federal Communications Commission*, 359 F.2d 994 (D.C. Circuit), March 25, 1966.

76. Kahn, op. cit., p. 233.

77. *Red Lion Broadcasting Co., Inc., et al. v. Federal Communications Commission et al.*, 395 U.S. 367 (1969).

78. The Fairness Doctrine and personal-attack rules go to the heart of the idea that the airwaves are public property. Formally written into FCC regulations in 1949, the Fairness Doctrine was perhaps the most controversial aspect of broadcast regulation for nearly forty years, until the FCC announced in August 1987 that it would abandon it.

   The Fairness Doctrine was broad, and during its life was applied to such things as advertising and political campaigns; but in general it required two things: broadcasters had to give reasonable time to the coverage of public issues; and such coverage had to be fair in the sense that broadcasters had to provide airtime for opposing points of view. Congress considered including something like the Fairness Doctrine in both the Radio Act and the Communications Act, but didn't. But the Federal Radio Commission had ruled in 1929 that the "public interest requires ample play for free and fair competition of opposing views, . . . not only to political candidates, but to all discussion of issues of importance to the public" (*Great Lakes Broadcasting Statement*, 3 FRC Ann. Rep. 32, 1929); the FCC later promulgated the Fairness Doctrine in 1949, in a long report on editorializing by broadcast licensees. In 1959, Congress amended Section 315 of the Communications Act to exclude news programming from the FCC's equal-time rule, but in doing so explicitly approved the principle behind the Fairness Doctrine, an approval that the Supreme Court later supported. In 1974, the FCC reviewed the Fairness Doctrine's application and decided that it worked well.

The Fairness Doctrine represented the single most dramatic and effective incursion by the FCC into programming, and broadcasters hated it, since it exposed them to charges from virtually anyone with a cause or grudge claiming they had not given enough attention to this or that public issue. As a consequence, broadcasters said, the Fairness Doctrine had the unintended effect of *discouraging* public affairs programming, since from a broadcaster's point of view the best strategy to avoid conflict was to avoid controversial subjects altogether. In this way, they argued, the Fairness Doctrine acted as an unconstitutional prior restraint on free expression; even more important, they said, it violated their basic right, protected by the First Amendment, to make independent editorial decisions.

The personal-attack rules involved in the *Red Lion* case and contained in a subsection of the Fairness Doctrine were considerably more specific about broadcasters' obligations. Still, most broadcasters objected to them on the same grounds they did to the doctrine generally.

79. *Red Lion Broadcasting*, at 389.
80. *Agreements Between Broadcast Licensees and the Public*, 57 FCC 2nd 42, 1975.
81. The best discussion of the ferment that surrounded commercial television in the 1970s is Kathryn Montgomery, *Target: Prime Time* (New York: Oxford University Press, 1989).
82. See *Report and Statement of Policy re: Commission en banc Programming Inquiry*, 25 Fed. Reg. 7291; 44 FCC 2303, July 29, 1960.
83. See *Writers Guild of America v. FCC*, 423 F.Supp. 1064 (1976).
84. Quoted in "Rewrite of Communications Act Serious Subject on Hill," *Broadcasting*, August 9, 1976.
85. H.R. 13015, *The Communications Act of 1978*, Subcommittee on Communications, Committee on Interstate and Foreign Commerce, U.S. House of Representatives, 95th Congress, 2nd Session, June 7, 1978.
86. Quoted in Erwin Krasnow, Lawrence Longley, and Herbert Terry, *The Politics of Broadcast Regulation* (New York: St. Martin's Press, 1982), p. 248.
87. Ibid., p. 252.
88. Quoted in "Broadcast Regulation: Plan Makes Waves," *The New York Times*, June 12, 1978.
89. Quoted in "Reactions," *The Washington Post*, June 13, 1978.
90. The two bills were S. 611, sponsored by South Carolina senator Ernest Hollings, and S. 612, sponsored by Arizona senator Barry Goldwater.
91. H.R. 3333, *The Communications Act of 1979*, Subcommittee on Com-

munications, Committee on Interstate and Foreign Commerce, U.S. House of Representatives, 96th Congress, 1st Session, 1979.

92. "Van Deerlin Refuses to Say Die," *Broadcasting*, September 17, 1979.

93. Mark Fowler and Daniel Brenner, "A Marketplace Approach to Broadcast Regulation," *Texas Law Review*, Vol. 60, 1982, pp. 209–10.

94. Ibid., pp. 242–47.

95. *Dissenting Statement of Henry M. Rivera, in re: Children's Television Programming Practices Report and Order in Docket No. 19142*, 96 FCC 2d 658, 1983.

CHAPTER 3

1. Mark S. Fowler and Daniel L. Brenner, "A Marketplace Approach to Broadcast Regulation," *Texas Law Review*, Vol. 60, 1982, pp. 253–54.

2. Diane S. Killory and Richard J. Bozzelli, " 'Fairness,' the First Amendment and the Public Interest," *Gannett Center Journal*, Winter 1988.

3. Quoted in "Barrett, Quello Oppose New Kids TV Regulations," *Electronic Media*, July 4, 1994.

4. "Washington Watch," *Broadcasting and Cable*, November 8, 1993.

5. "Taking Aim at Freedom," *Broadcasting and Cable*, October 25, 1993.

6. See particularly Erik Barnouw, *The Image Empire: From 1953*, Vol. 3 of *A History of Broadcasting in the United States* (New York: Oxford University Press, 1970), pp. 1–103.

7. Newton N. Minow, "How to Zap TV Violence," *The Wall Street Journal*, August 3, 1993.

8. Case law on this question has involved many different media, from student newspapers to the public airwaves. See, for example, *Hazelwood School District v. Kuhlmeier*, 484 U.S. 260 (1988), and *FCC v. Pacifica Foundation*, 438 U.S. 726 (1978).

9. See Margaret Blanchard, "Filling in the Void: Speech and Press in State Courts Prior to *Gitlow*," in *The First Amendment Reconsidered: New Perspectives on the Meaning of Freedom of Speech and Press*, ed. Bill F. Chamberlin and Charlene J. Brown (New York: Longman, 1982).

10. Benno C. Schmidt, Jr., "Pluralistic Programming and Regulation of Mass Communications Media," in *Communications for Tomorrow: Policy Perspectives for the 1980s*, ed. Glen O. Robinson (New York: Praeger, 1978), p. 197.

11. Walter Lippmann, "The Public Philosophy" (1955), in *The Essential Lippmann*, ed. Clinton Rossiter and James Lare (Cambridge, Mass.: Harvard University Press, 1982), p. 89.

12. This approach to the public interest is not confined to communications, but is common to almost all areas of public policy. It constitutes what in 1969 the political scientist Theodore Lowi called the "end of liberalism." Many other students of modern American democracy have made Lowi's point since, including journalists like E. J. Dionne and Jonathan Rauch, but none have stated the problem so succinctly or so well. In a democracy,

Lowi wrote, public policy must be based on moral decisions for which someone must be held responsible. Today, talking about what is fundamentally right and wrong in policy invites ridicule, and public responsibility has devolved into a finger-pointing contest between the right and the left.

13. Martha Minow and Richard Weissbourd, "Social Movements for Children," *Daedalus*, Winter 1993, p. 2.

14. William A. Galston, "Causes of Declining Well-Being Among U.S. Children," *Aspen Quarterly*, Winter 1993, pp. 52–55.

15. Ibid., p. 66.

16. Minow and Weissbourd, op. cit., p. 4.

17. See Jerry Muller, *Adam Smith in His Time and Ours: Designing the Decent Society* (New York: The Free Press, 1992), pp. 1–11.

18. Adam Smith, *Inquiry into the Nature and Causes of the Wealth of Nations*, Vol. 1 (London: George Bell and Sons, 1908), p. 265.

19. Rodney A. Smolla, *Free Speech in an Open Society* (New York: Alfred A. Knopf, 1992), p. 8.

20. Alexander Bickel, *The Morality of Consent* (New Haven: Yale University Press, 1975), p. 57.

21. *Globe Newspaper Co. v. Superior Court*, 457 U.S. 596 (1982) at 607. The *Globe* case involved a Massachusetts statute that excluded the press and general public from the courtroom during the testimony of a minor victim in a sexual-offense trial. The Court rejected a blanket policy on such exclusions, but upheld their use on a case-by-case basis.

22. See *Tinker v. Des Moines Independent Community School District*, 393 U.S. 503 (1969); *Hazelwood School District v. Kuhlmeier*, 484 U.S. 260 (1988); and *New York v. Ferber*, 458 U.S. 747 (1982).

23. Thomas I. Emerson, *The System of Freedom of Expression* (New York: Vintage Books, 1970), p. 496.

24. *West Virginia Board of Education v. Barnette*, 319 U.S. 624 (1943).

25. *Tinker*, at 506.

26. *Island Trees Board of Education v. Pico*, 457 U.S. 853 (1982).

27. *Hazelwood*, at 271.

28. In *Bethel School District v. Fraser*, for example, the Court upheld the suspension of a student who made generous use of sexual metaphor and innuendo in a campaign speech on behalf of a friend. "The undoubted freedom to advocate unpopular and controversial views in schools and classrooms must be balanced against the society's countervailing interest in teaching students the boundaries of socially appropriate behavior." 478 U.S. 675 (1986). And in *Broussard v. School Board of Norfolk*, the Court upheld the suspension of a girl who wore to school a T-shirt with the slogan "Drugs Suck!" emblazoned on the front in eight-inch-high letters. Slip. Op., Civil Action No. 2:92cv71 (E.D. Va., September 3, 1992).

29. *Ginsberg v. New York*, 390 U.S. 629 (1968). The Court has reinforced its position in *Ginsberg* several times. See, for example, *Miller v. California*, 413 U.S. 15 (173).

30. *Young v. American Mini Theatres, Inc.*, 427 U.S. 50 (1976) at 69.

31. *New York v. Ferber*, 458 U.S. 747 (1982).
32. *Osborne v. Ohio*, 495 U.S. 103 (1990).
33. *Ginsberg*, at 636, 637, and 641.
34. *Sable Communications of California, Inc. v. FCC*, 109 S.Ct. 2829 (1989), at 2836.
35. *Butler v. Michigan*, 352 U.S. 380 (1957) at 383.
36. *Erzoznik v. City of Jacksonville*, 422 U.S. 205 (1974), at 212–13.
37. *FCC v. Pacifica Foundation*, 438 U.S. 726 (1978), at 749.
38. Fowler and Brenner, op. cit., p. 229.
39. Jack Valenti, "Whose Children Are They Anyway?" *Los Angeles Times*, October 4, 1993.
40. *Action for Children's Television v. FCC*, 11 F.3d 170 (1993). See also "Indecency Regulations Overturned," *The Washington Post*, November 24, 1993. The possibility that the indecency ban may yet be upheld is still open. All eleven judges on the appeals court reheard the case on October 12, 1994; if the en banc decision reverses that of the original three-judge panel, the case may well go to the U.S. Supreme Court. At this writing there has been no decision.
41. Larry McGill, "By the Numbers—What Kids Watch," *Media Studies Journal*, Fall 1994, p. 98.
42. John Paul Stevens, "*The* Freedom of Speech," *Yale Law Journal*, Vol. 102, No. 6, 1993, p. 1301.
43. *Sable Communications of California, Inc. v. FCC*, 492 U.S. 115, 109 S.Ct. 2829 (1989) at 2837.
44. Ibid., at 2836, 2838.
45. 47 U.S.C. 223(b) et seq.
46. Cited in Carolyn Nielsen, "See No Evil: Is Television Robbing Our Cradles?," unpublished research paper, Northwestern University, 1994.
47. If the "child's First Amendment" is clear on any point, it is that the government's power to control adult speech is at its apex when that speech is directed toward children. This principle was established in *Ginsberg* (1968) and again in *Ferber* (1982).
48. See Thomas Krattenmaker and Lucas Powe, Jr., *Regulating Broadcast Programming* (Cambridge, Mass.: MIT Press; Washington, D.C.: AEI Press, 1994), pp. 196–202, 221.
49. Stevens, op. cit., p. 1307.
50. *Video Software Dealers Assoc. et al. v. Webster*, 968 F.2d 684, 8th Cir. (1992).
51. Various applied definitions of violence have included: "behaviors—both self-directed and interpersonal—that result in suicide, homicide, and nonfatal injuries" (Centers for Disease Control, 1991); "behavior by persons against persons that threatens, attempts, or completes intentional infliction of physical or psychological harm" (American Psychological Association, 1993); "behaviors by individuals that intentionally threaten, attempt, or inflict physical harm on others" (National Research Council [Britain], 1993). None of these definitions would include, say, football games, nature

specials, or most Saturday-morning cartoons. They may indeed capture *Hamlet*, though to date neither PBS nor any broadcast network has announced a Saturday-morning or after-school Shakespeare festival on its fall schedule.

52. Sissela Bok, *TV Violence, Children, and the Press: Eight Rationales Inhibiting Public Policy Debates*, The Joan Shorestein Barone Center on Press, Politics and Public Policy, Harvard University, April 1994, p. 14.

53. *Schenck v. United States*, 249 U.S. 47 (1919).

54. Douglass Cater, telephone interview with the authors, January 4, 1995.

55. Everette E. Dennis, "Curbing TV Violence: Matter of Self-Regulation," *Communiqué*, Freedom Forum Media Studies Center, New York, July-August 1993.

56. Robert Packwood, foreword to Edwin Diamond and Norman Sandler, *The FCC and the Deregulation of Telecommunications Technology* (Washington, D.C.: Cato Institute, 1983).

57. *Red Lion Broadcasting Co. v. FCC*, 395 U.S. 367 (1969). Today, there are no broadcast frequencies open in any of the United States' major market areas.

58. In July 1994 the Electronic Industries Association approved an electronic standard for the v-chip that will make it a part of many new television sets beginning in 1996. The standard is voluntary, however, and manufacturers are not required to adhere to it.

59. Quoted in Douglass Cater and Stephen Strickland, *TV Violence and the Child: The Evolution and Fate of the Surgeon General's Report* (New York: Russell Sage Foundation, 1975), p. 90.

CHAPTER 4

1. Adlai E. Stevenson, Miami, Florida, September 26, 1956.

2. Douglas Davis, "Who's Afraid of the Big, Bad Tube?" *Los Angeles Times Magazine*, March 14, 1993.

3. Robert Kubey, "The Case for Media Education," *Education Week*, March 6, 1991.

4. John Merrow, "Title Goes Here," in *America's Schools and the Mass Media*, ed. Everette E. Dennis and Craig L. LaMay (New Brunswick, N.J.: Transaction, 1992), p. 40.

5. Ibid., p. 46.

6. Theodore Lowi, *The End of Liberalism: The Second Republic of the United States* (New York: W. W. Norton, 1969), pp. 312–13.

7. Not only did Congress give itself special access to the airwaves in Section 315, it also required broadcasters to sell it to them at the lowest unit rate. Later the act was amended (Section 312(a)(7)) to require that time be sold or afforded to all federal candidates for office—by which they meant, principally, themselves.

8. Leo Bogart, *The Age of Television* (New York: Frederick Ungar Co., 1956), p. viii.

9. Douglass Cater, "The Intellectual in Videoland," *Saturday Review*, May 31, 1975.
10. See "The Telcos Are Coming," *Broadcasting and Cable*, March 1, 1993.
11. According to 1990 U.S. Census information, 15 percent of American homes had computers in them. The Children's Partnership reported that 35 percent did in 1994; see *America's Children and the Information Superhighway: A Briefing Book and National Agenda*, September 1994.
12. "Present at the Marriage of Phone and Cable TV: Britain Offers Encouraging Experience," *The New York Times*, May 18, 1993.
13. Ken Auletta, "Barry Diller's Search for the Future," *The New Yorker*, February 22, 1993.
14. See Joseph Garber, "Do-It-Yourself Television," *Forbes*, March 15, 1993.
15. Barry Diller, *Larry King Live*, CNN, April 12, 1993.
16. John Seabrook, "E-Mail from Bill," *The New Yorker*, January 10, 1994.
17. *Newsweek*, for example, characterized the age of SuperTube as "The Next Revolution" (April 6, 1993); *Time* invited readers to "Take a Trip into the Future on the Electronic Superhighway" (April 12, 1993).
18. "Big Brother's Holding Group," *Newsweek*, October 25, 1993.
19. Brandon Tartikoff, *The Last Great Ride* (New York: Delta Books, 1993), p. 209.
20. News clip broadcast on *Larry King Live*, CNN, April 12, 1993.
21. See "TV Shopping Hooks High-Toned Viewers," *The Wall Street Journal*, November 16, 1993.
22. Herb Brody, "The Home Front: Information Highway," *Technology Review*, August-September 1993.
23. See "Superhighway Planners Bet on Gambling," *Broadcasting and Cable*, December 13, 1993.
24. Cited in "Letters," *Chronicle of Higher Education*, September 6, 1994.
25. Quoted in "SuperHighway Patrol," *The Hollywood Reporter*," September 16, 1993.

CHAPTER 5

1. Sissela Bok, *TV Violence, Children, and the Press: Eight Rationales Inhibiting Public Policy Debates*, Joan Shorenstein Barone Center on Press, Politics and Public Policy, Harvard University, April 1994, p. 1.
2. Personal communication to the authors. See also David Kleeman, "The Children's Hour: A Future History," *Electronic Media*, July 19, 1994.
3. See "Grateful Man Leaves $5.6 Million to Federal Government," *The New York Times*, October 8, 1994.
4. Edward L. Palmer, *Television and America's Children: A Crisis of Neglect* (New York: Oxford University Press, 1988), pp. 122–26.
5. *Starting Points: Meeting the Needs of Our Youngest Children*, Report of the Carnegie Task Force on Meeting the Needs of Young Children, Carnegie Corporation of New York, April 1994, p. 36.

6. See Milton Chen, *The Smart Parent's Guide to Kids' TV* (San Francisco: KQED Books, 1994).

7. Patricia Marks Greenfield, *Mind and Media: The Effects of Television, Video Games, and Computers* (Cambridge, Mass.: Harvard University Press, 1984), p. 66.

8. Michael Kelley, *A Parent's Guide to Television* (New York: John Wiley & Sons, 1983), p. 65.

9. Jay F. Davis, "Five Important Ideas to Teach Your Kids About TV," *Media and Values*, Fall 1990/Winter 1991.

10. *Violence on Television: A Symposium and Study Sponsored by the Editors of TV Guide*, June 1992.

11. "What We Can Do," *TV Guide*, August 22, 1992.

12. David Bianculli, *Teleliteracy* (New York: Continuum, 1992), p. 165.

13. See Aimee Dorr, *Television and Children* (Beverly Hills: Sage Publications, 1986), p. 113; and Shari Roan, "Tuned In and At Risk," *Los Angeles Times*, March 10, 1993.

14. Randal Levenson, "Teaching Children to Say No to TV," *The New York Times*, March 24, 1993.

15. "Zap! The Smart Set," *The Washington Post*, August 29, 1992.

16. Larry McGill, "By the Numbers—What Kids Watch," *Media Studies Journal*, Fall 1994, pp. 95–97. According to Nielsen Media Research data from 1992 to 1993, men eighteen and older watch about twenty-nine hours of television a week; women in the same age category watch almost thirty-three hours.

17. Richard S. Leghorn, "The OKTV Program," memorandum of November 11, 1994.

18. Sanford McDonnell, letter to Newton N. Minow, September 15, 1994.

19. FCC commissioner Rachelle Chong has called the undertaking "staggering," not only in terms of cost but also in terms of planning. See *Telecommunications Reports*, October 17, 1994.

20. Quoted in *Academe*, September-October 1994.

21. Bok, op. cit.

22. Ibid., p. 15.

23. Quoted in Judy Mann, "Learning to Read TV," *The Washington Post*, September 3, 1993.

24. See Kate Moody, "Growing Media Smarts—The New Mexico Project"; and Renee Hobbs, "Teaching Media Literacy—Yo! Are You Hip to This?" *Media Studies Journal*, Fall 1994. See also Dorothy G. Singer, "Creating Critical Viewers," *Television Quarterly*, Winter 1994.

25. Robert Kubey, "The Case for Media Education," *Education Week*, March 6, 1991.

26. See Patricia Aufderheide, *Media Literacy: A Report of the National Leadership Conference on Media Literacy* (Washington, D.C.: The Aspen Institute, 1993), pp. 5–8.

27. Edward R. Murrow, address to the Radio and Television News Directors' Association Convention, October 15, 1958, reprinted in Harry J. Skornia, *Television and Society* (New York: McGraw-Hill, 1965), p. 237.

Index

ABC, 23, 25, 51, 59, 86, 89, 97, 128, 156–57
ABC Afterschool Specials, 51
Abel, John, 21–22
Action for Children's Television (ACT), 46–51, 53–54, 59, 99, 112, 161
advertising (radio), limitations on, 80
advertising (TV): Blue Book statement on, 92–94; children's inability to distinguish, from programs, 61, 166; code for, 167; exploitation of children by (*see* children's television); FCC attempt to limit, 92–94; increase in, 21, 53–54; preschool audience, 60–62; syndicate vs. network, 52–53; time limits on, 21, 45–46, 48–49, 52–53, 55, 57, 166–67

Advertising Age, 45
A&E, 39
aggressive behavior, and television violence, 28–34, 99, 133–34
airtime: adult vs. children's, 37–39; equal-time rule, 100–1, 141; family-viewing time, 99
airwaves: and political jurisdictions, 12–13; as public utility, 4, 73–74, 77, 88, 98, 101, 132; *see also* spectrum allocations; UHF; VHF
Alcoa Hour, The, 85
All in the Family, 99
American Academy of Arts and Sciences, 170
American Academy of Pediatrics, 172
American Bar Association, 78, 112
American Center for Children's Television, 156

LaVergne, TN USA
19 October 2010
201381LV00001B/22/A
0831